RESEARCH IN ECONOMIC HISTORY

Supplement 2 • 1982

VARIATIONS IN BUSINESS AND ECONOMIC HISTORY: ESSAYS IN HONOR OF DONALD L. KEMMERER

Indexed and Abstracted in:

Historical Abstracts. Part B: Twentieth Century Abstracts, 1914 to Present

America: History and Life. Part A: Article Abstracts and Citation

RESEARCH IN ECONOMIC HISTORY

A Research Annual

VARIATIONS IN BUSINESS AND ECONOMIC HISTORY: ESSAYS IN HONOR OF DONALD L. KEMMERER

Editors: BRUCE R. DALGAARD
Director, Center for Economic Education University of Minnesota

RICHARD K. VEDDER
Department of Economics Ohio University, and Economist, Joint Economic Committee, Congress of the United States

---

SUPPLEMENT 2 • 1982

JAI PRESS INC.

Greenwich, Connecticut *London, England*

36 Sherwood Place
Greenwich, Connecticut 06830

JAI PRESS INC.
3 Henrietta Street
London WC2E 8LU
England

ISBN: 0-89232-262-4

Manufactured in the United States of America

CONTENTS

LIST OF CONTRIBUTORS

Robert Ankli	Department of Economics, University of Guelph
Bruce R. Dalgaard	Director, Center for Economic Education, University of Minnesota
William J. Hausman	Department of Economics, College of William and Mary
Dana Hewins	Department of Economics, College of Arts and Science, Ohio University
John M. Hunter	Director, Latin American Studies Center, Michigan State University
Albro Martin	Oglesby Professor of American Heritage, Bradley University
E. Wayne Nafziger	Department of Economics, Kansas State University
Robert F. Severson, Jr.	Department of Economics, Central Michigan University
Robert J. Thornton	Department of Economics, Lehigh University
Richard K. Vedder	Department of Economics, Ohio University, and Economist, Joint Economic Committee, Congress of the United States

Richard K. Winkleman — Department of Economics, Arizona State University

Stephen T. Worland — Department of Economics, Notre Dame University

PREFACE

The idea for a *Festschrift* honoring Donald Kemmerer began to take shape in the year immediately following completion of my graduate study at the University of Illinois in 1977. I was Don Kemmerer's last graduate student. His teaching career had spanned five decades, and he had influenced scores of graduate students; his influence on me had been profound. I felt it was only fitting that I try to find some way to recognize the contributions this man had made to the professional development of so many students. As I talked with some of my classmates and met some of Don Kemmerer's former students, I realized that many others felt as I did about him and that they strongly supported the idea for a book of essays.

I first got to know Donald Kemmerer when I was an undergraduate student at Illinois. I enrolled in his course in American economic history in 1967. The demands of the course were somewhat overwhelming, but the professor was so well versed in the field that the students were inspired to complete the readings in order to take full advantage of his knowledge. Kemmerer's ability to weave the opinions of a variety of authors into an overall view of the evolution of the American economy was impressive. The breadth of information I gained encouraged me to enroll in his graduate-level course in European economic history. The work load in this course was even greater than in the undergraduate course, but long hours of library research and reading, combined with student involvement in class, made the learning process rewarding. Just before I left the university to begin teaching high school, Kemmerer indicated that if I ever decided to return to graduate school, he would be ready to assist me.

It was this offer of assistance which eventually drew me back to Illinois for further graduate work. Over the next four years Don Kemmerer taught me what it was to be an economic historian. He involved me in research projects and gave me advice on how to make sense out of seemingly disparate information by seeking out data, by looking for trends, and by identifying isolated events. He taught me a process rather than facts; he demonstrated a technique rather than requiring a specific viewpoint. While we often differed on sociopolitical events, he never allowed this to interfere with my education; he never forced me to accept his opinion.

What Don Kemmerer did for me he did, to varying degrees, for all of his students. His encouragement and scholarly example served to motivate many of us who studied with him. I realized how much his students thought of him when I first suggested the idea of a book of essays in his honor. The response was overwhelmingly favorable. Furthermore, his former students conveyed in letters to me their strong feelings about the scholarly ability and pedagogic impact of Don Kemmerer.

As drafts of essays began to come to me, I realized another characteristic of Don Kemmerer which may help to explain why so many feel so grateful to him. It was not just in me that Kemmerer instilled a real quest for knowledge; he had done this with all the former students whose essays are contained herein. And he had done it without dictating a specific economic philosophy or methodology. The diversity of the contributors' interests demonstrates that Kemmerer taught people *how* to think but not *what* to think. He encouraged his students to pursue a variety of paths of inquiry, not just those which interested him or complemented his current research. It is probably for this reason, more than any other, that he is so admired by his students, and that his students have found success through so many professional channels.

Don Kemmerer comes from a strong academic tradition; his father was a professor of international finance at Princeton University. Don Kemmerer received his formal education at Princeton. He earned the bachelor's degree in 1927 and was elected Phi Beta Kappa. He completed his doctorate in 1934. His first academic appointment was at Lehigh University, an institution to which I would follow him forty-two years later. In 1937 Kemmerer left Lehigh to accept an appointment in the department of economics at the University of Illinois. He was made full professor in 1949 and retired professor emeritus in 1973.

During his career, which did not end with his formal retirement, Don Kemmerer has distinguished himself in many ways. He was a Fulbright scholar to the University of Montpellier, France, in 1960 and was again awarded a Fulbright to the University of Munich, Germany, in 1964. He served as president of the Economists' National Commission on Monetary Policy from 1967 to 1970. Kemmerer's interest in the promotion of graduate study in economic and business history is evidenced by his twenty-three-year presidency of the Lincoln Educational Foundation, a group which supports graduate study with annual fellowships.

Despite these accomplishments, and the many others which are not mentioned here, I feel that this volume recognizes Don Kemmerer's most significant achievement—the training of scholars in economic history. Those of us contributing essays, as well as dozens of other Kemmerer students, feel indebted to Don Kemmerer for encouraging their scholarship and professional activities.

A great deal of cooperation went into the preparation of this volume. The idea for a book of essays honoring Don Kemmerer may have developed in 1977, but it was not until Richard Vedder became involved that the idea began to take shape. He provided the expertise necessary to allow the project to be completed. In addition to Dick Vedder, Paul Uselding must receive credit for providing a vehicle for the publication of this book. The Research in Economic History Series is the ideal publication outlet for these essays. My thanks go to both of these men.

Bruce R. Dalgaard
Minneapolis

FOREWORD

I first met Donald L. Kemmerer on the front steps of the Student Union building of Texas Christian University in the spring of 1973, during the Business History Conference. It was my first attendance at the conference, and I daresay it was at least Don's twenty-first. It was he and a few other midwesterners who decided after World War II to rescue the systematic study of business enterprise and its relationship to American society from the low level to which it had lapsed and founded the conference.

My teaching assistant at the American University, where I had begun my teaching career only three years before as a middle-aged "retread" to the academic world, had been an undergraduate at the University of Illinois and a student of Don's some years before and was working on a doctorate in the field of international finance. In a midnight discussion of what makes a good teacher—a common pastime of assistant professors and their teaching assistants—he had mentioned that a certain Donald

Kemmerer had been the best teacher he had ever had. That, I told Don upon meeting him, was a pretty good reputation to have preceding one.

I was never Don's student, in the conventional sense, but I have learned a few things from him in the ensuing years. At the center of his personality is a trait of great value to anyone who would stimulate and guide the thinking of younger people: a plain-spoken realism that emphasizes that nobody knows everything, that all wisdom is constantly on trial, and that history—the "logic of the actual," as Leonard Krieger has called it—shapes economic theory, and not the other way around. Descended though he may be from a long line of Pennsylvania Germans, Don Kemmerer has refreshed many a jaded fellow scholar's mind with his potent brand of English pragmatism, the only bulwark against that fatuous positivism which forever gnaws at our institutions.

Don's "field," as we say, is the history of finance. But such a generalization will not do. True, he had the most rigorous early training that one can get, and he learned well from his father, longtime professor of economics at Princeton and adviser to many nations during post–World War I reconstruction, the principles of the great monetary and financial issues that agitated Americans of his father's generation. He traveled to many places that most young men only dreamed about, and he built upon this solid foundation a broad cultivation in the humanities that reminds one of Joseph Schumpeter (whose work on entrepreneurial innovation had such an influence on Don)—a background that is so important in an economist and yet so seldom evident in the modern breed. Talking to Don, you want sometimes to remark how unusual it is that one can have been both a college professor and the son of a college professor and still sound so little like one.

Dealing with this kind of a man, it would have been a shame if this collection of recent work by some of his former students bore any resemblance to the usual *Festschrift*. It does not. Reading these papers, I was struck by how appropriate any of them would be for publication, on its own, in a prominent scholarly journal. Discussing these articles is somebody else's job, but I want to point out how pleased Don will be to find scholars—and especially his students—choosing to write on the subjects represented. He will be delighted to learn that scholars like Richard Vedder and Richard Winkleman are as well occupied at chewing the rag of monetary theory and policy as he ever was, and that they can show the Old Man a thing or two. He will be gratified at the global sophistication of scholars like Wayne Nafziger and John Hunter, who can write so confidently on such exotic places as Africa and Latin America, and he may reflect on how little has changed since his father tried to advance the world view in a period of gross isolationism.

No anti-institutionalist for all his theoretical armament, Don will admire

Robert Severson's fascinating and all-too-short article on the Civilian Conservation Corps as a form of "workfare" and Robert J. Thornton's study of early collective bargaining in the determination of teachers' salaries. These pieces reflect a Kemmerer brand of realism, no longer unstylish, in two categories of public-policy problems that will have to be reckoned with in the coming years. Robert Ankli's article on the Canadian newsprint industry will help many to a better understanding of the industrial economy of our neighbor to the north. William Hausman and Dana Hewins demonstrate the power of history to answer questions about the efficacy of government intervention in economic decision making that all the deductive theorizing in the world has failed to illuminate. And Stephen Worland, in his incisive exposé of the hidden cracks in both the method and the philosophy of the "new" economic history, points the way to a usable ethic of economic life that Don will cheer.

Whether Don will cheer Bruce Dalgaard's study of Professor E. W. Kemmerer's decline in vogue after 1929 is questionable, but there can be no doubt that he will find it moving. A true product of the Progressive era, E. W. Kemmerer never lost his faith that economic theory had reached the state of practical usefulness, even when everything around him seemed to prove that gold-standard orthodoxy was, after all, just another special case—the stuff that history, not "social science," is made of.

A rather cynical college teacher friend of mine once said that we were lucky to get one or two really good students in a lifetime. Don Kemmerer had at least twelve. I would say that he has been a lucky man—except that luck hadn't a thing to do with it.

Albro Martin
Oglesby Professor of the
American Heritage
Bradley University

THE CANADIAN NEWSPRINT INDUSTRY, 1900–1940

Robert E. Ankli

Several "new" and fast-growing industries—pulp and paper or newsprint, automobiles, hydroelectric power, and mining (together with the growth of wheat exports and the settlement of the prairies)—have dominated our perception of how the Canadian economy changed or grew early in the twentieth century. The study of these industries is important in its own right, but such study becomes even more interesting in determining whether there was a link between these industries and the severity of the depression and the failure of the Canadian economy to recover in the 1930s. In the only full-length study of the Canadian depression, A. E. Safarian argued that "several large and relatively new industries developed rapidly in the twenties. Their impact on the thirties was limited by the fact that investment opportunities had been so thoroughly exploited in the twenties. There were no extensive backlogs of

Variations in Business and Economic History:
Essays in Honor of Donald L. Kemmerer
Research in Economic History, Suppl. 2, pages 1–30.

ISBN: 0-89232-262-4

investment opportunity in major industries, old and new, to cushion the downswing and expedite the recovery."[1]

The purpose of this paper is to examine one of these industries—newsprint—during the first four decades of the present century. The paper is divided into three parts. It begins with a description of the industry and its growth. Output of newsprint rose more than tenfold between 1913 and 1929. This leads to an examination of the question of whether this large increase in capacity was justified. Both sides of the issue are looked at in the second section, but the question is not easily answered. So the last part attempts to measure "economic" capacity. It is concluded that there probably was too much "economic" capacity in the late twenties, but that it was not as large as many have suggested.

I. THE NEWSPRINT INDUSTRY AND ITS GROWTH

It is difficult to trace the early history of the pulp and paper industry or its largest component—newsprint—in Canada, because reliable and authentic records are simply not available. The industry appears to have begun in 1803 when the first paper mill was established in the Province of Quebec.[2] The earliest paper was handmade, from rags and other waste materials, so the industry was something of a scavenger, depending on some of the waste materials of society. It was not until after 1860 that wood began to be used for making paper in Canada.

There are two principal methods by which wood is converted into pulp: the mechanical process and various chemical processes. Spruce is most generally used, with hemlock and balsam fir also important, but other types are used as well.

The first groundwood mill was opened by Alexander Buntin at Valleyfield, Quebec, in 1866, the grinders for that mill being imported from Sweden. These grinders produced about two tons of pulp per day and utilized white maple wood. By contrast, Canada's largest groundwood mill today produces over 850 tons daily, and several newsprint mills produce considerably more for conversion into newsprint.

After the wood is barked, mechanical pulp or groundwood is produced by pressing the pieces of wood to the face of a large grindstone by means of hydraulic pressure. "The groundwood comes from the grinders in the form of slush, which is then screened in order to remove the coarser particles."[3] Mechanical pulp is not suitable for paper by itself because it "contains only about 55 percent of cellulose and the fibers are too short and stiff to felt or interlace together properly; hence it is mixed with a certain quantity of chemical pulp which is pure cellulose with fibers of greater length."[4]

The percentage of groundwood used in newsprint varies depending upon the quality of paper desired, but, on average, newsprint consists of about 80 percent mechanical pulp. Since sulfite, the chemical pulp used in the manufacture of newsprint, is more expensive than mechanical pulp, no more is added than is necessary. Various other ingredients are also included. Talc or china clay serves as a filler, making the paper more opaque and smoother. Liquid rosin "sizes" the paper so that the printing ink will not be absorbed and thus cause the impressions to become blurred. Red and blue aniline dyes are introduced, when obtainable, to make the paper white, and alum is also added to precipitate the rosin and the coloring matter upon the fibers.[5]

These ingredients are mixed together in the "beaters"—cylindrical rolls fitted with steel or bronze blades that revolve over stationary concave bedplates equipped with similar blades. After the beating has been completed the pulp is run off into a stuff chest, through a strainer, and "then onto a wire-screen belt consisting of fine copper wires, woven with 60 or 70 meshes to the inch. The length of this screen is often 75 feet and the width 150 or more inches, with much of the water draining through the mesh of the screen." Toward the end of the screen the "paper" moves over several vacuum boxes and then passes through a series of rolls and is dried as it travels over several cast-iron cylinders which are internally heated.[6]

The treatment of wood by chemical processes closely followed the invention of groundwood pulp, and the pulp produced by these means rapidly assumed great importance. The pulp resulting from the chemical treatment of wood has a longer fiber and considerably greater strength. Its use has gone far to replace the use of rags in the manufacture of book paper and many other finer grades. The first process to be developed was the soda process, so called because the wood was cooked in a solution of caustic soda. Hemlock is the chief wood used for this process, but a wide range of woods can be substituted. This was a more expensive process than the grinding method; the pulp produced was light and bulky (thick-fibered) and was of great use as a filler in combination with pulp from other sources. Soda pulp is used chiefly for book and writing paper. The soda process has undergone considerable development in the United States, but has not made very much headway in Canada, more attention having been paid there to the manufacture of mechanical and other chemical pulps. Prior to 1940 soda pulp rarely accounted for more than 1 percent of total Canadian pulp.[7]

The sulfite process for the manufacture of wood pulp was worked out in 1866–67 in the United States, but was not at first a commercial success. Later, in 1874, a Swede named Ekman overcame many of the difficulties in connection with the process and built the first sulfite mill in the world at Bergvik, Sweden. The Ekman process was introduced into the United States by C. S. Wheelwright and was put into operation at the plant of the Richmond Paper Company. Another method of producing sulfite pulp was developed by Rittner Kellner, an Austrian, and this process was used in the first sulfite mill established in Canada by J. R. Barber and Charles Riordon, at Merriton, Ontario, in 1887.[8] The sulfite process for making chemical pulp involves chipping the wood into small pieces and cooking the wood for about eight hours at a temperature of 365° under about 80 pounds of pressure in a solution of calcium of magnesium bisulfite and sulphurous acid. After coming out of the digester it is washed for about three hours. "Sprucewood pulp obtained in this manner contains about 88 percent of cellulose, while untreated spruce wood contains only about 55 percent."[9] Besides its use in paper, sulfite pulp has also become an important material in the manufacture of rayon, cellulose products, lacquers, and explosives.[10] The introduction of sulfite pulp opened up new fields for the paper manufacturer. The combination of sulfite pulp with mechanical pulp made possible a tremendous expansion in the newsprint industry, which is today the leading sector of the pulp and paper industry in Canada.

Sulfate-pulp production was not reported in the statistics of Canadian production until 1912. "Sodium sulfate is substituted for the more expensive sodium carbonate. . . . Sulfate pulp is used largely for the manufacturing of wrapping, cover and all other kinds of paper where strength is the most important factor, while the dark color of the paper is of no disadvantage."[11]

Canada's abundant forest reserves and accessible power sites were hardly developed before 1900. The forty-one mills in 1881, for example, employed only 1,588 employees and had an output valued at $2.5 million, consisting of pulp valued at $63,000 and paper valued at $2.4 million.[12] Domestic consumption of paper was only about five pounds per capita, and a good deal of that was imported. Nearly 75 percent of the wood pulp produced in Canada in 1901 was mechanical pulp or groundwood, the rest being mainly sulfite pulp with a smaller quantity of soda pulp.

About 1900 began the rapid expansion of the industry that has brought it to the leading position among the manufacturing industries of Canada. At that time almost twice as much pulpwood was being exported in the raw state as was being manufactured into pulp and paper. In 1911 the number of mills in Canada reached fifty-four, and the production of wood pulp was 497,000 tons. Of these fifty-four mills, twenty-eight were in the Province of Quebec. It was not until 1913 that domestic consumption of wood pulp exceeded the amount imported. Table 1 illustrates the trend in the domestic consumption and the export of wood pulp.

Table 1. Canada: All Pulpwood Production (Millions of Cords)

Year	*Total Production*	*Total Exports*	*Apparent Domestic Consumption*	*Percentage Domestic Consumption*
1908	1.3	.8	.5	36.4
1909	1.6	.9	.6	39.9
1910	1.5	.9	.6	38.8
1911	1.5	.8	.7	44.2
1912	1.8	1.0	.9	46.8
1913	2.1	1.0	1.1	51.7
1914	2.2	.9	1.2	55.7
1915	2.4	.9	1.4	59.7
1916	2.8	1.1	1.8	62.3
1917	3.1	1.0	2.1	67.4
1918	3.6	1.3	2.2	62.1
1919	3.5	1.1	2.4	69.4
1920	4.0	1.2	2.8	69.0
1921	3.3	1.1	2.2	66.6
1922	3.9	1.0	2.9	74.2
1923	4.7	1.4	3.3	70.3
1924	4.6	1.3	3.3	71.4
1925	5.1	1.4	3.7	72.0
1926	5.6	1.4	4.3	75.2
1927	5.9	1.5	4.4	74.0
1928	6.3	1.5	4.8	75.7
1929	6.5	1.3	5.2	80.2
1930	6.0	1.3	4.6	77.7
1931	5.2	1.1	4.1	78.4
1932	4.2	.6	3.6	85.3
1933	4.7	.7	4.0	84.9
1934	5.8	1.0	4.8	82.3
1935	6.1	1.1	5.0	81.8
1936	7.0	1.2	5.8	82.4
1937	8.3	1.7	6.6	79.5
1938	6.4	1.8	4.7	72.8
1939	6.9	1.5	5.4	77.7
1940	8.5	1.5	6.9	81.7

Source: Pulp and Paper Industry, 1951, p. H-22.

The domestic-consumption figures are a good index of the growth of the industry in Canada, since this output would be used in the newsprint industry. Detailed statistics were first published by the Forestry Branch of the Department of the Interior between 1908 and 1917 when the work was taken over by the Dominion Bureau of Statistics, which has issued an annual census report since that time. Unfortunately, the Forestry Branch reports were concerned only with raw pulpwood and the manufacture of pulp and gave no information on paper. Therefore, there are no authentic records of the production of paper until 1917, by which date the industry was well established. In the earliest years, however, newsprint was the principal grade of paper manufactured, as it is today.

There were two very important causes for the rapid expansion, particularly from 1908 to 1929. One was the prohibition of the exportation of pulpwood from Crown lands, which was put into force by the provincial authorities in 1910. This action gave great impetus to the domestic manufacture of wood pulp and paper and led to the establishment of many new mills in this country. The second factor was the rescinding of the tariff on wood pulp and newsprint paper by the United States, which threw open the doors to that market. In 1907 there was considerable worry among publishers in the United States about the high prices of newsprint, and this pressure resulted in a tentative agreement on general trade reciprocity with Canada. The agreement was rejected by the Canadian Parliament, but this was only a temporary setback for the industry, for the United States amended its tariff in 1913 to admit wood pulp and printing paper (valued at no more than 2½¢ per pound) free of duty. With the largest market in the world open to Canadian pulp and paper exports the future of this industry was assured, and Canadian exports of wood pulp and paper have increased steadily since that time. Table 1 shows that until 1913 total exports of wood pulp exceeded apparent domestic consumption, but in that year production rose by almost 200,000 tons while total exports of wood pulp dropped, and newsprint manufacture (or apparent domestic consumption) far outdistanced exports.

In 1917 the first complete census of the pulp and paper industry of Canada was issued by the Dominion Bureau of Statistics (DBS). This report gave various items of information which before that time had not been published.

The 1917 census indicated that eighty-three pulp and paper mills were in operation in Canada with a total production valued at $96.4 million. The capital investment represented by these mills in 1917 was given as $186.8 million; the average number of wage earners was 21,400, and salary and wage payments totaled $20.4 million.[13]

World War I apparently increased the demand for newsprint as the populace of the two countries clamored for news about the war. The first estimation of newsprint production, made in 1910, was 215,000 tons, or approximately 43 percent of total pulp production. By 1913 Canadian output had risen to 350,000 tons. Three years later its manufacture was almost three-fourths greater, and by 1920 output was 876,000 tons.[14] Table 2 provides data on the output of newsprint estimated by the News Print Service Bureau, together with its value based on the Three Rivers, Quebec, contract price. The production of other grades of paper was not recorded before 1917, but its total must have been small; these products did not figure prominently in Canadian international trade.[15]

Prices shot up during the war and its immediate aftermath. Table 3 shows the average price of newsprint for the years 1915–39.

The Three Rivers price is the net price obtained by a mill in the Three Rivers area. In the next column "average freight rate" means the average rate per ton of newsprint from Three Rivers to New York. The columns bearing the captions f.o.b. New York and f.o.b. Chicago contain the resulting price for delivery in those cities. The column headed f.o.b. Iroquois represents the price received by Abitibi for newsprint shipped from the mill at Iroquois Falls (Ontario). The next column—"average freight rate"—denotes the cost of shipping a ton of newsprint from Iroquois to Chicago.[16]

It is true, of course, that costs to the newsprint industry rose during this period, but it should be noted that the U.S. Federal Trade Commission found that 1917's prices rose more than costs would have jus-

Table 2. Market Value and Production of Canadian Newsprint, 1913–1938 (Based on Average Three Rivers Contract Price)

Year	*Production (000 tons)*	*Value (000 $'s)*	*Year*	*Production (000 tons)*	*Value (000 $'s)*
1913	350	14,000	1926	1,882	122,330
1914	415	16,600	1927	2,087	135,655
1915	489	18,582	1928	2,381	144,527
1916	608	29,184	1929	2,729	150,641
1917	686	41,160	1930	2,504	138,221
1918	735	44,100	1931	2,221	111,494
1919	803	59,422	1932	1,914	78,723
1920	876	91,980	1933	2,017	68,679
1921	808	83,830	1934	2,599	86,287
1922	1,082	75,740	1935	2,753	91,400
1923	1,266	94,950	1936	3,191	109,132
1924	1,353	100,122	1937	3,648	130,234
1925	1,522	106,540	1938	2,625	113,400

Source: Coughlin, p. 60, from News Print Service Bureau.

Table 3. Average Price of Newsprint for the Years 1915–1939

Year	*F.O.B. Three Rivers*	*Average Freight Rate*	*F.O.B. New York*	*F.O.B. Iroquois*	*Average Freight Rate*	*F.O.B. Chicago*
1915	$ 38.00	$3.78	$ 41.78	$ 37.00	$4.21	$ 41.21
1916	48.00	3.78	51.78	37.00	4.10	41.10
1917	60.00	3.78	63.78	65.00	4.37	69.37
1918	60.00	4.30	64.30	70.50	5.29	75.79
1919	74.75	5.40	80.15	75.00	6.10	81.10
1920	105.00	7.60	112.60	95.00	6.20	101.20
1921	103.75	7.60	111.35	103.50	8.10	111.60
1922	70.00	6.80	76.80	70.00	8.35	78.35
1923	75.00	6.80	81.80	75.00	7.90	82.90
1924	74.00	6.80	80.80	74.00	7.90	81.90
1925	70.00	6.80	76.80	70.00	7.90	77.90
1926	65.00	6.80	71.80	65.00	7.90	72.90
1927	65.00	6.80	71.80	65.00	7.90	72.90
1928	60.70	6.80	67.50	58.15	7.70	65.85
1929	55.20	6.80	62.00	54.30	7.70	62.00
1930	55.20	6.80	62.00	54.30	7.70	62.00
1931	50.20	6.80	57.00	49.30	7.70	57.00
1932	41.13	7.20	48.33	40.81	8.10	48.91
1933	34.05	7.10	41.15	32.00	8.00	40.00
1934	33.20	6.80	40.00	32.21	7.79	40.00
1935	33.20	6.80	40.00	31.37	8.63	40.00
1936	34.20	6.80	41.00	32.86	8.14	41.00
1937	35.70	6.80	42.50	34.54	7.96	42.50
1938	43.20	6.80	50.00	42.04	7.96	50.00
1939			50.00			50.00

Source: Coughlin, p. 98. First three columns, News Print Service Bureau, New York. Last three columns, Abitibi Power and Paper Co., Ltd., Bondholder Representative Committee, Exhibit A-8.

tified. As a result, seven U.S. newsprint manufacturers were indicted under the Sherman Act, and five pleaded nolo contendere.[17] The Canadian government intervened in the Canadian industry by fixing the domestic price at a lower level than the export or American price. Producers consequently attempted to export as much as they could, a practice that resulted in some shortages for Canadian newspapers during the period. The government naturally set up a Royal Commission to investigate the problem and also appointed a paper controller, but it is fair to say that all parties were dissatisfied until prices crashed in 1921.[18] Consumption of newsprint continued to increase in 1919 and 1920, partly because of the general postwar prosperity. "By 1920, consumption had so taxed the capacity of producing units, that some lots of newsprint were sold in the open market in June at $270 per ton although the bulk of it was supplied on contract at $112. Throughout 1920, reports of the United States Federal Trade Commission showed that an average price of $102.76 was maintained."[19]

Expansion was also aided by the unsettled conditions in Europe after World War I. Because the Scandinavian countries and Germany were not in a position to supply their former markets with pulp and paper products, Canadian goods were in great demand throughout the world to make up the deficiency. This led to a large increase in the capacity of the mills and in production which continued until 1921, when the worldwide postwar boom collapsed with the results that caused a relatively (i.e., relative to 1929–36) minor setback in industry everywhere, newsprint not being an exception. Toward the end of that year, however, the pulp and paper industry recovered and expanded at an explosive rate until the depression. Canada became the world's leading exporter in 1923 and the leading producer in 1925, positions she holds at the present. By the late 1930s the pulp and paper industry employed 16.2 percent of all gainfully occupied workers in Canada. It stood first in value of production from 1925, when it replaced flour mills, until 1935, when nonferrous-metal smelting and refining overtook it.[20]

The pulp and paper industry continued its rapid growth during the 1920s. Newsprint production grew from less than one million tons in 1920 to 2.7 million tons in 1929,[21] while the New York price of newsprint fell by almost one-half between those years (see Table 3 above). Yet (or consequently) by 1931 this industry was in great difficulty despite the fact that at no time during the 1920s did the price of newsprint fall to within ten dollars of the prewar price. "Mills having 58 percent of total Canadian capacity [were] in bankruptcy or receivership, or [were] passing, or [had] recently passed through, some form of reorganization. Furthermore, all these companies failed at a time when both the price of newsprint and the volume of production were substantially higher than today [1934], and they included five out of eight of the large newsprint manufacturers in North America."[22] What happened? Was overbuilding the problem, as C. P. Fell seems to suggest in the quote just above? In other words, is it a supply-side phenomenon, or is the depression somehow the key, with the failure of demand taking center stage? The next section investigates the industry and seeks to provide insight into its problems during the late 1920s and early 1930s.

II. OVEREXPANSION?

Table 4 provides output and output/capacity ratios between 1920 and 1938. These ratios are based on rated capacity, which attempts to measure capacity based on wood supplies, power supplies, etc. There are

Table 4. Estimated Rated Capacity, Production, Operating Ratio, and Excess Capacity of Canadian Newsprint Mills, 1920–1938

Year	*Total Rated Capacity*	*Production*	*Operating Ratio*
1920	917	876	95.5
1921	1,097	808	73.5
1922	1,134	1,082	95.2
1923	1,266	1,266	100.0
1924	1,474	1,353	91.8
1925	1,610	1,522	94.5
1926	1,931	1,882	97.4
1927	2,475	2,087	84.4
1928	2,993	2,381	79.7
1929	3,225	2,729	84.5
1930	3,600	2,504	69.5
1931	3,825	2,221	58.0
1932	3,840	1,914	49.7
1933	3,847	2,017	52.0
1934	3,861	2,599	67.3
1935	3,914	2,753	70.2
1936	3,921	3,191	81.4
1937	4,050	3,645	90.0
1938	4,204	2,625	62.4

Source: Coughlin, p. 82, from Newsprint Association of Canada.

other capacity ratios which have been reported and differ somewhat in level, but all show the same relative changes.[23] Rated capacity more than doubled between 1920 and 1926, but production rose as rapidly, so that the output/capacity ratio was actually higher in 1926 than in 1920. After that, capacity continued to grow, while increases in output lagged. Is this the evidence of overexpansion which so many others have cited? The problem is that the newsprint manufacturers had to make some projection of demand. The topic made for lively debate during this period. As early as 1921 Premier Taschereau of Quebec argued that overproduction was close at hand,[24] but that year appears to have been abnormal, and the industry went on expanding as output rose. The argument becomes more relevant as the middle 1920s are approached. The *Financial Post* quoted one manufacturer in 1925: "We newsprint manufacturers have been expecting overproduction in the industry for a long time, but it never seems to come—perhaps it never will."[25] Since it took between one and three years to bring a new mill into operation,[26] such a sentiment could easily lead to overcapacity if demand failed.

A 1925 headline in the *Financial Post*[27] read, "Warns of Overexpansion in Pulp and Paper." The article continued, "There seems to be no doubt whatever that this increase of, say, 50 percent [in capacity] will not be met by a corresponding increase in world consumption." Two weeks later, however, the *Post*'s headline read,[28] "Increased Consumption Big Factor in Newsprint Outlook. Bigger demand in States and curtailed exports from Europe may take care of larger production of Canadian mills." This attitude continued throughout the late 1920s. Howard Smith, the president of Howard Smith Paper Mills,[29] argued that, "while the expansion has, in a measure, been obliged to operate at less than rated capacity for the first time in a period of about seven years, the aggregate production of all lines of pulp and paper has been the greatest on record. There is reason to believe, too, that having withstood conditions brought about by this over-expansion for the year just closing [1927], the future can be faced with still greater confidence. The market demand is now on the upswing. The period of abnormal expansion has about run its course. From now on, the indications are, demand will gradually overtake ability to supply. The situation, in fact, is altogether hopeful." Capacity ratios declined in 1928, but rose in 1929, so that the *Financial Post* foresaw the need for expansion in the newsprint industry:

> One must bear in mind that in the thirty-two month period since 1925 rated capacity increased by 43 percent while the rise in demand during the same period was somewhat greater. This is significant because the spread between capacity and demand has steadily grown less. If new installations are at present kept to a minimum it will not be long before demand accounts for 90 percent of capacity. This, of course, is a mathematical promise and does not make allowance for the many disadventures which might crop up.[30]

Capacity rose in 1930 and 1931, but then remained almost constant until 1937. Production reached its low point in 1932 and regained its 1929 level in 1935. By 1937 the operating ratio was back up to 90 percent, but by then the price of newsprint was very much less than it had been ten years earlier.

In contrast to the day-to-day observers of the 1920s, just about everyone who has written on the topic since 1929 believes that there was overexpansion in the 1920s. C. P. Fell (1934) argued that "problems of the newsprint industry [in the depression] have been partly a result of rapid expansion in the post-war period."[31] E. A. Forsey (1935) believed that "one root cause of the trouble was over-expansion in the pre-depression years."[32] V. W. Bladen (1956) pointed out that "production did not increase quite as rapidly as capacity to produce. This expansion in production had a derpessing effect on prices."[33] Bladen also, however, listed all the technical improvements which reduced costs. A. E. Safarian

(1959), already quoted in the introduction, argued that investment opportunities in general had been thoroughly exploited in the 1920s. Specifically, with respect to the newsprint industry, he noted that operating ratios fell after 1926. "This decrease in operating ratios reflected the fact that the rise in capacity was more rapid than that in sales. The capacity of the industry was doubled from 1925 to 1930. Profits had been large, sales were rising, funds were readily available, and provincial governments made it easy to secure timber rights. Although prices were falling, costs also fell because of technological improvements."[34] This seems to be a careful statement, yet in his conclusion Safarian writes, "In newsprint, over-expansion had occurred."[35]

As early as 1932 Stanley T. Frame, writing in the *Harvard Business Review,* argued that "facilities for the manufacture of newsprint paper in continental North America have expanded rapidly since the World War until existing capacity far outstrips any reasonable demand which may be projected for as distant a date as 1940."[36] He ascribed this condition to ruinous prices, predatory competition, heavy capital losses, and reorganizations precipitated by the failure to earn charges on funded indebtedness. Clifton Coughlin, writing in 1939, argued:

> Serious mistakes have been made in the past. The speed in which the newsprint industry shifted to new areas in its search for more abundant supplies of raw material led to the duplication and over-extension of production facilities, over-capitalization and inevitably to the financial breakdown of the largest producers. Competition has been reckless, operations have been extravagant and there has been a general lack of coordination. Unreplaceable forest resources have been depleted without profit. Each and all of these have played their part in the instability of the newsprint industry.[37]

L. Ethan Ellis (1960), a longtime observer of the newsprint industry, also felt there was overinvestment in the 1920s:

> The enormous prices of 1916–1917 and 1919–1920, coupled with the ever-increasing appetite of the American public for news, attracted investment capital to the Canadian industry. This movement was stimulated by provincial authorities in Quebec and Ontario, anxious to exploit domestic resources of wood and water power and rivals in Dominion industrial development. Hovering on the fringes were the stock promoters so characteristic of the 1920s, not unwilling to inject a modicum of their peculiar brand of "water" into a situation ripe for speculative development. Under these stimuli Canadian output increased. . . . Supply soon exceeded demand, with consequent falling prices.[38]

Finally, John A. Guthrie, an outstanding student of the newsprint industry, also argues that there was too much expansion and that it was recognizable by 1925 or 1926:

> The most pressing problem facing the industry today [1941] is heavy excess capacity. This excess capacity is due to errors in judgement and short-sighted optimism on the part of provincial governments and executives of newsprint companies who, assisted and encouraged by financial promoters, sought to build a mighty industry without reckoning the future needs of newspaper publishers. The inevitable result was an over-built and heavily over-capitalized industry. From the vantage point of a decade or more later, it is easy to see and criticize the errors of the post-war period. But even in 1926 the inevitable outcome of feverish mill-building *must have been clearly apparent* [my italics]; and five years after that date new mills were still coming into operation. Little can be said in defense of the provincial governments, who vied with one another to grant new timber limits; and still less can be said for the activities of financial promoters.[39]

Guthrie argues that the provincial premiers of Ontario and Quebec clearly saw the dangers of overexpansion in 1925 when they announced that new timber leases would be granted only to existing firms. When defaults and receiverships began in 1931, industry spokesmen blamed the provincial governments who sought additional revenues for timber limits, to start new industries, and to create more employment. The provincial governments blamed the industry for capitalizing anticipated future profits and creating too much capital in the process.

So there is a disagreement between the industry spokesmen of the 1920s and the commentators since then who argue that there was overexpansion before the depression—that, in fact, it was an ex ante overexpansion and was not a result of the depression. Such a case can indeed be made, but, as will be shown below, it is not necessarily persuasive.

When the output figures are compared with the capacity ratios, the case for overproduction is greatly diminished. The usual argument is that, if producers had stopped expanding in 1926, they would not have gotten into the trouble they did. Thus Coughlin writes:

> The mills were operating at about 97 percent of capacity in that year [1926] and earnings were satisfactory. Had there been a pause for breath in 1926 all would perhaps be well today [1939], or at least not as serious as it is. The mills operating in 1926 plus those under construction and completed by the middle of 1927, had sufficient productive capacity to supply almost the total Canadian output up until 1935. But there was no pause.[40]

The problem with this argument is that it has shifted from ex ante to ex post. If there had been no depression then surely the production reached in 1936 and 1937, greater than 1929's rated capacity, would have come much sooner. In fact, the large increases in capacity in 1930 and 1931 combined with 1937's output would have left the industry with a capacity ratio (1937 output/1931 capacity) of .95, which is comparable to the ratios of the early 1920s.

Yet there is still an ex ante case to be made. Sometimes during the 1920s it seemed that manufacturers and bankers were more interested in the "paper" profits to be made through mergers and the issuance of new securities than in the profits to be made by producing paper.

It would be tedious to trace the many mergers and amalgamations of the 1920s. It is sufficient to note that, by 1930, the three largest companies—Abitibi (17.3 percent), Canadian International Paper (14.7 percent), and Canadian Power and Paper (20.8 percent)—controlled 52.8 percent of total newsprint-mill capacity in Canada.[41] This, in turn, was partially responsible for the poor financial performance in the early 1930s, which saw over half the industry in bankruptcy or receivership, or just having passed through some kind of reorganization. Too much of the expansion and too many of mergers were financed by bond sales. E. A. Forsey reports that "between 1925 and 1929 total investment in pulp and paper rose by almost $194 million, of which over $94 million, or 48½ percent, came from bonds or debentures, and over $44 million or 22½ percent, from preferred stocks.[42] The result was that, by the end of 1930, the aggregate capitalization of the thirteen largest firms (North America) was as follows: bonds, 31.0 percent; preferred stock, 14.0 percent; common stock, surplus, reserves, 48.5 percent; current liabilities, 6.4 percent.[43] Table 5 provides data on individual firms.

Table 5. How North American Newsprint Companies Finance Their Net Assets December 31, 1930

	Bonds	*Preferred Stock*	*Common Stock Surplus, Reserves*	*Current Liabilities*
Abitibi Power & Paper Co.	33.6%	24.1%	37.3%	4.9%
Canadian International Paper Co.	40.3	0	52.8	6.9
Canada Power & Paper Co.	48.6	16.3	24.7	10.4
Price Bros. & Co.*	16.2	9.3	69.3	5.2
St. Lawrence Corp.	13.2	47.8	32.9	6.1
Minnesota & Ontario Paper Co.	33.1	4.2	54.9	7.8
Great Northern Paper Co.	0	0	98.1	1.9
St. Croix Paper Co.	0	7.9	90.2	1.9
Consolidated Water Power & Paper Co.	8.8	0	85.2	6.0
Crown Willamette Paper Co.	30.0	0	63.4	6.6
Spruce Falls Power & Paper Co.	36.7	34.0	26.9	2.4
Bathurst Power & Paper Co.	0	0	99.5	0.5
Pacific Mills, Ltd.	20.2	9.8	66.8	3.2

Note:
* Year Ending February 28, 1931.
Source: Frame, p. 448.

It is seen that the big three in Canada—Abitibi Power and Paper (2,013 daily tons of capacity), Canadian International Paper (1,817 tons), and Canada Power and Paper (2,444 tons)—had significantly larger portions of their assets financed by bonds and preferred stock than did other companies in the United States and Canada. When prices and output declined during the depression, they were unable to pay interest and preferred dividends. The result was that Canada Power was acquired by Consolidated Paper in 1931 and had its capitalization scaled down.[44] Abitibi went into receivership,[45] and in 1937 International Paper reduced its preferred dividend accumulation by about $20 million and reduced the interest on its preferred stock to 5 percent.[46]

The capital intensity of the industry was a further problem for the industry. In a fully self-contained newsprint operation with its own supply of raw materials, the capital-output ratio may be five or six to one.[47] Guthrie estimates that, under normal circumstances, fixed costs absorbed about 40 percent of total costs.[48] This meant there was a large margin available for a firm to at least cover variable costs. Combined with an inelastic demand for newsprint, this situation led to ruinous price competition during the early 1930s.

The low ratio of variable to total costs combines with other pricing peculiarities which added to the difficulties. Price and demand are not necessarily inversely related in this industry. A reduction in the price of newsprint will not lead to an increase in demand for newsprint, for it is unlikely that a newspaper could increase its circulation even if the reduction in newsprint cost were sufficiently large to lead to a reduction in the price of the newspaper. Conversely, an increase in newsprint costs will not lead to a reduction in demand. Hence, neither producer nor publisher affects the demand, and, somewhat surprisingly, neither does the final consumer. Most important is the advertiser, since a newspaper normally contains 40–50 percent advertising matter.[49] Of course, the amount of advertising will bear some relationship to the number of readers.

A second peculiarity of the pricing system was the unusual type of contract. Buyers and sellers of newsprint signed an agreement extending for five or ten years with the amount of paper, but not the price, specified in the contract. Ninety-eight percent of American production in 1929 was disposed of under this system.[50] The contract used was an interlocking one in which the seller agreed to meet the lowest price that any seller with at least 100,000 tons of capacity established.[51] This price was then determined at six- or twelve-month intervals. Usually the price adopted was a figure agreed upon by certain large "price-fixing companies, including International, Great Northern, Abitibi, Price Brothers, and Consolidated Paper in the East."[52] In fact, International Paper usually fixed the price between 1923 and 1928, but had considerably more difficulty after that.[53] Needless to say, newsprint manufacturers did not like this pricing arrangement, and by the late 1930s no more than 5 percent of contracts retained the interlocking clause.[54] Table 3 showed these prices.

There were two major attempts at price fixing in the late 1920s. While they do not prove there was excess capacity, they certainly indicate that it was a possibility. The first attempt was a joint sales company, the Canadian Newsprint Company (Ltd.), which comprised the largest Canadian mills and which came into being on May 1, 1927. Its purpose was to make all sales contracts for member firms and allocate production on an equitable basis.

The weakness of the organization was that not all producers joined and thus were in a position to undercut Canadian Newsprint's prices. Abitibi later argued that it lost 125,000 tons of business because of this. The company (Canadian Newsprint) did get a large contract with the Hearst chain for a long period of time at a specified price, but as soon as other consumers found out about the lower price, the Newsprint Company was forced to reduce its price under the terms of the interlocking contracts. In any case, it would have been forced to lower prices or lose business to nonmember firms. A new executive for CN refused to fulfill the Hearst contract. Hearst sued, member firms dropped out, and by December 1928, the Canadian Newsprint Company ceased to exist, but this did not solve the producers' problems.[55]

International's role as price setter came to an end in 1928. It had announced a price of $65 per ton for 1929, but in the scramble for the Hearst contract it was forced to reduce its price to $57. Canadian manufacturers, unwilling to meet this price, protested to the premiers of Ontario and Quebec. The result was the Newsprint Institute of Canada, which was formed in December 1928. In effect, this was another selling pool, but this time it was on a larger scale. International did not join either attempt because of fear of prosecution under the Sherman Antitrust Act, but, after a protracted debate, a price of $62 was set.[56] Bitterness continued between the Institute and International for the next few years. Institute mills also earned the ill will of their customers during the period by trying to keep prices up. The result was that Institute mills operated at much lower rates of capacity than did non-Institute mills, as Table 6 makes clear.

The differences were particularly large in 1930 and 1931. In 1931, for example, Institute mills operated at 45 percent of capacity, while non-Institute mills operated at almost 91 percent. Price Brothers, one of the soundest and most conservative members, left the Institute in 1931. Others concluded they would be better off outside the organization, so

Table 6. Rate of Capacity at Which Newsprint Mills in North America Operated, 1929–1931

Year	*Canadian Institute Mills*	*Canadian Non-Institute Mills*	*Total Canadian Mills*	*Newfoundland Mills*	*United States Mills*
1929	81.0%	98.0%	86.4%	104.5%	80.0%
1930	59.3	93.0	70.1	101.1	76.0
1931	45.4	90.8	58.0	98.0	65.4

Source: Coughlin, p. 128 from News Print Service Bureau.

it ceased to be a factor in the newsprint industry by early 1931.[57] Other attempts were made in the early thirties to stabilize prices and shares of output, but all ended in failure.[58]

Up to this point, questions have been raised which suggest that the case for ex ante overcapacity is not as strong as many have believed. The case can be made more directly. The idea of profit maximization at least suggests that we must be very careful in proposing that firms did not act in their own best interests. Trevor Dick calculated the return to capital in the pulp and paper industry, broader than the newsprint industry, between 1919 and 1929. He found net income as a percentage of capital to be 10.4 percent in 1921 and 11.1 percent in 1929. The 1924 rate was 11.3, the 1925 rate was 13.2, and the 1926 rate was 13.0 percent, so the 1929 rate was somewhat lower, but it was still a good return.[59]

A second point is that capacity is not a once-and-for-all contract. Some excess capacity may disappear under certain conditions. "Much of what appears to be excess capacity at any one time may actually be obsolete plant which embodies old, uneconomic technology. In this case, a major increase in demand could be temporarily met by bringing old plant back on the line, but after a while producers will replace this plant with newer plant embodying up-to-date technology."[60] In this respect C. P. Fell provides data from an unspecified time in the early 1930s which show that of a daily capacity of 11,945 tons, 12 percent was rated high-cost, 38 percent less efficient, and only 50 percent efficient.[61]

A related point is that capacity is a very slippery concept. A mill may have effective machine capacity but no wood. Another mill may have wood but lack immediate water for power. A third mill might not be able to cover variable costs at the going price for newsprint and be therefore maximizing its profit (minimizing its loss) by remaining idle.[62]

A third reason for not accepting the overcapacity arguments insofar as they are based upon the decline in price of newsprint during the 1920s is that the decline in price may have been due to scale economies. This industry, like many other industries, was subject to significant economies of large-scale production techniques. The possibility of adoption of these cost-saving techniques became especially important during the 1920s as each of the various firms had to increase its efficiency in order to remain competitive in the face of falling prices. V. W. Bladen lists the following cost improvements:

> In the woods tractors and chutes supplanted horses, and railways penetrated into regions not well supplied with natural water transportation. The method of storing the vast stocks of pulpwood made necessary by the seasonal character of operations in the woods was improved. In making mechanical pulp artificial stones of uniform quality displaced the natural grindstones which frequently had defects. "Magazine" and "pocket" grinders were introduced to increase the capacity of grindstones. New methods in sulphite production decreased the cooking time and increased the yield of cellulose. Economy of power was practiced: the peak load was reduced, electric steam boilers were introduced, and surplus power was sold in increasing quantities, thus providing additional revenue. Improved methods of removing water in the paper machine permitted higher speed production of wider sheets. The maximum speed was increased from about 1,000 feet of newsprint per minute in 1920, to 1,350 in 1940. . . . In 1910 machines with a speed of 500 feet per minute were not common; in 1900 the maximum speed was 150 feet per minute. The widest sheet was not much over 200 inches in 1920; it was 264 inches in 1928. . . . In 1910, 120 inches was not common. The average daily capacity of the machines was only 10 tons in 1880; by 1940 it was nearly 200 tons. The cost of transporting pulpwood to the mill, and paper to the market, was reduced by the development of special ships adapted to these tasks.[63]

Such a change in supply conditions would allow only the lower cost or more efficient firms to remain in business.

It is likely that International set the pricing during the 1920s at a level allowing the most efficient firms to capture economic rents with other firms hard pressed at the margin. In such a situation, new capital investment may be a necessity. For example, as the lower-cost firms pass on their reduction in costs to the consumer in the form of lower prices, the firms closest to the margin must either innovate or go out of business. Therefore, in a growing market, a highly capitalized firm will remain more competitive than one with low fixed costs. This point must be emphasized since often it is the case that a hypothesis of excess capacity or overinvestment is made from a purely technical relationship (the ratio of production to capacity output). The technical relationship is completely inappropriate as a measuring rod of excess capacity. From a firm's point of view, the relationship between production and capacity output depends upon two economic factors:

1. the expected rate of growth in demand as compared to the gestation period of investment expenditures. For example, since investment decisions take at least two years to materialize, then, if the rate

of growth in demand is expected to be very rapid, the firm on the lower short-run average total-cost curve is at an advantage over the firm on the higher-curve one, even though its technical production capacity ratio is significantly lower than one.

2. the extent of market imperfections. For example, in an oligopoly situation a few low-cost firms might share 50 percent of the market while the high-cost firms share the remainder. This could give a production capacity ratio much lower than one. Yet from an economic-theory viewpoint the situation is viable as price leadership has been established.[64]

The ex ante argument for overcapacity is also weakened by the introduction of radio. The dramatic increase in the number of radios in the late 1920s caused advertisers to switch from newspapers. "While general business in 1937 had recovered to within 8 percent of the 1929 level, newspaper advertising lineage was only 74 percent of the pre-depression figure. In 1929 radio obtained approximately 3 percent of the American advertiser's dollar whilst it 1937 in obtained 13 percent. Over this same period the share spent on newspaper advertising declined from 69 percent to 60 percent."[65] Perfect foresignt would have overcome this problem, but, combined with the depression, it proved very serious indeed to the industry.

Finally, a wholesale index of the price of newsprint compared to the wholesale price of all commodities shows that newsprint prices were really not out of line until 1933. Up to that time newsprint prices may even have been a little higher, as Table 7 indicates.

Overall, this section may be concluded by arguing that, although different opinions have been expressed about whether there was overcapacity, the problem has not been solved.

III. A TEST OF OVERCAPACITY

In an attempt to draw some conclusions from these many strands, some type of definition of capacity must be used to test for overcapacity. In many studies the question of "overcapacity" is analyzed purely in terms of technical data. The engineer derives some measure of theoretical capacity; actual output is compared to this and a capacity ratio is found. But the economist may properly question this figure. If we believe that cost curves are approximately U-shaped, then the point of lowest average total cost will come far before a "theoretical" capacity limit is reached. "Rate capacity," the concept used in Table 4, is more than a simple technical concept, but it still does not take account of such economic factors as the cost of capital or wage rates. It should also be noted that

Table 7. Canadian Index Numbers of Wholesale Prices of All Commodities and of Newsprint, 1913–1938 (1926 = 100)

Year	*All Commodities*	*Newsprint*
1913	64.0	56.9
1914	65.5	58.5
1915	70.4	57.9
1916	84.3	59.2
1917	114.3	76.4
1918	127.4	90.2
1919	134.0	104.8
1920	155.9	151.9
1921	110.0	155.1
1922	97.3	108.1
1923	98.0	113.9
1924	99.4	111.5
1925	102.6	106.3
1926	100.0	100.0
1927	97.7	100.0
1928	96.4	97.7
1929	95.6	84.9
1930	86.6	84.9
1931	72.1	77.2
1932	66.7	66.8
1933	67.1	52.6
1934	71.6	51.1
1935	72.1	51.1
1936	74.6	52.6
1937	84.6	58.1
1938	78.6	68.0

Source: Coughlin, p. 202, from Dominion Bureau of Statistics, *Prices and Price Indices* (Ottawa: The King's Printer).

for the concept of overinvestment to be meaningful it is necessary to establish that the overinvestment occurred ex ante. It is true that there was too much capital in various industries in the early 1930s, once income had collapsed, but that does not mean there was too much investment in the 1920s. Overinvestment would be proved only if it were shown that there would have been too much investment even if income had continued to grow at the same rate as in the 1920s.

Recently, Bert Hickman developed a technique for measuring economic capacity using the stock-adjustment model.[66] L. J. Mercer and W. D. Morgan then applied this model to the American automobile industry in the 1920s and 1930s.[67] This paper follows their model to estimate capacity for the pulp and paper industry, not the newsprint industry, because of lack of data. The basic stock-adjustment equation makes net investment some function of the difference between desired capital stock this period and actual capital stock last period. So

$$I_t = \gamma\,[K_t^* - (1 - \delta)\,K_{t-1}] \tag{1}$$

$$I_t = \text{gross investment in period } t$$

where

$$K_t^* = \text{desired capital stock in period } t$$
$$K_{t-1} = \text{actual capital stock in period } t-1$$
$$\gamma = \text{speed of adjustment function.}$$

If $\gamma = .5$, then half of the difference between desired capital this period and actual capital last period will be closed in this period. Equation (1) becomes slightly more complicated by positing that investment will also depend on the real cash flow available for investment. Thus,

$$I_t = \gamma_1\,[K_t^* - (1 - \delta)\,K_{t-1}] + \gamma_2\Pi_t \tag{2}$$

where Π_t = real cash flow available for investment.

The problem with estimating this equation is that there is no acceptable capital-stock series. To overcome this problem, Equation (2) is transformed following a procedure used by Robert Coen[68] and later adopted by Mercer and Morgan,[69] which transforms capital, using the net-investment series, by substituting the definition of past investment for actual capital stock:

$$K_{t-1} \equiv \sum_{i=o}^{\infty} (1 - \delta)^i\, I_{t-1-i}. \tag{3}$$

After subtracting I_{t-1} from both sides of Equation (2), the final specification of the model becomes

$$I_t - \gamma_1\,[K_t^* - (1 - \delta)\,K_{t-1}^*] + (1 - \gamma_1)(1 - \delta)\,I_{t-1} + \gamma_2\,[\Pi_t - (1 - \delta)\,\Pi_{t-1}]. \tag{4}$$

In order to estimate this equation, specification of K_t^* becomes necessary. K_t^*, desired real capital stock, is made a function of output and a ratio of wage/capital cost. Thus

$$K_t^* = a_o + a_1 Y_t + a_2\,\frac{\Delta W_t}{\Delta P_{ct}} \tag{5}$$

where Y_t = gross value of product from *Historical Statistics of Canada* (*HSC* hereafter), Series K175, deflated by the wholesale price index for wood and wood products, *HSC*, Series J39, using 1926 as a base.

ΔW_t = the percentage change in the wage rate, *HSC*, Series K170 and K171, converted to an hourly rate assuming a work year of 2080 hours.

ΔP_{ct} = the percentage change in the price of capital goods (*Px* interest rate). *P* is the price of producers' equipment, *HSC*, Series J66, and the interest rate is *HSC*, H591, the corporate bond yield.

This equation tells us that, if the real gross value of product (*Y*) increases, manufacturers would like to increase real capital. Likewise an increase in the wage rate or a decrease in the price of capital goods would also increase desired capital.

Real cash flow was defined to be gross value of production minus salaries and wages, fuel and electricity, and cost of materials deflated by the producers' goods wholesale price index.[70]

The difference in desired stocks from Equation (4) is defined as

$$K_t^* - (1 - \delta)\, K_{t-1}^* = \delta a_o + a_1\, \Delta Y_t + a_2 \frac{\Delta W_t}{\Delta C_t} \tag{6}$$

where for any variable X, $\Delta X_t \equiv X_t - (1 - \delta)\, X_{t-1.}$

Substituting (6) into (4) and adding a stochastic error term yields the Equation (7) to be estimated

$$\begin{aligned} I_t = {} & \gamma_1 \delta a_o + \gamma_1 a_1\, \Delta Y_t + \gamma_1 a_2 \frac{\Delta W_t}{\Delta C_t} \\ & + (1 - \gamma_1)(1 - \delta)\, I_{t-1} + \gamma_2 \Delta \Pi_t + U_t. \end{aligned} \tag{7}$$

The depreciation rate, δ, was assumed to be 5 percent.[71] Various weighting schemes were tried for *Y* and Π. The equation performed best when *Y* was defined as Y_{t-2}. This implies that desired capital in time *t* would depend on income two years earlier.

The equation was then estimated for the years 1921–40, using ordinary least squares with *t* values in brackets.

$$\begin{aligned} I_t = {} & \underset{(-0.01)}{-\,39.71} + \underset{(1.58)}{.105\, \Delta Y_{t-2}} + \underset{(1.47)}{1472.31} \frac{\Delta W_t}{\Delta P_{ct}} \\ & + \underset{(6.33)}{.842\, I_{t-1}} + \underset{(.92)}{.146\, \Delta NV_t} \end{aligned} \tag{8}$$

$$\overline{B}^2 = .7177 \quad df = 15 \quad SEE = 9170.4 \quad DW = 2.36 \quad \min RHO = -.01$$

The next step is to estimate capacity output. The analysis follows Mercer-Morgan. The equation derived above makes output, relative prices, and cash flow the determinants of investment. But these variables may also be used to determine a measure of "economic" capacity. "The investment equation used here implies a precise relationship between capital and the cost concept of capacity where capacity output is that of minimum total unit cost."[72] Capacity output (*Yc*), using end-period capital and adjusting resources to obtain minimum cost, is found by substituting actual capital for desired capital in Equation (5). The result is

$$Yc_t = \frac{K_t - a_o - a_2 \dfrac{\Delta W_t}{\Delta Pc_t}}{a_1} \tag{9}$$

This measure of capacity assumes that investment is a function of the difference between expected and capacity output and reverses the original hypothesis that investment is a function of the difference between desired and actual capital stock. This means that the capacity figures are only as good as the original investment equation.[73]

At this point we can no longer finesse the lack of a capital series. The capital-stock series used was calculated from figures obtained in Hood and Scott's *Output, Labour, and Capital in the Canadian Economy,* a study for the Royal Commission on Canada's Economic Prospects. The appendix provides the details on these estimates. The estimates seem to give us a capital stock series that behaves well. The major discrepancy between the actual series and the estimates derived here would probably be the result of fluctuation in the depreciation rate.

Table 8 gives us "economic" capacity utilization rates based on Equation (7) where actual and capacity output are denominated in real dollars. A capacity ratio of one indicates that the industry is producing at the bottom of the U-shaped cost curve, or at the point of lowest average total cost. A ratio greater than one means that firms are producing above lowest average total costs on the rising portion of the cost curve, which is a signal to expand. Likewise a ratio less than one indicates that the industry has excess capacity and does not need to expand. The results in Table 8 indicate that the industry should have been expanding through 1926. In 1927 the ratio dropped to .91. The next year it dropped to .79, but rose slightly to .81 in 1929. The ratio dropped slightly in 1930, but then dropped precipitously in 1931 and 1932, when it reached a low of .57. After that it began to increase, and was over one—the signal to expand—in 1936 and the remaining years of the decade with the exception of 1938.

Table 8. "Economic" Capacity Ratios in the Pulp and Paper Industry, Growth of Production in Pulp and Paper and Newsprint, and "Rated" Capacity in the Newsprint Industry.

Year	*"Economic" Capacity: Pulp and Paper*	*Growth Output: Pulp and Paper*	*Growth Output: Newsprint*	*Growth "Rated" Capacity: Newsprint*
1921		−21.0%	−7.8%	19.6%
1922	1.62	38.8	33.9	3.4
1923	1.42	15.2	17.0	11.6
1924	1.28	−0.4	6.9	16.4
1925	1.10	12.5	12.5	9.2
1926	1.02	16.5	21.3	19.9
1927	.91	1.5	10.9	28.2
1928	.79	10.0	14.0	20.9
1929	.81	11.5	14.6	7.8
1930	.77	−10.0	−8.2	11.6
1931	.62	−12.5	−11.3	6.3
1932	.57	−15.9	−13.8	0.4
1933	.69	11.9	5.4	0.2
1934	.85	22.0	28.9	0.3
1935	.88	6.4	5.9	1.4
1936	1.07	16.0	15.9	0.2
1937	1.13	14.7	14.2	3.3
1938	.92	−28.7	−28.0	3.8
1939	1.05	13.6	9.7	
1940	1.40	27.0	19.7	

Sources: (1) *HSC,* Series K175 and Equation (7)
(2) *HSC,* Series K148
(3) Table 4, Column 2
(4) Table 4, Column 1

The difficulty with interpreting these results is that the "economic" capacity ratio refers to the pulp and paper industry, while most of the discussion has focused on the newsprint industry. This is not a serious problem, for newsprint made up over half of total pulp and paper production.[74] Nevertheless, to facilitate interpretation, the growth outputs of both pulp and paper and newsprint are provided in Table 8. It is seen there the two growth rates move in approximate harmony.

The "economic" capacity ratios basically confirm the analysis developed in the second section of the paper and may be compared to total "rated" capacity, which is a measure of what firms actually did. The early 1920s were years when production was steadily bumping against capacity, but there was a two- or three-year lag between increased production and the time when new capacity came on line. In 1926 or 1927 capacity caught up with production, but with the lag in putting new capital into place, it is not surprising that new investment continued at a very rapid rate, even though our "economic" capacity ratio indicates that the industry should not have been expanding.

While some justification can be made for the increased capital expenditures in 1927 and 1928, there seems little reason to have continued such a rapid enlargement of facilities in 1929, 1930, or 1931. It is true that the growth of output remained strong in 1928 and 1929, but that did not make expansion a necessity, especially in view of the just-completed substantial expansion in 1927 and 1928. This is well confirmed by our "economic" capacity ratio, which fell below one after 1926. After 1931 there was little growth in capacity until 1937, when, again, "economic" capacity moved above one in 1936, which was the signal to expand.

I conclude from this analysis that there was, indeed, ex ante overexpansion in the late twenties, something that I was more or less unwilling to accept until this analysis was performed. Yet this does not mean that the collapse of demand should be ignored. If demand had remained strong (no depression or no switch of advertising) the newsprint industry would have weathered its excess optimism much better than it did.

IV. CONCLUSION

This paper has examined the pulp and paper industry between 1900 and 1940. The first part traced the growth of the industry over this period. Next, the question of overexpansion was considered in the context of ex ante supply-side changes versus ex post demand collapse. A slight presumption was put forward that demand was more important. Finally, a test of "economic" capacity was made. Here, it was assumed that desired capital was a function of output, cash flow, and the relative price of capital and labor. The results indicated that there was indeed ex ante overexpansion in the late 1920s. But the argument concludes that the industry would not have been in nearly as much trouble during the eary 1930s if demand had not collapsed.

APPENDIX

In order to estimate capacity output in the pulp and paper industry it is necessary to estimate both a capital-stock and an investment series from 1920 to 1940. Gross new investment in the pulp and paper industry from 1926 to 1940 is found in the Dominion Bureau of Statistics *Private and Public Investment*. Table 9 shows the detail. For the years 1920–25,

Table 9. Gross New Investment in the Pulp and Paper Industry (Millions)

Year	*Construction*	*Machinery and Equipment*	*Total*
1926	$21.4	$22.5	$43.9
1927	23.7	23.7	47.4
1928	31.8	17.2	49.0
1929	16.0	9.6	25.6
1930	4.4	20.8	25.2
1931	11.3	1.9	13.2
1932	2.1	1.2	3.3
1933	0.1	0.7	0.8
1934	0.8	2.7	3.5
1935	2.2	2.4	4.6
1936	1.5	3.6	5.1
1937	4.2	6.4	10.6
1938	2.6	4.6	7.2
1939	3.9	2.2	6.1
1940	5.1	9.8	14.9

Source: Private and Public Investment, p. 160.

imports of pulp and paper machinery for fiscal years ending March 31 are all that is available. They appear in various *Canada Yearbooks.* These figures were adjusted to calendar year estimates using the formula:

$$\text{Imports}_{ct} = .75 \text{ imports}_{ft+1} + .25 \text{ imports}_{ft}$$

where

$$ct = \text{calendar year } t$$
$$ft = \text{fiscal year } t.$$

The calendar-year import series was then blown up to real gross investment using the relationship between imports and gross investment in 1926.

Finally, the whole series was deflated by *HSC,* Series J65, the producer's goods wholesale index.

ACKNOWLEDGMENTS

This study was made possible by a grant from the Canadian Social Science and Humanities Research Council. I would like to thank Robert E. Gallman and John J. Madden, who read earlier drafts. Jane Forster, Baiba Grant, and Mike McDermott provided research help. The final draft of this paper was written while I was visiting associate professor at the University of North Carolina–Chapel Hill.

NOTES

1. Safarian (1959), p. 15.
2. Coughlin (1939), p. 7.
3. United States Federal Trade Commission (1917), pp. 26–27.
4. *Ibid.*, p. 26.
5. *Ibid.*
6. *Ibid.*, pp. 29–30.
7. Burley (1970), p. 335.
8. Coughlin (1939), p. 7.
9. United States Federal Trade Commission (1917), pp. 27–28.
10. Burley (1970), p. 337.
11. Reich (1925 or 1926), p. 11. Burley (1970), p. 348, includes a section from *The Report of the Royal Commission on Pulpwood,* Ottawa (1924), which estimates output figures for selected years.

Production of Wood-Pulp in Canada

Year	*Ground Wood Tons*	*Sulfite Tons*	*Sulfate Tons*	*Soda Tons*	*Total Tons*
1908	278,570	82,311	—	2,178	363,079
1912	499,226	142,978	33,469	6,959	682,632
1916	827,258	363,972	100,977	3,877	1,296,084
1920	1,090,114	675,733	188,487	5,768	1,960,102
1922	1,241,185	678,878	217,862	793	2,150,251

12. Canada, Dominion Bureau of Statistics, *The Pulp and Paper Industry, 1936,* p. 9.
13. *Ibid.*
14. Coughlin (1939), p. 190.
15. See note 11.
16. Coughlin (1939), p. 97.
17. Guthrie (1946), p. 198.
18. See Travis (1979), pp. 29–54.
19. Coughlin (1939), p. 53. Prices might vary from the established price. Guthrie (1941) writes (p. 117), "Unofficial reductions and rebates are at times granted. It is also possible to give secret rebates under the guise of damage to rolls in transit." He suggests (p. 109) that this happened after the peak in 1929. It should also be noted that Canadian firms gained in the early 1930s when Canada devalued, while U.S. firms did not. Since prices were quoted in U.S. dollars, the Canadian dollar return increased to these manufacturers.
20. *Pulp and Paper Industry, 1938,* p. 2.
21. Coughlin (1939), p. 82.
22. Fell (1934), pp. 50–51.
23. Other capacity ratios appear in Urquhart and Buckley (1965), K174 and 175; Bladen (1941), p. 159; and Bladen (1956), p. 182.
24. Ellis (1960), p. 131.
25. *Financial Post,* November 27, 1925, p. 1.
26. Federal Trade Commission (1917), p. 12, one–two years; Ellis (1960), pp. 197–98, about two years; Guthrie (1941), p. 125, two–three years.
27. *Financial Post,* October 30, 1925, p. 1.
28. *Ibid.*, November 13, 1925, p. 1.
29. *Monetary Times,* January 6, 1928.
30. *Financial Post,* September 26, 1929, p. 22.

31. Fell (1934), p. 40.
32. Forsey (1935).
33. Bladen (1956), 181.
34. Safarian (1959), p. 44.
35. *Ibid.*, p. 235. Safarian also writes (p. 44), "The industry had obviously over-expanded and would have required considerable adjustments even without a depression."
36. Frame (1932), p. 441.
37. Coughlin (1939), p. 3.
38. Ellis (1960), p. 125.
39. Guthrie (1941), p. 228.
40. Coughlin (1939), p. 74.
41. Guthrie (1941), p. 65, and chapter 5 for a list of mergers. J. G. Cummins, "Concentration and Mergers in the Pulp and Paper Industries of the U.S. and Canada," unpublished Ph.D. dissertation, Johns Hopkins, 1960, pp. 41 and 62 (as reported in Dick, 1973, p. 7), finds fewer mergers of newsprint firms between 1922 and 1932 than either before or after.
42. Forsey (1935), p. 502. "The Canada Power and Paper merger involved issue of $35,466,700 of new debentures for common stock of Laurentide and Wayagamack, and the Abitibi mergers increased preferred stocks by $16,012,300. While total investment rose by 28½ percent, interest on funded debt rose by almost $7,000,000, or 82 percent, and preferred dividend requirements by almost $3,500,000 or 79 percent." In 1934 (?) the debt charges per ton at various operating ratios were as follows when the f.o.b. mill price was between $33.20 and $33.60.

	Abitibi	*Can. Int. Paper*	*Consol-idated**	*Donna-conna*	*Great Lakes*	*Lake St. John*	*Price Bros.*
At 60 percent	$5.95	$5.96	$8.27	$8.74	$9.52	$9.90	$3.63
At 75 percent	4.77						
At 100 percent	3.57	3.57	4.95	5.25	5.71	6.34	2.17

Note:
* After a 34 percent reduction in funded debt.

43. Frame (1932), p. 448.
44. Guthrie (1941), p. 68.
45. *Ibid.*, p. 67.
46. *Ibid.*, p. 67.
47. Coughlin (1939), p. 18.
48. Guthrie (1941), p. 116.
49. *Ibid.*, pp. 18–19, 48.
50. Guthrie (1941), p. 102.
51. Coughlin (1939), p. 20.
52. Guthrie (1941), p. 107.
53. *Ibid.*, pp. 107–8; see Federal Trade Commission (1930), pp. 40–48, for a good discussion of pricing.
54. Safarian (1959), p. 44n.
55. Coughlin (1939), pp. 114–17.
56. Federal Trade Commission (1930), pp. 38–44.
57. Coughlin (1939), pp. 118–30.
58. *Ibid.*, pp. 130–39.
59. Dick (1973), p. 50.

60. Branson (1972), p. 214.
61. Fell (1934), p. 51.
62. Bladen (1941), p. 159.
63. Bladen (1956), p. 181.
64. The Abitibi Power and Paper Company acquired the Murray Bay Paper Company, but it was never operated by Abitibi since it was an inefficient mill. See Bladen (1956), p. 185.
65. Coughlin (1939), p. 175.
66. Hickman (1964).
67. Mercer and Morgan (1972).
68. Coen, pp. 200–211.
69. Mercer and Morgan (1972), pp. 1217–18.
70. Urquhart and Buckley (1965), Series K171, 172, 173, 175, and J65.
71. Calculated depreciation rates were 4.9 percent—1937, 5.9 percent—1938, 5.1 percent—1939, and 5.3 percent—1940; hence 5.0 percent was adopted.
72. Mercer and Morgan (1972), p. 1221.
73. *Ibid.*
74. Table 1 showed that domestic consumption of newsprint increased from about 70 percent of total production in 1920 to about 80 percent in 1940. Newsprint totaled 72 percent of paper production in 1920, 85 percent in 1930, and 81 percent in 1940. See *Pulp and Paper Industry, 1951,* p. H-12.

REFERENCES

Bladen, V. W. (1941), *An Introduction to Political Economy*. Toronto: University of Toronto Press.

——— (1956), *An Introduction to Political Economy,* revised edition. Toronto: University of Toronto Press.

Branson, William H. (1972), *Macroeconomic Theory and Policy*. New York: Harper and Row.

Burley, Kevin, ed. (1970), *The Development of Canada's Staples, 1867–1939: A Documentary Collection*. Toronto: McClelland and Stewart.

Canada, Dominion Bureau of Statistics (1947), *Private and Public Investment in Canada*. Ottawa: The King's Printer.

Canada, Dominion Bureau of Statistics, *The Pulp and Paper Industry*. Ottawa: The King's Printer, various years.

Canada, Royal Commission on Canadian Economic Prospects (1957), William Hood and Anthony Scott, *Output, Labour, and Capital in the Canadian Economy*. Ottawa: The Queen's Printer.

Coen, Robert (1968), "Effects of Tax Policy on Investment in Manufacturing. *The American Economic Review* 58(May):200–211.

Coughlin, Clifton Rexford (1939), "The Newsprint Industry in Canada." Unpublished M.A., McGill University.

Dick, Trevor (1973), "A Model of Early Twentieth Century Industrial Expansion with an Application to Canadian Newsprint." Unpublished paper, Department of Economics, University of Western Ontario.

Ellis, L. Ethan (1960), *Print Paper Pendulum: Group Pressures and the Price of Newsprint*. New Brunswick, N.J.: Rutgers University Press.

Fell, C. P. (1934), "The Newsprint Industry." In H. A. Innis and A. F. W. Plumptne (eds.), *The Canadian Economy and Its Problems*. Toronto: The Canadian Institute of International Affairs.

The Financial Post. Toronto: Maclean-Hunter, various issues.

Forsey, E. A. (1935), "The Pulp and Paper Industry." *The Canadian Journal of Economics and Political Science* 1 (August):501–509.

Frame, Stanley T. (1932), "Planning for the Newsprint Industry." *Harvard Business Review* 10(July):441–452.

Guthrie, John A. (1941), *The Newsprint Paper Industry: An Economic Analysis*. Cambridge, Mass.: Harvard University Press.

——— (1946), "Price Regulation in the Newsprint Industry." *Quarterly Journal of Economics* 60:194–219.

Hickman, Bert G. (1964), "On a New Method of Capacity Estimation." *Journal of the American Statistical Association* 59(June):529–549.

Mercer, L. J. and W. D. Morgan (1972), "Investment, Demand Capacity, and Capacity Utilization." *The Journal of Political Economy* 80(Nov./Dec.):1124–1231.

Monetary Times. Toronto, various issues.

Reich, Nathan (1925 or 1926), *The Pulp and Paper Industry in Canada*. Toronto: The Macmillan Co. of Canada, n.d.

Safarian, A. E. (1959), *The Canadian Economy in the Great Depression*. Carleton Library Series, No. 54. Toronto: McClelland and Stewart, reprinted 1970.

Travis, Tom (1979), *Canadian Manufacturers and the Federal Government, 1917–1931*. Toronto: University of Toronto Press.

United States Federal Trade Commission (1930), *Newsprint Paper Industry*. U.S. Senate (71st Congress, Special Session of the Senate, Document 214 [1930]), Washington, D.C.: U.S. Government Printing Office.

——— (1917), *Report of the Federal Trade Commission on the Newsprint Industry*. Washington, D.C.: U.S. Government Printing Office.

Urquhart, M. C., and K. A. H. Buckley (1965), *Historical Statistics of Canada*. Toronto: The Macmillan Co. of Canada Ltd.

E. W. KEMMERER: THE ORIGINS AND IMPACT OF THE "MONEY DOCTOR'S" MONETARY ECONOMICS

Bruce R. Dalgaard

I. INTRODUCTION

The quest for a proper definition of "money" is not an esoteric pursuit of an abstract notion. It is extremely practical, especially today. "Money," whatever it may be, is used by the government as one of its main tools to move the economy toward the goals of full employment, maximum growth, a stable price level, and continuing prosperity. One of the reasons that achievement of these goals seems to escape government planners is that the tool which they are using is anything but a precision instru-

Variations in Business and Economic History:
Essays in Honor of Donald L. Kemmerer
Research in Economic History, Suppl. 2, pages 31–44.

ISBN: 0-89232-262-4

ment. The problem of how to define "money" has plagued economic theorists for most of the present century.

Nor is another problem which is threatening today's world—the decaying of monetary systems of many lands—a new development. It too has attracted the attention of monetary theorists for a long time.

Among those who wrestled with these two problems for many years was Professor Edwin Walter Kemmerer of Princeton University, known in his day as the "money doctor." From his pioneering studies in quantitative economics to his financial advisory missions, E. W. Kemmerer had "a career in the application of economic doctrine to public affairs which . . . has few if any parallels" ("E. W. Kemmerer Obituary," March 1946).

For over two decades, from before World War I to the 1930s, Kemmerer was one of the most prominent economists in America and around the world. To this day he is still renowned in a number of foreign countries. Kemmerer's early writings gained him prominence, but his financial advisory missions made him the "money doctor" to much of the world.

His career as an applied economist began with his appointment as a financial adviser to the U.S. Philippine Commission in 1903. He went on to serve as adviser to Mexico (1917), Guatemala (1919 and 1924), Colombia (1923 and 1930), South Africa (1924–25), Chile (1925), Poland (1926), Ecuador (1926–27), Bolivia (1927), China (1929), Peru (1931), Turkey (1934), and Liberia (1936). In 1922 he was a U.S. trade commissioner in South America and in 1924 he accompanied the Dawes Commission to Europe.

Kemmerer's financial advisory missions did not prevent scholarly and literary activities. During his career he wrote over a dozen books and scores of articles for learned journals as well as many for popular periodicals. He also served as managing editor of the *Economic Bulletin,* predecessor to the *American Economic Review,* from 1908 to 1910 and was a member of the board of editors of the *American Economic Review* from 1911 to 1913. Economists recognized Kemmerer and his accomplishments when they elected him president of the American Economic Association in 1926.

Of mainly German ancestry, Kemmerer was born in Scranton, Pennsylvania, in 1875 and graduated from Wesleyan University in Middletown, Connecticut, in 1899. At Wesleyan he majored in economics, taking all the courses taught by Willard Clarke Fisher, whom he later described as an "economist with high standards of scholarship who . . . in his monetary philosophy was an international bimetallist and a great admirer of Francis A. Walker."[1] In his senior seminar with Fisher, Kemmerer chose to investigate the quantity theory of money.

II. ATTITUDES TOWARD THE QUANTITY THEORY IN THE 1890S

The quantity theory was a timely topic in the latter 1890s. The basic notion is ancient, but in recent centuries it has appeared in the works of Jean Bodin, John Locke, David Hume, David Ricardo, John Stuart Mill, and many others. Their quantity theory was essentially the crude formula $P = M/N$ (price level equals the supply of money divided by the supply of goods and services), which remained the widely accepted version during the nineteenth and twentieth centuries. But as financial systems became more sophisticated, individuals began to ask questions. Does money include anything more than coin and paper money? What is the best way of measuring the price level? (Price indices were not well developed.) How does one get a total for goods and services? (The gross national product had not yet been invented.) Is the rate of turnover (velocity) of money important?

As early as 1821 one American economist, Condy Raguet (1784–1842), contended that demand deposits (against which the holder may write checks) were a significant part of what is currently called M_1 (chiefly currency and demand deposits; Raguet, 1839:193). As the century progressed, Americans transacted more and more business by checks. By 1853 demand deposits were half of M_1; by the 1890s they were about 85 percent of it. Were demand deposits really money? A growing number of economists were saying so. Or was this just some professorial hairsplitting?

The quantity theory was a suitable topic for political reasons too. After thirty years of falling prices, from 1865 to 1896, the farmer-debtor classes, whom falling prices penalize, felt that they had a legitimate complaint against the nation's monetary system. William Jennings Bryan, the Democratic candidate for president in 1896, was their leader, and the quantity theory was the economic basis of his campaign.

What were the causes of the falling price level and what steps should be taken to remedy the situation? Under the crude quantity theory, as many viewed it, the falling prices were caused by a too-slow growth in the money supply in a rapidly expanding economy. That, they believed, was because since the 1870s the money supply had been based on gold, and not on both gold and silver, as had been true earlier in the century. The public did not think of demand deposits as filling some of the gap. The remedy, therefore, was to restore silver to its former role with gold as part of the money base. Freedom to coin silver, as well as gold, into money was the issue in the presidential campaign of 1896, which Bryan lost. But the controversy was not immediately stilled.

Very few persons voiced the view that the tremendous increase in productive efficiency on the farms, in the factories, and on the railroads might be the major cause of the falling prices in a largely competitive economy. Milton Friedman and others have done much to confirm this explanation in recent years (Friedman and Schwartz, 1963:92–94).

Back in the 1890s a number of economists questioned Bryan's explanation of the cause of falling prices and hence his remedy. For one thing, what should be included under the heading of money? How well did the quantity theory explain the falling price level of the previous thirty years? Among the notables in this group were J. Laurence Laughlin, Francis Walker, and Wesley C. Mitchell.[2]

III. KEMMERER'S REVISION OF THE QUANTITY THEORY

One of the first articles on the quantity theory that Kemmerer read was by Sarah McLean Hardy (Hardy, 1895:145–68). Hardy's ideas impressed him, and in the first outline of the senior thesis he prepared for Willard Fisher he "tried to disprove the quantity theory of money along the general lines of Miss Hardy's discussion."[3] He recalled,

> When, however, I talked the matter over with Fisher in our first conference, he punctured my balloon completely by asking me one very simple question. He said something as follows: "Miss Hardy's figures seem to show that commodity prices did not move up and down with the increase and decrease in the supply of money, but the quantity theory is a question of supply and demand and what are you planning to do to measure the demand?" Well, I went back and started all over again and began particularly digging into the writings of Francis A. Walker. (Bornemann, 1940:71–72)

Thenceforth Kemmerer became more favorably inclined toward the quantity theory.

His senior essay won him a scholarship to Cornell University, where he worked closely with Jeremiah W. Jenks and laid the foundation for a statistical method to delve further into the quantity theory. He received his Ph.D. in 1901 but did not publish his book, *Money, Credit Instruments and Prices,* until 1907. In it he redefined the old quantity theory to include demand deposits and money and deposit velocities and demonstrated statistically that this gave a more accurate reading of price-level changes (Kemmerer, E., 1901:76, 89n). He concluded, however, that:

> The value of money is determined like the value of other commodities, by the fundamental law of demand and supply, but *ceteris paribus,* a change in market prices can only find expression and thus only take place, through proportionate changes in the relative supply of circulating media; furthermore, that inasmuch as

> the check circulation, business confidence remaining the same, is a function of the monetary supply, the extensive use of checks in our modern industrial regime does not alter the essential truth of the old quantity theory as that theory was held by the fathers of political economy and is still held by the majority of its students.[4]

Kemmerer specified variables where others had only generalized. He gave the demand for money as much consideration in the determination of prices as the supply. And he provided empirical evidence that went beyond what had been published up to that time.

In 1911, four years after Kemmerer's book appeared, Irving Fisher published his *Purchasing Power of Money* with his version of that equation.[5]

Kemmerer's contribution to the understanding of the role of money is seldom cited. Joseph Schumpeter later argued that Kemmerer's *Money, Credit Instruments and Prices* was a "brilliant performance that had the misfortune of being overshadowed by the greater one of Fisher" (Schumpeter, 1968:1089n). Another explanation for the neglect of Kemmerer's contribution is that Kemmerer devoted a large part of his subsequent career to practical measures for preventing and curing rising price levels, whereas Fisher wrote several books on ways to create a monetary system that would ensure an almost perfectly stable price level.

In his later years Kemmerer's favorite definition of money was "Money is as money does." It is not an easy idea to grasp, but those who do grasp it will understand his lifelong attitude toward the constantly evolving concept of money. The definition emphasizes that at different times and places different things have served as a medium of exchange, including commodities of many kinds, precious-metal coins, and demand deposits. Were he alive today Kemmerer would probably add savings deposits promptly convertible into demand deposits. Peering into the future, he might privately conjecture that money might someday be electronic recordings that could be transmitted only at the will of the owner.

IV. THE WORK OF THE MONEY DOCTOR

On receiving his doctorate from Cornell, Kemmerer accepted a teaching position at Purdue University. Two years later he was invited to join a financial advisory team working in the Philippines. Henceforth his career would be a mixture of teaching and foreign advisory missions. In the Philippines he assisted in the replacement of the old silver-standard currency with a new gold-standard currency to stabilize the monetary system. This was to be the first of many instances in which he suggested financial reforms which stabilized the currency by placing the country on a gold or gold-exchange standard.

On his return from the Philippines, he accepted a professorship at Cornell University, where he taught from 1906 to 1912 before moving to Princeton University. During his Cornell years he did a study of seasonal variations in the relative demand for money and capital for the National Monetary Commission. It was part of the investigation of currency and banking which contributed to the formation of the Federal Reserve System. Also, he began a third book, based on his personal experiences in the Philippines and his knowledge of the financial reforms in India, Puerto Rico, the Straits Settlements, and Mexico. This study was published in 1916 under the title *Modern Currency Reforms*. The procedures he outlined in this work were to a certain degree a blueprint for the financial advisory missions that were to follow.

He repeatedly emphasized to the nations that he advised that a sound monetary system was a prerequisite for economic growth. As he pointed out in his American Economic Association presidential address, most of the countries which sought his advice were "on a depreciated and depreciating money basis where money is passed on quickly to avoid the loss of further depreciation. . . . This gives the money . . . an abnormally high rate of turnover." The result was unusually high interest rates, inflation, minimum capital formation, and a no-growth economy, a situation similar to that existing in the United States today. The Kemmerer plan of attack was to establish a central bank to coordinate monetary activities and to institute some form of a gold-based currency system. The gold reserve was essentially a "regulator fund" which served to "adjust the supply of currency and circulating bank credit to the changing demands of trade" (Kemmerer, E., 1927:9–12).

On his early missions he worked almost alone or with one assistant or specialist but of course in cooperation with the officials of the nation being advised. Starting with the missions in the mid-1920s, he usually put together an advisory team of experts whose task was to diagnose the country's economic ailments and to prescribe remedies. The remedies proposed included changes in banking laws, government budgeting procedures, and accounting procedures. Improved administration of state agencies, including the state-owned railroads, was occasionally part of the package. The advisory team did not remain to implement the prescribed remedies, although now and then individuals from the team might stay on as consultants at the request of the government.

In Colombia in 1923 and again in 1930 Kemmerer's recommendations led to the adoption of the gold standard, the establishment of a central bank, and a complete reorganization of the federal government's accounting and tax systems (Dalgaard, 1980:98–104). On his 1924 Guatemala mission he recommended a new currency unit, the quetzal, on a modified-gold-standard basis, to replace the depreciated peso and reduce monetary instability. From its establishment in 1926 the quetzal has almost continuously maintained parity with the U.S. dollar.

In South Africa in 1924–25 Kemmerer, along with Gerard Vissering, governor of the Bank of the Netherlands, recommended establishment of a central bank and South Africa's return to gold. The government accepted the proposals almost immediately, the Kemmerer-Vissering recommendation that South Africa return to gold, independently of England, sped up British efforts to reestablish its gold standard (Dalgaard, 1981).

V. THE CHANGING VALUE OF MONEY

Meanwhile Kemmerer's friendly rival, Irving Fisher, was still primarily concerned with improving the accuracy of price-level measurements and with devising ways to prevent rising or falling price levels, especially in the United States. In the 1920s Fisher spearheaded the formation of three successive stable-money associations. Kemmerer served on major committees of each of these and was president of the third one, the Stable Money Association, for one year. Repeatedly Fisher sought to have these organizations adopt his plan of altering the gold content of the dollar in order to maintain the same level of purchasing power at all times. He was not successful. Nor did he make substantial progress with this idea in Congress or in persuading the Federal Reserve System to support it (Kemmerer, D., 1977:112, 116, 118).

The continued interest among economists in finding ways of achieving a stable price level is readily understandable. Those taking part in the search for stability during the late nineteenth and early twentieth centuries had been born between 1840 and 1880. The older ones had seen prices more than double in the Civil War. The price level was cut in half between 1865 and 1896, then rose by 20 percent from 1896 to 1914. There followed a more-than-doubling of prices during and just after World War I, and finally a sharp drop of 40 percent in one year's time in 1920–21. Fisher, the perfectionist, was quite critical of the gold standard because the United States had been on it during most of these years—from 1897 to 1917 and again from 1919 to 1933. Yet, ironically, the 1920s were an era of very stable prices except in stocks and real estate, and this seeming monetary stability misled many experts and lulled the politicians to sleep.

Kemmerer was one of the exceptions. By the 1920s he had seen at close hand the inflation going on in many Latin American nations, especially in those whose governments he had advised. He taught his classes that inflation and deflation, with their various economically disruptive and unjust effects, were both undesirable, but that inflation was by far the more common and the more damaging of the two. All of his "patients" suffered from inflation. "Money doctor" Kemmerer could foresee the dangers to national economies from unbalanced budgets and overexpansion of the supply of money and credit. His favorite "prescription" was the adoption of the gold standard, which placed some limits, not easily circumvented by politicians, on the expansion of the supply of money and credit.

VI. THE ROLE OF GOLD

Kemmerer would not say, however, that a gold standard would ensure a stable price level. He had seen both rising and falling price levels under gold standards. But he often said that the gold standard was the best money standard that had been devised, certainly far better than any inconvertible paper-money standard. He did not believe that any nation would break with tradition to the point of adopting something as untried as Fisher's plan. In a political world the gold standard was the best that could be achieved.[6] Nearly all of his contemporaries in the realm of money and banking agreed, with the exception, of course, of those under the influence of Irving Fisher.

World financial leaders meeting in Brussels in 1920 and in Genoa in 1922 were only too ready to urge that all nations return to the gold standard as soon as practicable. This was the mood of the 1920s. In that decade the "money doctor" urged eight of his "patient" nations to do so, and all did, although several used the gold-exchange standard.

Then in the early 1930s the fashion in monetary standards changed swiftly. The Panic of 1929 set off the Great Depression; business failures and unemployment shot up, prices plummeted, and savings and investments fell off sharply. Poorer nations, particularly in Latin America, found that monetary and economic reforms no longer attracted foreign investments as they previously had. In 1931 first Austria, next Germany, and finally, to the surprise of most, England abandoned the gold standard. England's departure pulled the dominions and several other dependent nations off the gold standard. To justify the move, some of her leading economists blamed the gold standard for Britain's prior economic difficulties.[7]

Would the United States be the next to depart? There were fears that it would when between August of 1931 and June of 1932 about 20 percent of the country's gold reserves flowed out. And in the three years from 1929 to 1932 the consumer price level dropped 20 percent. No longer inflation but now deflation was the problem. As in the 1890s, the farmers and debtors, as well as unemployed workers, complained bitterly. The old proposal of free coinage of silver reappeared. Irving Fisher's basic idea of a dollar tailored to have a stable purchasing power now had greater appeal. Governor Franklin D. Roosevelt, whom the Democrats chose in July 1932 as their presidential candidate against incumbent President Herbert Hoover, began listening to economic advisers who believed that the monetary standard needed a drastic overhaul.

On October 4, 1932, President Hoover implied that if the Democrats won the election the Treasury would not be able to remain on the gold standard. And Kemmerer, to whom Hoover had several times turned for advice, made the same prophecy to some friends and colleagues. Democratic Senator Carter Glass of Virginia, the presumed choice for Secretary of the Treasury, was indignant at the suggestion that "there was the remotest chance of anything of the kind" (*New York Times*, 1932). But in December, after further talks with Roosevelt and his advisers, Glass surprised everyone by declining the secretaryship. A series of bank moratoriums, which had started in October, grew into a national crisis in March as Roosevelt took office. A few weeks later the United States left the gold standard (i.e., established a noncirculating-gold-reserve system) and Congress enacted legislation that seemed to give the new president the power to halt the deflationary slide.[8]

In the spring of 1933, President Roosevelt's political adviser Louis M. Howe came to Princeton University to give a luncheon talk at the faculty club. Howe told of the new administration's many money and banking problems. When a member of the faculty asked him why the administration did not consult Princeton's "money doctor," Howe responded, "We know about him and we don't want his kind of advice."[9]

Obviously the Kemmerer type of monetary reforms was no longer politically attractive. As 1933 progressed that was increasingly evident. Congress declared gold-clause contracts nonenforceable in June, and in July the president announced that the United States would take steps to have a dollar whose purchasing power would remain stable over time. This implied, and it proved to be true, that he would purposely inflate the dollar, which had undergone deflation since 1929. The so-called Gold Purchase Plan to help bring about that inflation began in October and continued until it blossomed into the devaluation of the dollar on January 31, 1934. Irving Fisher was pleased with many of these developments.[10] But anxiety grew in the minds of many leading economists. Would the government be able to halt the inflation once it had been set in motion? An artificially caused inflation to counterbalance a previous deflation was the kind of remedy that William Jennings Bryan had advocated in 1896, but he had been defeated. Now, following the 1929–33 deflation, a Bryan type of remedy was being put into effect. A determined group of monetary experts rose to the challenge.

VII. KEMMERER AS PART OF THE LOYAL OPPOSITION

On November 17, 1933, Kemmerer and several others organized the Economists' National Committee on Monetary Policy (ENCMP). The group included Ray Westerfield of Yale, the first president; H. Parker Willis of Columbia; O. M. W. Sprague and Frank Taussig of Harvard; Jacob Hollander and George Barnett of Johns Hopkins; Walter E. Spahr of N.Y.U.; Ernest Bogart of Illinois; Neil Carothers of Lehigh; W. W. Cumberland; John Parke Young; and many other monetary experts of that period. There were at one time in the 1930s eleven ex-presidents of the American Economic Association among the eighty or so ENCMP members (Spahr, 1942:1). They felt that the year 1933 "will always stand out in American history as a field day for monetary crackpots" (Spahr, 1942:5–6) and that it was their responsibility to offer the Roosevelt administration advice on every major money and banking issue that came along. Their advice was seldom requested.

A natural question at this point is why E. W. Kemmerer, a respected financial adviser, was not involved as an adviser in his own country. Louis Howe was quite explicit in rejecting the Kemmerer point of view in his comments at Princeton University. Paul Samuelson also recognized the issue during his 1961 American Economic Association presidential address. He said, "He who picks his doctor from an array of competing doctors is in a real sense his own doctor. The Prince often gets to hear what he wants to hear" (Samuelson, 1962:17).

This viewpoint is supported by John Parke Young. Young was one of Kemmerer's graduate students at Princeton and was part of several financial advisory missions. Young later went on to serve in the State Department. Young commented that Kemmerer "did not go along with Roosevelt's money maneuvering. He made some statements about Roosevelt that made it impossible for Roosevelt to use him. . . . From then on [Kemmerer] wasn't in the limelight nearly as much as he had been."[11] According to this explanation, Kemmerer was politically unacceptable to an administration that brought economists into government on a large scale. As a policy-oriented economist without access to the political power structure, Kemmerer was forced to function as part of the "loyal opposition."

Kemmerer became even more steadfast in his opposition to any economic policy which promoted inflation. The New Deal's economics, with its emphasis on putting more money into circulation to stimulate the economy, its minimizing the dangers of inflation, and its disparagement of the gold standard, irritated him. These policies were all too reminiscent of false economic doctrines that he had heard before and whose consequences he had seen and had to cope with.

Actually the economic disaster flowing from unbalanced budgets and inconvertible paper money that the classical economists prophesied was not developing during the 1930s. Nevertheless, on January 28, 1936, Kemmerer wrote a former student,

> Personally I can see nothing in sight that is likely to stop our drift in the inflation current. The politicians will not stop or prevent heavy expenditures because these expenditures have votes and it is with votes they are most concerned. For the same reason they will not provide the revenue for meeting these expenditures through increasing taxation. Under such conditions, the public will not buy government bonds at rates of interest that are politically possible and pay for those bonds out of their savings.
>
> If these assumptions are true, and unless we have a powerful recovery, which is not likely to happen in Washington, the only course that is left is a continuation of our present extravagant financing policy under which funds are obtained by forcing government obligations down the throats of the banks and having the banks pay for them by credit secured by these obligations. That is inflation pure and simple and there can be only one end of such a policy.

Forty years later Detroit banker Henry R. Bodman discovered this statement in a bundle of letters he had kept, and *Barron's National Business and Financial Weekly* published it twice as a prophecy largely come true (*Barron's*, 1975 and 1976).

In 1938 Kemmerer became president of the Economists' National Committee on Monetary Policy, and that organization increased its efforts to warn Congress and the American people of the likely consequences of the monetary policies in operation. He accepted many speaking invitations, wrote articles and books,[12] and testified frequently at hearings held by Senate and House committees on proposed money and banking legislation. He was highly critical of the 1935 revision of the Federal Reserve Act and later of the charter and powers of the International Monetary Fund (IMF). He claimed that both institutions would stimulate further inflation.

VIII. A KEMMERER LEGACY?

It is not difficult to understand why such an outspoken critic of Roosevelt's programs would be forced out of the political and economic picture. It is somewhat more difficult to understand two other issues. Why is Kemmerer not part of the mainstream in the history of American economic thought? And why did Kemmerer's monetary economics not adjust to the "state of the art" during the 1930s?

A response to the first question may in fact be related to the very reason he was so widely recognized during the early part of the century.

Kemmerer was an applied economist, a practitioner. And, while he was influential in American monetary affairs through the 1920s, the main thrust of his activities was in foreign countries, largely peripheral or developing countries. His main theoretical contributions, relating to the quantity theory of money and the components of the money supply, were made early in his career and were overshadowed by the work of other economists, Irving Fisher being the most obvious one. Furthermore, the "money doctor" was unswerving in his conviction that economic prosperity was intimately tied to monetary stability and that monetary stability was best achieved via the maintenance of a gold or gold-exchange standard. Such a conviction did not fit into the changing pattern of economic theory.

The reason that Kemmerer did not adjust his thinking to match that of mainstream economic theory is in part explained by his moralistic approach to the issue of monetary policy. To him any policy which promoted inflation was as foolish and evil as indulgence in drugs. But beyond this, one must again look to his success as a "money doctor." In country after country his recommendations were readily accepted and he was hailed as the world's leading monetary authority. In most cases also his reform recommendations accomplished their intended purposes. With the constant reinforcement of policymakers, Kemmerer's convictions were supported and strengthened. Aside from the continuing debate over the proper formula for monetary stabilization, the repeated vindication that Kemmerer received as financial adviser was sufficient to keep him steadfast in his views. A less successful man might have sought refuge in the conformity of the new economics. Kemmerer felt no such need.

E. W. Kemmerer's contribution to economic theory is considerable, regardless of whether he is ever accorded more recognition than he has so far received. But the efforts of Kemmerer the "money doctor" are perhaps more significant. The significance of his work lies in his efforts to provide a mechanism for monetary stability and a procedure for effecting economic change via monetary reform. The Kemmerer financial-reform missions to the developing countries of the 1920s and 1930s provide contemporary policymakers with a practical, albeit controversial, approach to monetary restoration. As such they surely merit review and discussion.

NOTES

1. Kemmerer (n.d.), p. 19. See also James (1973), pp. 413–14.
2. For a brief, clear discussion of the debate see Hirsch (1967), pp. 822–43.
3. E. W. Kemmerer letter quoted in Bornemann (1940), p. 71.
4. Kemmerer (1901), p. 150. Kemmerer summarized the relationship with the equation

$$P = \frac{MR + CR_c}{N + N_c}$$

in which P is the general price level, MR is the circulation of monetary supply narrowly defined, CR_c is check circulation, N is the volume of monetary transactions, and N_c is the volume of check transactions.

5. It is not easy to say who was the initial exponent of this version of the quantity theory. Kemmerer started his work in the late 1890s and completed it under Jenks at Cornell in 1901. Irving Fisher laid the foundation for his work in the early 1890s as part of his doctoral work in mathematics, but it was not until 1905 that his interest found application in economics, and it was not until 1911 that he published his *Purchasing Power of Money*.

6. These comments were made by E. W. Kemmerer on many occasions during conversations with his son, Donald L. Kemmerer, and conveyed to this author by the latter during an interview, July 9, 1980.

7. Economist John Maynard Keynes had opposed Britain's return to the gold standard from the outset, even before 1925.

8. The Thomas amendment to the Agricultural Adjustment Act, May 12, 1933, gave the president authority to do any or all of the following: (1) devalue the dollar by up to 50 percent; (2) issue \$3 billion of greenbacks; (3) put the nation on the bimetallic standard; and (4) have the Federal Reserve purchase as much as \$3 billion of U.S. government obligations in the open market. Krooss and Samuelson (1969), pp. 2719–22.

9. Unpublished paper given by D. L. Kemmerer at the Economic History Society meeting in Urbana, Illinois, May 25, 1979.

10. Fisher still talked of a "standard" under which the government altered the "price" of gold up or down from time to time to endeavor to keep the price level stable. President Roosevelt's refusal to negotiate an accord with other nations at London on the relative par value of their currencies, Fisher said, was "the most important Presidential decision" since Lincoln's Emancipation Proclamation; this time it was "the abolishing of debt slavery which comes from the great depression." Fisher saw the decision as an advance but with ample room for improvement. "Recommendations from Professor Irving Fisher on Monetary Policy, July 7, 1933," cited in Krooss and Samuelson (1969), pp. 2770, 2772.

11. John Parke Young interview with Bruce R. Dalgaard, Pasadena, California, October 1978.

12. Two books in particular deserve mention: *The ABC of Inflation: With Particular Reference to Present Day Conditions in the United States* (New York: McGraw-Hill Co., 1942) and *Gold and the Gold Standard: The Story of Gold, Past, Present and Future* (New York: McGraw-Hill Co., 1944). Both are out of print.

REFERENCES

Barron's, New York, December 1, 1975, and January 5, 1976 (Mailbag).

Bornemann, Alfred (1940), *J. Laurence Laughlin: Chapters in the Career of an Economist.* Washington, D.C.: American Council on Foreign Affairs.

Dalgaard, Bruce R. (1980), "Monetary Reform, 1923–30: A Prelude to Colombia's Economic Development." *The Journal of Economic History* 40(1):98–104.

——— (1981), *South Africa's Impact on Britain's Return to Gold, 1925*. New York: Arno Press.

"E. W. Kemmerer Obituary" (1946), *American Economic Review* 36(1):219.

Fisher, Irving (1911), *Purchasing Power of Money*. New York: Macmillan.

Friedman, Milton and Anna J. Schwartz (1963), *A Monetary History of the United States, 1867–1960*. Princeton, N.J.: Princeton University Press.

Hardy, Sarah McLean (1895), "The Quantity Theory of Money and Prices, 1860–1891: An Inductive Study." *The Journal of Political Economy* 3(2):145–68.

Hirsch, Abraham (1967), "Wesley Clair Mitchell and the Quantity Theory of Money." *The Journal of Political Economy* 75(6):822–43.

James, Edward T., ed. (1973), *The Dictionary of American Biography*. New York: Scribner's, Supplement 3.

Kemmerer, Donald L. (1977), *The Life of John E. Rovensky*. Champaign, Ill.: Stipes Publishing.

Kemmerer, E. W. (n.d.), "Autobiography of a Money Doctor. Unpublished manuscript.

——— (1909), *Money and Credit Instruments in Their Relation to General Prices,* 2d ed., New York: Henry Holt and Company.

——— (March 1927), "Economic Advisory Work for Governments." *American Economic Review* 17(1):9–12.

Krooss, Herman E. and Paul E. Samuelson (1969), *Documentary History of Banking and Currency in the United States*. New York: McGraw-Hill Book Company, vol. 4.

New York Times, October 7, 1932.

Raguet, Condy (1839), *A Treatise on Currency and Banking*. London: Ridgway.

Samuelson, Paul (1962), "History of Ideas." *American Economic Review,* 52(1):17.

Schumpeter, Joseph A. (1968), *History of Economic Analysis*. New York: Oxford University Press.

Spahr, Walter E. (1942), "History, Nature, Purposes and Responsibilities of the Economists' National Committee on Monetary Policy." New York: Economists' National Committee.

GOVERNMENT AND BUSINESS IN EIGHTEENTH-CENTURY ENGLAND: ANTICOMBINATION ACTS AND THE STABILITY OF THE NEWCASTLE COAL CARTEL, 1700–1750

William J. Hausman

By 1700 London was almost totally dependent upon coal shipped from the northeast (primarily the area around Newcastle, but including other areas of Northumberland and Durham contiguous to the Tyne and the Wear) to supply its energy needs. The rapid development of the city and the coal trade in the eighteenth century created perceived problems which caused Parliament to concern itself with regulation of the mining and distribution of this vital commodity. In fact, between 1695 and 1770 over eighty statutes relating directly to the coal trade were enacted by Par-

Variations in Business and Economic History:
Essays in Honor of Donald L. Kemmerer
Research in Economic History, Suppl. 2, pages 45–70.

ISBN: 0-89232-262-4

liament.[1] The major obstructions to trade were thought to be the periodic attempts of producers, dealers, shippers, and other middlemen to form combinations or cartels in order to restrict supply and raise the price of coal to the consumer.

Two major types of policy were forthcoming from Parliament in response to such perceived obstructions. First, there were attempts to regulate the industrial structure of the trade through anticombination laws. These were directed primarily against producers, shippers, and the major London dealers and factors. Second, Parliament resorted to direct price regulation. The form of this legislation was generally to instruct or permit (depending on specific conditions) the Lord Mayor and Court of Aldermen of the City of London to set a ceiling price on coal, and to enforce this ceiling through Middlesex Justices of the Peace. Since the second form of regulation was unequivocally unsuccessful,[2] this paper will focus on the first branch of public policy, where the results are subject to differing interpretations.

The first indication of the existence of formal agreements between Newcastle producers and London dealers in the eighteenth century came from an investigation begun in 1702.[3] On October 27, not long after the outbreak of the War of the Spanish Succession, a Parliamentary committee was appointed "to enquire into the Reasons of the excessive price of Coals . . . and to consider of some Means, for lowering the same."[4] The citizens of London had a valid reason for concern. The average price of coal to the large consumer in 1702 reached thirty-eight shillings per chaldron. This was five shillinqs above what the price had been in 1701, and ten shillings above the 1700 price. It would not be until after 1750 that the average yearly price would again reach this peak.[5]

The committee appointed to examine the coal trade reported its findings on November 7 (*JHC,* vol. 14:19). Addressing the question of the causes of the high price for coal, the committee came to two conclusions. The first reason was high wages paid to seamen in the trade. This was a natural result of wartime activity. With enlistment reducing the number of able-bodied seamen, the wages of the remaining men would naturally be higher because of supply conditions in the factor market. Furthermore, a higher wage would have to be paid in order to induce seamen who remained with the colliers to run the risk of impressment that was occasioned by calling on ports, especially at London, where press gangs were most active. But there was a second reason for the high price suggested by the committee:

> But, that a further Reason appeared also to the Committee, from a certain Contract . . . between several Owners of Collieries at Newcastle, and the Body of Lightermen at London; whereby the Proprietors oblige themselves to pay the Lightermen 3d. per Chaldron, for all Coals, they should sell for them; in Consideration of which

> Reward, the Lightermen are to pay the Proprietors Six-pence per Chaldron, for all other Coals, they shall at any time sell, before the Proprietors Coals are sold off.

This system of rebates was a feature of the coal trade that was to occur intermittently throughout the century.[6] In return for a premium of three pence per chaldron, a group of mine owners at Newcastle were guaranteed a quick delivery of their coals at London. This in turn made their coals more popular with the ship masters. The lightermen received the rebate and, as a pledge of support, offered to return double that rebate if they unloaded the coals of any nonparticipating owners in preference to those of participating owners. Enforcement was quite difficult, of course, and breaches of faith occurred on both sides, causing considerable difficulties, as will be demonstrated below. The mine owners were said to have raised the price at Newcastle to make up for this added charge at London. The committee proposed two resolutions: (1) that the agreements between Newcastle proprietors and London dealers be declared a discouragement to trade and (2) that a competent number of seamen be allotted to the coal trade (and that convoys be assigned to protect the east-coast trade). A bill entailing the recommendations of the committee was ordered to be prepared, but the matter was subsequently dropped and no bill was presented.

Pressure was still being put on the authorities to act, however. On April 23, 1703, a petition of two London citizens, Ambrose Cox and Abraham Jaggard, was presented to the Lord Mayor and Court of Common Council of London. One of the major complaints was the failure of the government to provide protection for the colliers: "Delay is occasioned for want of a convoy."[7] Cox and Jaggard claimed that coal was available and that the ships merely needed good winds and adequate protection to reach London and relieve the city of some of the hardships caused by the excessive price of coal. The perceived sensitivity of the price to expectations can be demonstrated in the following statement by Cox and Jaggard:

> That the very Expectation of this fleet of Coals had lowered those prices to five and thirty or six and thirty shillings the chaldron and it was judged by all that they would come to two and thirty shillings the chaldron but now are risen to four and forty shillings the chaldron. (*London Journals,* vol. 53:f. 740)

Their petition claimed that the price would reach sixty shillings per chaldron if convoys were not sent. There is no evidence that the price ever reached this level—380 ships carrying over 68,000 chaldrons entered London in May and June of 1703.[8] A total of 296,000 chaldrons were imported in 1703, a slight increase over the previous year, and the average price remained at just under thirty-eight shillings per chaldron.

Again, in November of 1703, there was pressure to act. Queen Anne in her address to Parliament (*JHC,* vol. 14:211) requested it "to make some Regulations, for preventing the excessive Price of Coals," and she specifically noted combinations in the trade. Investigation by the House of Lords commenced on November 17, 1703. The Lord Mayor and Court of Aldermen stated the following:

> That they conceive the occasion of the excessive price of coals at this time is from the want of a timely and sufficient convoy for the frequent convoying the ships trading in coals to and from Newcastle, and the pressing of seamen out of the said ships lying there and in the river Thames. (Historical Manuscripts:254)

The city authorities requested that six frigates be assigned to convoy the coal trade, that seamen involved in the coal trade be exempted from impressment, that the trade be permitted to use foreign seamen (which would have required temporary suspension of the Navigation Acts, for which there was precedent), and that crimps and brokers in the coal trade be prohibited from purchasing coal on their own account. A report from the Justices of the Peace for Middlesex placed the blame for the excessive price of coal more squarely on a particular group of middlemen. It stated,

> Plain it is, that Billingsgate has been and ought to be a free and open market for all consumers and retailers of coals to apply themselves to the several masters of ships, from whom they may be satisfied of the sorts, prices and goodness thereof. And as plain it now is, that the same is altered and restrained by a small number of lightermen, whose business properly is to lighter coals and other merchandizes from ships to the several buyers, and such only was their former practice.[9]

The testimonial went on to accuse the lightermen of abusing their charter and of conspiring with the northern mine owners:

> From the agreement they have made with some owners of coal pits, though perhaps it does not amount to a monopoly, yet it is evident all other coalowners and ship masters as do not freight within the contract find from the lightermen great discouragement, both in price and time of delivery. (Historical Manuscripts:237)

The Justices of Middlesex suggested that to control such practices every contract between ship master and buyer be registered on the coal meter's certificate and be left open for inspection at the meter's office.[10] This at least would have made the prices the dealers were paying part of the public domain.

Even with this major investigation, there is no evidence that a bill was ever prepared. The reason could be that despite the continuing war, 1704 saw a significant recovery in shipments of coal to London. In the summer months alone (June, July, and August), over 1,350 ships carrying 214,000 chaldrons of coal arrived at London, and the price fell to thirty-six shillings per chaldron. The total shipments for the year were over 380,000 chaldrons. Prices continued to fall during 1705 and 1706, with total shipments leveling off at around 340,000 chaldrons per year. Prices again peaked at about thirty-seven shillings per chaldron during the period from 1708 to 1710, but little agitation for controls was forthcoming until the very end of that period, perhaps because this was near the height of the war effort (as measured by the number of men armed).[11] Throughout the period from 1700 to 1710 no statute concerning combinations in the coal trade was passed even though there had been considerable agitation, including that from the queen, for such a law.

It was the city of London which initiated new investigations into the coal trade in 1710. On May 16, a committee was established to "call before them some of the Principal Dealers in Coals and any others who they shall think fit, and by the best means they can to inform themselves what agreements or other Contracts have been made and by whom in relation to the enhancing the price of Coals."[12] There was no mention this time of the problems of convoying or impressment. The average price per chaldron had remained at thirty-seven shillings for three years, and this was thought excessive, especially since the yearly imports had risen to over 370,000 chaldrons in both 1708 and 1709. On May 25, the committee was informed that 450 ships were laid up at Harwich, and that there existed a combination among masters of ships to restrict artificially the sailing season:

> They have agreed that the ships of the greatest Burthen employed in that trade shall be laid up from the end of October to the beginning of March and the rest of said ships from the end of October to the beginning of February.[13]

The purpose of such a policy would be to extend by about a month the time ships were laid up, which normally included the winter months of December, January, and February. For the period from 1706 to 1710 about 4 percent of the total yearly shipments were delivered during those three months (generally by the smaller, more intrepid ships), and weather undoubtedly had more to do with those figures than the organized efforts of the shipping interest. Still, the committee complained "that this Procedure hath already raised the Price of Coals from twenty-four shillings the Chaldron to Thirty shillings the Chaldron in the Poole which must of necessity not only enhance the Price much higher, but also deprive the Manufacturers and Poor" (*London Reps,* vol. 114:f. 235). An important point to note is for whom the committee expressed concern—not the general householder, but the manufacturer. This was so because it was the large consumers of coal who could put pressure on the city authorities to act, and the concern for the poor was probably added merely for effect. The only positive action which emanated from this investigation was a resolution urging masters of ships not to delay and to make speedier trips to and from Newcastle (*London Reps,* vol. 114:f. 304).

One interesting proposal (subsequently rejected) was put forth by Sir Gilbert Heathcote, later Lord Mayor of London. He proposed that the city "should buy the value of 2000 worth of Coals at Newcastle and freight 20 Ships therewith to bring them to London as a means to break the Combination amongst the Coal Owners and Lightermen" (London, *Minutes,* 1710). The city authorities, however, did not wish to get into the coal business at this time, and even if they had, it would have been difficult to argue that twenty shiploads would have broken any combination (for example, 348 ships entered London in June of 1710).

Attention by the national government was not diverted from the trade for long, because on March 3, 1711, the House of Commons ordered that a bill to dissolve present combinations and prevent future combinations in the coal trade be prepared for Parliament (*JHC,* vol. 16:551). The bill was presented on March 16, and was read the first time on April 4; meanwhile, committee hearings were being conducted on the bill.

The timing of this particular investigation was probably prompted by events taking place in Newcastle, although complaints against local London dealers had hardly diminished. Discussions among the larger Newcastle mine owners had begun in 1708, and it is certain that a formal "regulation" was in effect by early 1709.[14] The regulation included the major Newcastle proprietors and many of the local fitters (or factors). The group was controlled by five men—Sir Henry Liddell, Mr. Clavering, Alderman White, Mr. John Ord (agent of Mr. Wortley), and Mr. Wilkinson—known as "the Five," with William Cotesworth acting as chief executive officer and secretary. Operations of this group were financed out of a fund of £1000, raised by assessment. Meetings among the Five were held monthly from June of 1710. The major concern of the regulation was to limit output by proportioning the vend among themselves. The Five also attempted to control the fitters and sought to deal directly with the major London dealers—known not so imaginatively as "the Ten"—members of the London Lightermen's Company who, because of their control over the Thames lighters and their marketing facilities, had a near-monopoly of the London retail coal trade. That the two groups carried out an active correspondence was made clear during the committee hearings.

It was obvious from the very beginning of the investigation by the House that no group in particular was being pursued, but that the members were at least vaguely aware of the combinations in all branches of the trade. When first ordered on March 3, 1711, to bring in a bill, the groups specifically mentioned were "Combinations of Coalowners, Lightermen, Keelmen, Masters of Ships, and others, [seeking] to advance the Price of Coals, in Prejudice of the Navigation, Trade and Manufactures, of the Kingdom" (*JHC,* vol. 16:531). During the committee hearings, each group in turn sought to direct attention from itself by laying the blame squarely on one or more of the other groups involved in the trade.

At a meeting of the Five on March 12, the owners planned their strategy. It was decided

> That Mr. Cotesworth propose to Mr. Hedworth [MP for County Durham] a meeting of the coal owners of both rivers in order to consider of what may be proper at this juncture to be done for the common good of the coal trade. That he write to Mr. Liddell that money will be raised without loss of time for defraying the charge that shall acrew in soliciting the coal trade now depending in Parliament: 1d per cha. is the sum talked of and proposed. That Mr. Cotesworth be desired to go forthwith to London to negotiate and to solicit the coal trade depending before the Parliament. (Hughes, 1952:176)

An important point to note is that the coal owners did not regard the Parliamentary inquiry casually; they were very seriously concerned with the outcome of the investigation. On April 13, Sidney Wortley and Henry Liddell presented a petition to Parliament on behalf of all mine owners, formally asking to be heard in the matter. They were subsequently called before the committee.

Relations between the Five and the Ten had not been without friction. Apparently, the Five were in arrears on their payments (premiums similar to those mentioned in the 1702 controversy) to the London lightermen. As Henry Liddell stated in a letter to Cotesworth:

> . . . the Consequences of not keeping Touch with the Dealers would prove very dangerous and occasion such a Confusion as would shake the Agreement more than all other Artifices that our Enemys could practice. I design for the Gate [the coal market at Billingsgate] tomorrow to see if I can stopp their mouths by fair promises, but I doubt I shall not succeed since they are a sort of people that will not be fed with words alone. (Hughes, 1952:178)

Liddell seemed annoyed that the premiums had not been paid. In a subsequent letter he again warned Cotesworth:

> Should you quarrel with the Dealers att this time, you may guess att the disturbance and interruption they would unanimously give to the Trade and though you were to ingage all the other Dealers in your interest, yet they are most of them people of little or no substance. (Hughes, 1952:180)

The controversy between the two groups was brought to a head at the committee hearings.

On April 14, Cotesworth was called before the committee. He did not deny the fact that an agreement had been reached among the mine owners, but he stated that no monopoly was intended: "The reason of the Gentlemen coming into the Regulation was occasioned by a complaint of masters and dealers of base mixtures discovered by the Consumers" (Hughes, 1954:184). The somewhat ironic rationale for the combination was to protect the London consumer. Cotesworth then tried to convince the committee that the combination was not very powerful. He pointed out that they controlled less than half of the total output of the Tyne and the Wear. The following statement by Cotesworth demonstrated his basic strategy of attempting to shift blame to the London dealers: "That the Lightermen in January last . . . had £1250 for unloading the Contractors' coals and for dispatching their business the quicker when they came to London" (Hughes, 1952:186). If the Five were going down, they were determined at least to take the Ten with them.

The masters of ships were also brought into the matter. It should be remembered that they had been accused of combining in 1710 by the city investigation carried out in that year. The masters, like the mine owners before them, admitted that they had attempted to control the trade in the previous year, but they also had an excuse. Mr. Bowell, a master,

> Owned the Contract at Harwich and that the reason of their stay there was by the ill-usage of the Coal Owners at Newcastle and Lightermen at London for at Newcastle the language was 'you will load in the Contract or out,' and if they buy outside the Contract the Lightermen will not come on board at London by reason of the large Premiums they have from the Coal Owners at Newcastle. (Hughes, 1952:188)

Since the masters actually acted as merchants, purchasing the coal at Newcastle and selling it at London, their concern at being pinched at both ends was understandable. An important point to note from the testimony of Bowell is that it is clear that in order for the system to be successful there had to be mutual support from both ends of the trade, and Liddell's concern to please the London dealers was very real and necessary to the effective operation of the combination at Newcastle. Conversely, if premiums were to be collected from mine owners some sort of stable organization at that end of the trade was necessary.

The first anticombination law of the century was passed on May 19, 1711 (9 Anne c. 28). The justification of the bill was that having coal in London,

> at cheap and reasonable prices, tends greatly to the improvement and increase of the trade and navigation of this kingdom, by breeding and employing many thousands of skillful mariners for the service of her Majesty, and defense of the realm, and

> to the relief of the poor; and for that end, and for the better advancing the duties upon coals granted to her Majesty for carrying on the present war, . . . it is necessary the same should not be monopolized.

The act was comprehensive; the first section dealt with combinations among and between groups. It was enacted that,

> all and every contract . . . whether heretofore made or entered into, or hereafter to be made or entered into, by or between any coal-owners, lightermen, fitters, masters, or owners of ships or vessels, crimps, coal factors, or other person or persons . . . are hereby declared to be illegal, null, and void.

The penalties were graduated: coal owners, £100; fitters, £50; masters or ship owners, £20; clerks or agents, £20. In order to open up the trade Newcastle fitters were instructed to record for each loading the date, the quantity, and the names of the collieries from which the coal had been obtained, as well as the price paid. The certificates were to be registered at the London cocquet office and to be open for inspection. A fine of £10 was to be paid for not registering or for fraudulent statements on the cocquet (similar to bills of lading). Any salary or gratuity received by a lighterman, crimp, master, or factor from any coal owner, fitter, or master was declared illegal, and a fine of £50 per offense was levied. This provision was meant to end the practice of coal owners' giving premiums to the London dealers. It was also enacted that ships laying up for more than seven days at any port between Newcastle and London for any unnecessary reason (with such events as inclement weather, lack of convoys, and need for repairs excluded) would be fined £50. In order to enforce the law, any person bringing suit was to receive half of the fine collected, the other half going to the Crown. The law was to be in force for three years, but was made perpetual in 1715 (1 George I c. 26).

It is difficult to measure the direct impact of the law. From the letters exchanged between Cotesworth and Liddell, it is clear that the Newcastle owners were quite concerned about the publicity of their actions in front of the Parliamentary inquiry, and when Cotesworth returned to Newcastle in July, the meetings of the owners continued. But the organization was already in trouble. They controlled somewhat less than half of the output of the northeast, and several of their own members were exceeding their assigned vends (especially the larger and more powerful members like the Wortleys). There was serious competition from the Sunderland owners and the nonregulated owners of Newcastle. And it is certain that the inquiry held in 1711 did not enhance their relationship with the London dealers. In 1712 Liddell stated in a letter:

> You observe right that these vermin will prove in some measure worse than gift [a reference to being forced to give gift coal to masters], were it only on this account

> that they squeeze the poor masters as well as the owners. I wish, therefore, that any expedient could be thought of to bring them within bounds. (Hughes, 1952:198)

The Parliamentary inquiry and the resulting statute may have speeded up the disintegration of the Newcastle combination, which was effectively dead by 1712, even though they continued to meet after this time.

The year 1712 was the last year of the War of the Spanish Succession, and demobilization had already begun. Coal shipments had increased to 370,000 chaldrons and the average price had fallen by five shillings to thirty-two shillings per chaldron. The years after 1712 were ones of expansion with shipments reaching the range of 410,000 to 440,000 chaldrons per year for the years 1716–20. The average price had leveled off at around twenty-nine to thirty shillings per chaldron. It would be saying too much to attribute this expansion to the passage of the anticombination law in 1711. These were relatively peaceful years (with the exception of the Jacobite Rebellion in 1715), and it is not at all clear that the statute reduced the effective control of the trade at London by the lightermen. But at least the act was held in enough esteem so that it was made perpetual in 1715.

Interest in the coal trade was again aroused in March of 1717. The Aldermen of London exhibited concern and stated: "This Court taking notice of the excessive Price of Coals, doth order, that a Court be summoned . . . to consider thereof, and that some of the Principal Lightermen, Woodmongers, and Crimps do attend for this Court's further Information therein" (*London Reps,* vol. 121:f. 161). This was another indication that the activities of the London dealers had gone unchecked. Although 1716 had been a very good year with over 412,000 chaldrons imported at an average price of thirty shillings per chaldron, 1717 had started off badly, with March a particularly difficult month. Only forty-four ships carrying a little over 3,000 chaldrons entered in that month (compared with 39,000 chaldrons in March 1715, and 29,000 chaldrons in March 1716), and the price at the docks rose to about thirty-eight shillings per chaldron.[15]

The city inquiry placed the blame primarily on the lighterman. The problem arose "from a Clause in an Act made in the eleventh and twelfth Years of the Reign of the late King William the Third (cap. 21) whereby the Working of or in any Lighter is restrained only to such Lightermen and their Servants who shall register their Names according to the said Act."[16] The city Remembrancer was instructed to prepare a bill to submit to Parliament repealing the clause. On July 9, a representation was made to the king, but the matter was subsequently dropped. Events probably overtook the inquiry. The summer of 1717 was one of the best in the century for the coal trade (at least from the consumer's standpoint), with

221,000 chaldrons imported. The price at the docks fell to about twenty-six shillings per chaldron, and the average price for the year was twenty-nine shillings per chaldron. Still, the evidence brought out during the inquiry relative to the continued domination of the London trade by the lightermen was important. But it was equally clear that an inquiry could not be sustained when the trade was expanding.

An attempted combination by masters of ships in 1718 illustrates a major aspect of combinations in the coal trade: it was necessary for one group to enlist the help of at least one other group in the trade in order to assure any measure of success. There were four major points in the articles of agreement drawn up by the masters in 1718: (1) no coal was to be loaded before the first of March or after the twenty-ninth of September, (2) a stated margin was to be established between the cost of coal at Newcastle and the sale price at London, (3) all ships were to load in turn and deliver in turn, and (4) each transaction, including price paid, was to be registered.[17] If the proposed articles were to be enforced, the help of the mine owners was essential, and the masters made clear their intentions in letters to Cotewsorth, Colonel George Liddell, and the Lord Mayor of Newcastle. The owners supported the masters, but chose not to enter directly into agreements. They preferred instead to act through the fitters. In a letter of April 18, 1718, Cotesworth wrote to Liddell:

> It is the opinion of most here that the Masters project or Regulation ought to be encouraged. The way of doing it will not, as we take it, subject us to any censure from superior powers. . . . I think the Masters laying their injunctions on the fitters will be a means to make them much more observant than they would otherwise be and is taking the odium a good deale off the coal owner. (Hughes, 1952:209)

It is likely that the 1711 act remained in the thoughts of the owners, and the reference to "superior powers" is interesting. The statute clearly made overt agreements more difficult than they otherwise would have been. After a conference with Mr. Ord, Cotesworth again put the agreement in perspective: "He agreed with me that the scheme would be lookt upon as an unlawful combination, but to act and support the Masters as much as we could 'without breach of the law' " (Hughes, 1952:210). The owners feared the disruptions in their dealings caused by Parliamentary concern. The dilemma was explained in a letter of April 20, 1718:

> I have had a very difficult part to act, least by opposing the measure the Masters were concerting when others were for coming into them I should disoblige them, or the other hand, by coming into those measures to incense the Dealers and perhaps make you or myself lyable to the censure of Council or Parliament. (Hughes, 1952:212)

The measures taken did incense the Billingsgate dealers, who reacted to the high price demanded by the masters, not by requesting an inquiry, but by slowing down the delivery of ships, so that Liddell commented, "If they do not lower their price, they must break of course for as all staiths are full the whole country would be in Rebellion if ships should not be dispatched as soon as they came in" (Hughes, 1952:215). The dealers were successful in breaking the combination (over 99,000 chaldrons imported in July alone), and the average yearly price rose a modest two shillings above the previous year to thirty shillings per chaldron. The masters were equally unsuccessful in limiting shipments in the winter months. Winter coal imports as a percentage of shipments in the rest of the year rose steadily from 1718, when they were about 3 percent, to 12 percent by 1729–33. Although no legislation arose from this incident, it was an important event, in that evidence concerning the attitudes of the coal owners toward legislation already in existence was provided. The owners tended to act in a cautious manner so as not to bring the trade under further public scrutiny. The incident also demonstrated the fact that the masters, even with the implicit aid of the coal owners, could not control the trade without the additional compliance of the powerful London dealers.

The years 1719 to 1726 were relatively free from formal agreements, although the masters continued to press their demand of being allowed to load and deliver in turn. Yearly imports ranged from 421,000 to 511,000 chaldrons, and the average yearly price fluctuated between twenty-seven and thirty shillings per chaldron. These were also fairly peaceful years (a short war with Spain was just ending at the beginning of the period), and the added disruptions caused by war were not present, so that a moderate expansion in the trade might have been expected.

In the middle of 1726, a new formal agreement among the Newcastle owners came into being. This group called themselves the "Grand Allies," and Sweezy has said of them, "At no time before or since have the mines been so closely held or the trade so completely dominated by a small group of owners" (Sweezy, 1938:26). The intent of the agreement was the same as that of the 1709 regulation—to proportion the vend in order to control competition and regulate price. Many of the participants in the agreement were also involved in the 1709 regulation, including Sir Henry Liddell, Edward Wortley, and George Bowes. The agreement was to be in effect (at least in a formal sense) for the next twenty-five years, also a time of intense interest in the coal trade on the part of Parliament.

By 1729, the year of the next formal inquiry, relations among and between the various sections of the coal trade had become quite complex. As Raymond Smith has noted,

> The Lightermen had a private war with the [mine] owners, and a public one with the Woodmongers. The ship-owners were trying to squeeze what they could out of the owners, but looked upon the Lightermen as the real peril. The coal-owners were in difficulties amongst themselves, but had a collective feud with the Lightermen and a grievance against the ship-owners for being so indiscreet as to cause their affairs to be dragged into the limelight. The coal-owners and Lightermen were at each other's mercy on account of the illegal premiums that were extracted by the Lightermen from certain owners. The brewers and distillers of London and the Hostmen fitters of Newcastle were all embroiled in the affair, and in fact there was no one engaged in the coal trade whose interests were not implicated. (Smith, 1961:43–44)

The government stepped into this perplexing situation in an attempt to stimulate the trade.

As in several of the earlier controversies, the city of London began its own inquiry before Parliament acted. On February 11, 1729, Mr. Oldner, Mr. Blunkett, and several other lightermen and dealers were called before a committee and asked to explain the reason for the "high" price of coal. The dock price in February had risen to over thirty-two shillings per chaldron—six shillings over the January price and eight shillings over the price in the previous February. Only 13,000 chaldrons were imported during that month. The dealers claimed that there was "an agreement or Combination among the Coal Owners and Fitters at Newcastle" (*London Reps,* vol. 133:f. 181) and that the Newcastle faction was delaying the loading of coal until the third of March. They suggested that John Gibson, Benjamin Horne, and Joseph Merryman (all coal dealers or factors) could give a better description of those combinations, but they were not called by the committee. Instead, on February 18, Sir Henry Liddell, Edward Wortley Montague, and several others ("proprietors or owners of most of the great Collyaries") addressed the committee. They gave evidence that there were "great Quantities of Coals ready to be delivered and that they were ready and willing to deliver them to such persons as would purchase them" (*London Reps,* vol. 133:f. 190). Not too long ago they had formed the Grand Allies, and they sought to divert attention from themselves to the fitters and masters of ships, whom they accused of combining to the detriment of the entire trade. The ploy seemed to work, at least for the time being, because on April 22, the Court took note of "the dearness and scarcity of coals occasioned as is alleged by a Combination or agreement carved by some persons in this City with the Fitters at Newcastle and with most of the Masters and Owners of Ships" (*London Reps,* vol. 133:f. 292). There was no mention of the owners of the collieries. The Court decided to apply to Parliament for relief.

On the following day Parliament acted:

> Complaint being made to the House, of Combinations entered into, to enhance the Price of Coals; Ordered, that a Committee be appointed, to enquire, and examine, if any, and what, Combinations have been entered into, to enhance the Price of Coals; and that they do report the same, as it shall appear to them, to the House. (*JHC,* vol. 21:345)

The composition of the committee was such as to stimulate open debate on the matter; among others appointed were all members of London, Middlesex, Surrey, Kent, Essex, Durham, and Northumberland, a guarantee that all the major interests would be represented.

Parliament began its investigation early in May. Liddell acted as the owners' principal spokesman, and sat in on all of the hearings. In a letter of May 4 he explained how matters were progressing:

> This Morning we had a great deal of Wrangle at the Committee and a great deale of Dirt thrown and among the rest by Mr. Carr's [MP for Newcastle] means the premium brought upon the stage and it made a great noise. . . . The Dealers are exasperated and say they will produce severall of the Fitters' letters to show that they were in the Combination and at the instance of the Masters, I hope to prevent it. I cannot yet be certain when I can leave this place. . . . I am quite jaded. (Hughes, 1952:227)

On May 9, the ship owners presented a petition to Parliament, complaining of the combination of buyers at London. They freely admitted the accusations placed against them concerning loading in turn, but attempted to justify their actions:

> . . . the Regulation, which the Petitioners have entered into, for disposing of their Coals in Order, as their Ships arrive, is only to protect themselves from the Impositions of the Lightermen, . . . and that, if they are not allowed to employ Agents, or Factors, to dispose of their Coals, they cannot carry on their Trade. (*JHC,* vol. 21:366)

The attempt was to shift attention to the London dealers. During these inquiries the rule quite clearly became "every man for himself."

Most of the evidence given to the committee was by the lightermen and masters (or owners) of ships. The lightermen chose to emphasize the operations of the masters. Maltis Ryall, a prominent lighterman, explained the procedure of loading in turn:

> . . . the Masters came to an Agreement to take Turns; and accordingly two Men were employed to send up Word, what Ships, and what the Masters Names were, that passed by Greenhith; and those, that passed by first, took Turn first; for which Purpose there was an Office kept by Mr. William Ward, and others, who received

> One Penny per Chaldron, for which they receive a Certificate, to justify, that they have conformed to the said Agreement: That if Ships went to Newcastle without a Certificate, he had heard, they have been denied by the Fitters to have any more Coals, till such time as they had one. (*JHC,* vol. 21:369)

When asked if the coal owners were involved in the combination, Ryall said that he knew of none who were. His testimony was corroborated by William Williford, another major coal dealer.

The masters complained of the oppressions of the coal dealers. The above-mentioned Ward stated, "the Coal-buyers and Lightermen are opulent, and few in Number; who meet, and set what Price they please on Coals" (*JHC,* vol. 21:370). He did not deny the scheme for loading in turn, but insisted that there was no agreement to raise the price of coal. Thomas Watson, master, complained of ill treatment: "the Lightermen have given him Notes, payable in Forty Days, but not for value received" (*JHC,* vol. 21:371). John Watson, master, complained of great delays in unloading: "That he has had great Hardships from the Lightermen, and has lain Three Weeks in the River, and a Week in Turn, yet has not sold near his Cargo" (*JHC,* vol. 21:372). Others complained of being forced to unload before the price had been determined, only to have the price dictated by the lightermen.

On May 12, Liddell noted the final outcome of the investigation:

> Yesterday the Report was made from the Coale Committee when the City Members spoke smartly to the Combination among the Masters and Agents. . . . Sir Wm Strickland and some others defended the Masters with great Zeale and Charged the Lightermen with much more than they ought to bear. Some would have brought in both Fitters and Coal Owners but the first was prevented and the Ctee declared that nothing appeared to them that the Coal Owner was any way concerned in any Combination. (Hughes, 1952:227–28)

Liddell had been quite successful in keeping the Newcastle owners out of the limelight, and a subsequent resolution of the committee touched only the masters of ships and lightermen. On May 20, the Court of Aldermen and Common Council of London issued a decree to be published and posted at Billingsgate. It stated that

> . . . if the Masters of Ships concerned in the Coal Trade shall continue their Combination of unloading their Ships in Turn or if any persons shall continue or enter into any other Combinations relating to the Trade this Court upon Information thereof will prosecute such persons with the utmost severity. (*London Reps,* vol. 122:f. 347)

Prosecution could presumably have proceeded under the 1711 act. No further action by Parliament or city was immediately taken.

The year 1729 was quite vigorous, so far as quantities shipped were concerned. Just under 496,000 chaldrons were imported at an average price of twenty-eight shillings per chaldron. It is possible that the turmoil caused by the 1729 investigation had the effect of reducing some element of monopoly in the market, at least temporarily, thereby benefiting the consumers in London. But there is some qualitative evidence to the contrary. A pamphleteer made the following assertion:

> It was reasonable to suppose that such a Censure, from the Honorable House of Commons, shou'd terrify all Persons concern'd in such Combinations, and break all their illegal Contracts: but on the Contrary it appears, that the Masters of Ships continue more resolute than ever, employing the same Agents, and paying them one Peny per Chaldron as before, keeping their Turns strictly, and openly Report, that they have positive Assurances from Newcastle, &c. that no Ships shall be loaded without Certificates; they are so daring as to threaten if the Lord-Mayor, &c, prosecute their Agents, or any Person, on account of their Contract, the City should pay for it before Michaelmas next; and that if the Parliament shou'd take Notice of them, they will lay up their Ships. (Philalethes, 1729:9–10)

These were certainly daring assertions by the masters, if, in fact, they were made. The pamphleteer concluded with a vigorous defense of the lightermen, leaving no doubt about his loyalties. What this pamphlet suggests is that the government's decrees earlier in the year may have been ignored.

It was not long before complaints were again heard. On February 26, 1730, a petition of masters and owners of ships of the port of Scarborough was presented to Parliament. The shipping interests again complained that they were not making a decent living and that the coal trade would be ruined if some kind of relief were not given. Their primary target was again the lightermen:

> . . . one of the greatest Disadvantages they conceive to arise by the arbitrary and oppressive Proceedings of the Lightermen, since their Incorporation: And praying that the Coal Trade may be laid open, and the Market freed for all Buyers and Dealers in Coals.[18]

Similar petitions by the owners of ships of Whitby, Newcastle, Sunderland, and Great Yarmouth were later added. This time the masters had some support in other areas. On February 27, a petition of several woodmongers and wharfingers dealing in coal and other goods was presented, which accused the coal dealers of giving unfair measure and called for the opening up of the trade. Yet another committee was set up to investigate the matter.

The 1730 committee issued its report on March 25. The committee had examined three owners and masters, four factors, and several dealers not affiliated with the lightermen. No lightermen or coal owners were brought before the committee. The masters complained that for the past twelve years they had not "made more than 1 and $1\frac{1}{2}$ Cent [return on capital invested]," due to the control of the trade at London by fifteen lightermen (*JHC,* vol. 21:516). This year the masters asserted that no regulation existed among themselves, but that the trade would be improved if a statutory method of delivering in turn were instituted. The masters claimed that twenty-five shillings per chaldron was the minimum price at which they could sell coal and still recover their costs.

Two crimps, Caleb Smith and Benjamin Horne, who acted as agents between masters and lightermen claimed that the trade was quite restricted, "for One half of the Coals, brought to London, are bought up by about 12 lightermen, and the other half by about 40 more; but all of them insist on a Premium of Six Pence, or Nine Pence, per Chaldron, from the Coal Owners or their Agents" (*JHC,* vol. 21:517). Again the matter of rebates was brought up. The factors made the following assertion:

> If the Coal Trade was laid open, other Dealers could supply their Customers in London as cheap, as Lightermen; which now they can't do: If other Persons buy Coals at Billingsgate, those Persons are obliged to make use of a Lighter, belonging to such Lightermen, who, in such Case, demand and take a Premium, and also 1s. per Chaldron besides, for Literage.[19]

These crimps did see some benefit from the previous Parliamentary inquiry. They stated that the premiums normally given by owners to lightermen "have not lately been so regularly paid, as they were formerly, by reason of an Enquiry that was made last Session of Parliament" (*JHC,* vol. 21:517). Smith and Horne further noted that the lightermen acted as factors for the masters of about one-third of the 400 ships in the trade. Horne claimed to be concerned in about 40 ships himself, worth over £48,000, on which the return was less than $1\frac{1}{2}$ percent per year, not including insurance.

After reviewing the report of the committee, the whole House resolved

> That some of the Lightermen . . . have exacted unlawful Premiums, or Rewards, refused to give their Notes for Value received, for such Coals as they buy, and are become Crimps or Factors, to the Masters of Ships; at the same time they are Buyers of Coals on their own Account, and have used unfair Practices, to the Prejudice of the Coal Trade. (*JHC,* vol. 21:518)

Leave was given to bring in a bill embodying the resolution of the committee. On April 10, the bill was read a second time, and twelve days later a petition of the lightermen was offered to the House, but a vote to accept it was defeated. A clause added to the bill to register "all Bargains, Contracts, and Agreements, relating to coals imported" (*JHC,* vol. 21:555) was similarly defeated, and the bill was passed into law on April 28, 1730 (3 George II c. 26).

The primary purpose of the new act was to open up the trade by reducing the power of the lightermen. It was enacted that:

> it shall and may be lawful to and for any person or persons, who now do or hereafter shall keep any wharf or wharfs on the river Thames, . . . and for any other person or persons, who now do or hearafter shall trade or deal in coals or other goods, to keep, use and imploy their own lighters, barges, and other craft, in and for the carrying of coals and other goods, to and from any ships or other vessel, in the river Thames, and to and from any Wharf, dock, creek or other place.

This statutorily ended the company's monopoly of lighters which had been granted in 1700. The only stipulation was that any craft so used would have to be registered with the Lightermen's Company for a fee of five shillings. It was also enacted that "no lighterman or other buyer of coals for sale, . . . shall act as a crimp, agent or factor, for any master or owner of any ship or vessel importing coals into the port of London." A fine of £200 was assessed for acting otherwise. The section of 9 Anne c. 28 dealing with accepting premiums was reiterated, and a £500 fine was attached to receiving such gratuities (a significant increase over the £50 fine enacted by 9 Anne c. 28). In order to make enforcement of the new law somewhat easier, it was decreed that all contracts between buyers and sellers had to be recorded in the factor's notebook, each party to the transaction receiving a copy. Any fraud in these entries would receive a £50 fine. A £100 fine was attached to lightermen not giving masters notes for "value received in coals." Informants bringing successful suit were again awarded half of the fines exacted.

Besides permitting nonmembers of the Lightermen's Company to operate lighters, the most notable provision of the act was the increased penalty for breaking the law. It was certainly felt that this would provide added incentive for prosecution under the act. It was hoped that the bill would greatly benefit the shipping interest, without harming the London consumer. The Newcastle faction was uncertain about its probable effects. Liddell wrote that he was "satisfied it will not answer the Masters' expectations and I wish that the Coal Owners may find more good than harm from it" (Hughes, 1952:231). Certainly it had an impact on the lightermen. It shifted some power from them to other wholesalers and woodmongers and to the independent factors. Raymond Smith stated,

> *Pari passu* with the rise of the factors the lightermen lost the dominance of the market they had achieved in 1700. . . . It was the factor who supplied the coal buyer

> who succeeded the lighterman, and the coal merchants who succeeded the coal buyer. . . . Twenty years later the Society of Coal Factors was in being, and there can be little doubt that the rise of the factors to collective power dates from 1730, when they were given legal status, authority, and duties. (Smith, 1961:48)

That the factors became as close-knit as the lightermen showed that although the act shifted relationships within the coal trade, it did not open up the trade, which was the express purpose of the act.[20]

It is doubtful whether this law greatly improved the lot of the shipping interest. Colonel George Liddell had earlier pinpointed the major problem in that sector of the trade. He wrote:

> They Rayle with great violence at the Dealers as the only means of beating down the price of coales, whereas 'tis greatly owing to their being too many Ships in the Trade and many of those Ships having Masters of great passions and little Reason. They should, therefore, endeavour to reduce the number of these Ships, rather than raise the price of coales too high, by which means they will get more profit and the consumer be less agrieved. (Hughes, 1952:218)

Liddell was not alone in his assessment of the conditions in the shipping sector of the coal trade. A pamphleteer stated,

> The extraordinary Fall of the Profit of Coal-Shipping seems to be owing, in great Measure, to a piece of Mismanagement . . . tho' that might not possibly have had so bad an Effect, had not they been also overdone with Numbers. That they are too numerous, they themselves are ready to allow; but they seem to think, nevertheless, that their Usefulness to the Public requires something to be done, that they may be supported. (*A Letter,* 1730:9)

The writer suggested that if the government could find a way to reduce the number of ships, it would greatly benefit the shipping interest as a whole, but he feared that it was something "not easily to be done to any good purpose by Authority." He preferred to leave the job to "useful Experience, the only Instructress of Fools" (perhaps an early and rather crude statement of the working of the Invisible Hand).

If the masters and owners were pleased with the 1730 act, the satisfaction could not have lasted very long. On April 23, 1731, a petition of glassmakers, brewers, distillers, sugar bakers, smiths, dyers, and other large consumers of coal was presented to Parliament. They complained of evasions taking place under the 1730 act, and noted also that the masters had reinstituted the procedure of loading in turns. On April 26 a new regulation was passed (4 George II, c. 30). It was entitled "An act for rendering more effective . . . An Act for the better preventing the enhancing the price of coals in the river of Thames by keeping of turn in delivering coals there." Loading in turn received a fine of £100.

A fine of £50 was attached to failing to deliver the ship's cocquet within four days after passing Gravesend, so that the masters and owners of ships were again brought under stricter regulation.

The legislative activities of 1729–31 suggest that the government undoubtedly had problems enforcing the various extant acts concerning combinations in the coal trade. The average yearly price of coal in 1730 was thirty-two shillings per chaldron, up four shillings over the previous year. Quantity imported in 1730 fell by 36,000 chaldrons from the previous year to 460,000 chaldrons. The year 1731 witnessed a slight recovery—imports up 18,000 chaldrons to 478,000 chaldrons and price down by three shillings to twenty-nine shillings per chaldron. Combinations may have been rampant in these years, but the data do not indicate that a truly dramatic increase in price or restriction of output occurred. It may well be that the almost constant attention of the government to the coal trade during this period kept the various sectors in such turmoil that no truly effective regulation by the industry could take place.

The years 1732–37 were ones of relative stagnation in the trade. Quantities imported ranged from 450,000 to 515,000 chaldrons, and the average price remained fairly stable, fluctuating between twenty-nine and thirty-one shillings per chaldron. This may have been due to general economic stagnation[21] or it may have been due to the firm control of the Newcastle end of the trade by the Grand Allies (or some combination of both). But if London had been expanding rapidly, and if the Grand Allies had been effectively restricting the expansion of output at Newcastle, the price of coal in London would probably have risen much more than it did. A closer examination of the affairs of the Grand Allies during this time would be helpful.

The possibility of regulating the trade was never absent from the minds of the Newcastle mine owners. As early as 1722 (when no formal regulation existed) Colonel Liddell wrote to Cotesworth, "I think it very necessary (if not absolutely so) to have a Confederacy formed to save the coal trade from destruction and the neighborhood of the River of Tyne from oppression" (Hughes, 1952:233). No progress was made until the summer of 1726, when the first agreement was written. The document was signed by Wortley, Liddell, and George Bowes. As Sweezy noted, "The various signatory parties were joining hands to prevent the opening of new collieries by buying up land, royalties, and wayleaves. Any coal property which they could not directly get hold of they proposed to block off from an outlet to the river (Sweezy, 1938:24). They also agreed to drop all legal suits against each other. There was no plan for proportioning the vend as yet, and there is evidence that no effective regulation of this kind existed until after 1730 (Hughes, 1952:236–39).

By February of 1731 new negotiations had begun, this time including some of the Sunderland owners. Apparently there was concern about overexpansion in the trade. Liddell wrote:

> The owners on Weare are Alarmed and Stunned and so ought those of our River. If they will not, as the disease is desperate, so must be the remedy. 'Tis true many Thousand pounds will be lost, and for which nobody will thank you; but when that is done, as a great many Collierys will be laid in and many of their Owners Shaken, it will make people a little more Cautious for the future how they burn their Fingers by meddling with Collierys. (Hughes, 1952:241)

It is certain that by 1735 some agreement had been reached, because the vend was formally proportioned in that year and again in 1738 (although neither year was anomalous in terms of price or quantity shipped). George Nixon discussed the operations of the Grand Allies. He explained that they

> have engrossed into their Hands great Numbers of Collieries. . . . They have got into their possession by one Means or other, so large a Share of all the Vends adjoining to the River Tine, that they have almost totally debarred all other Persons from Access to it with Coals. . . . Great Numbers of wayleaves, the Grand Allies have engrossed into their own Hands, and pay dead Rents for many of them not to use them, but to exclude everybody else. (Nixon, 1739:13–14)

Still, problems existed for the Grand Allies. The Company of Hostmen complained that several large consumers were attempting to circumvent the control of the Grand Allies by instructing masters of ships to load only specified coal at Newcastle. They noted:

> As several masters on their arrival at Newcastle give the preference to some particular sorts of coals, which is very much to the prejudice of the trading Fitters in general, as they have done everything in their power to contribute to the good of the trade in general, they hope the ship owners will in return use such means as will effectually remove that complaint. (Dendy, 1901:196)

Loading in turn would have stopped such a practice, and there are indications that this was attempted.

An additional way to control the quantity and quality of coal loaded at Newcastle was to control the delivery of coal to the staiths. Nixon (1739:13–14) stated,

> . . . it is well known that, whenever the better sorts which have a quick vend, have got beforehand with their quantity their carriages have been laid off, and their delivery of coals entirely stopped for several days, if not weeks together, without any other apparent reason than to give room to the owners of the inferior sorts to force off their share.

This practice, along with mixing inferior with high-quality coal and loading in turn, were all part of the attempt to establish firm control of the trade at Newcastle.

The activities of the Grand Allies are not well documented during the years from 1739 to 1749.[22] That they were experiencing serious difficulties by 1745 is certain. In January of that year Matthew Ridley, one of the more reluctant members of the combination, wrote:

> But in Truth this has been the worst year I ever saw, the Coal Trade having met with many repeated Obstructions and the ugly Differences among the persons concern'd here has occasioned lowering of prices or advance of Measure which has been great Drawbacks from the profits. (Hughes, 1952:247)

By June of 1746 Ridley was more hopeful that some accommodation could be reached. He wrote to one of his creditors: "if a Regulation happens, which I think must take Effect in a very short time, I may be able in the next half year's payment to make you an Additional Remittance" (Hughes, 1952:248). By April of 1747 a formal regulation had been achieved. Ridley again wrote:

> In order to bring the several Persons concern'd in the Coal Trade into a Regulation as to Price and Measure it was necessary that every one should fix a settled proportion for his Share of the Delivery, which Delivery should always be in proportion, so that when any one exceeded what was set to him and another fell short, the person over, agreed to forbear selling any more till the short was brought up. (Hughes, 1952:248)

The 1747 regulation lasted for three years. William Brown, colliery engineer, wrote in 1749:

> To the situation of affairs in our part of the world the most material at present is wither or no the contract as it is termed with us subsists any longer. . . . The Contract . . . has been the three years past, inviolably and justly observed, notwithstanding the express acts to the contrairy. . . . Their has been two meetings of the gentlemen in order to settle the said regulation for three years more but has not yet agreed. (Sweezy, 1938:30)

The mine owners could not agree to a new regulation, and the trade opened up by 1751. In July of that year Brown reported that "the coal trade in our river is still at a very low ebb and as yet there is no likelyhood of any regulation to amend it" (Sweezy, 1952:31). The next formal regulation of the trade by the Newcastle and Sunderland owners did not materialize until the Limitation of the Vend in 1771.

CONCLUSION

Throughout the first half of the eighteenth century the government regularly intervened in the coal trade in an attempt to bring the price of coal to the London consumer down to what it considered to be a reasonable level. Exactly what this level should be was never discussed. Intervention usually took place in times of crisis, when the feeling of the London population, expressed usually through the large London consumers, was the simple notion that the price was too high and ought to be lowered. Government sought to disband combinations in the trade by making them illegal (with the goal of stimulating production and shipments to London to lower the price). The conclusion of most economic historians has been that public policy was singularly unsuccessful in achieving these ends. T. S. Willan stated,

> Throughout, the government was not very successful in its intervention in the coal trade. It was unable, in time of war, to ensure an adequate supply or a reasonable price, and even in times of peace it allowed a monopoly to grow up which was not in the best interests of either the trade or the state, for that monopoly diverted profit from the carrying branch which was essential to both. (Willan, 1967:59)

The existence of anticombination laws did not prevent the northern mine owners from attempting to establish formal regulations. An examination of the letters of several of the owners makes it clear, however, that the anticombination acts did influence their behavior, making overt actions much more difficult. The mining faction feared the publicity attendant upon Parliamentary inquiries, and it seems that the inquiries themselves often disrupted relations in the trade enough to contribute to the breakdown of certain agreements, especially those between two or more groups in the trade. It was not possible for any faction, acting alone, to successfully control the trade. The mine owners, shippers, and London dealers relied heavily on one another, and bringing their dealings into the open often caused a breakdown in cooperation (for instance, in the payment of premiums). In this sense public policy in the form of anticombination laws was successful in preventing a consistent monopolization of the trade at all levels in the chain of distribution.

NOTES

1. This figure includes statutes relating to the taxation of coal.
2. See Hausman (1976), pp. 80–92.
3. There is evidence that mine owners had attempted to band together to restrict the supply of coal to London as early as the sixteenth century, but it was not until the eighteenth century that the London dealers were brought into the regulation in a systematic way. See Sweezy (1938), chaps. 1–3.

4. *Journals of the House of Commons* (hereafter *JHC*), vol. 14, p. 10.

5. All references to the average coal price are to the price paid by the large consumers. See Hausman (1976), pp. 251–53.

6. The conclusion of the committee that these agreements existed in 1702 was concurred with by testimony given at a separate investigation undertaken by the House of Lords a year later. Historical Manuscripts, vol. 5, p. 237.

7. London, *Journals of the Court of Aldermen and Common Council* (hereafter *London Journals*), vol. 55, f. 740. The Lord Mayor of London presided over the "Courts" of the city. Two of the most important governing bodies were the Court of Aldermen and the Court of Common Council. There were twenty-six aldermen elected for life by freemen ratepayers of the twenty-six wards of the City. From these ranks (i.e., one of the aldermen) came the Lord Mayor. The aldermen exercised, both within their ward and collectively as a court, powers very much like those invested in Justices of the Peace. The Court of Common Council included the Lord Mayor and his fellow aldermen and about two-hundred commoners, also elected by the freemen of the wards. The Court had assumed both legislative and administrative functions by the eighteenth century. It was here that the major work of the city was conducted. See Webb and Webb (1908), vol. 3, pt. 2, pp. 574–77.

8. All import figures are from London, *Collector's Returns* (1695–1774). A London chaldron is approximately $1\frac{1}{3}$ tons.

9. Historical Manuscripts, p. 236. Charles Povey (1700, p. 4) had previously written, "There is a certain Combination of Men, and I have good reason to believe, that most of them go under the Denomination of Coal-Merchants, who according to their mutual Compact have united themselves together, with a full Resolution, . . . that it is a Cheat to be just, and Just to Cheat."

10. Coal meters were government agents whose job it was to record the amount of coal unloaded from each ship.

11. See Ashton (1959), p. 187.

12. London, *Repertories of the Court of Aldermen* (hereafter *London Reps*), vol. 114, f. 220.

13. *London Reps,* vol. 114, f. 235. A major strike by the keelmen of Newcastle in the spring of 1710 further complicated the issues. The months of March, April, and May saw only 47,000 chaldrons unloaded at London, the lowest spring figure for the entire century.

14. This discussion is based on Hughes (1952, pp. 166–77). Hughes's information came from the uncalendared Cotesworth-Ellison manuscripts.

15. All references to monthly dock price are for "Bear Key" from Rogers (1902).

16. *London Reps,* vol. 121, f. 165. The act 11 & 12 William III c. 21 incorporated the lightermen into the Watermen's and Lightermen's Company of the City of London and gave exclusive privilege to the company for operating craft in the Thames. Said one pamphleteer not favorable to them, "the Lightermen were incorporated into the Company of Watermen, with such exclusive privileges, as to the Use of Lighters, that other Persons trading in Coals have been greatly Injured and Oppressed thereby. The Lightermen . . . have been able to Monopolize and Engross the principal Part of the Coal Trade into their Hands." *The Case of Many Persons Keeping Wharfs* (1729).

17. This account is taken from a letter which the Whitby masters dated December 30, 1717, and is reproduced in Hughes (1952), pp. 203–4.

18. *JHC,* vol. 21, p. 465. Several years later a pamphleteer commented on the methods of the lightermen: "When a fleet of Ships was expected in, fifteen of the most considerable of these Upstart-Engrossers used to hold a Cabal, in which having first settled the Market-Price to their own Minds, everyone staked a moidore by way of Gage, that he would not

make a Breach in the Combination, by giving more for his Coals than the Standard here agreed upon." *Frauds and Abuses* (1744), pp. 7–8.

19. *JHC,* vol. 21, p. 517. The lightermen answered many of the charges against them in a pamphlet. They stated, "The only exclusive Privilege to which the Company of Lightermen are intitled, is that of keeping and working Lighters for Hire, all other Persons being at Liberty to keep Lighters, &c for their own use. . . . The said Lightermen have no Advantage in Buying, above any other Dealers in Coals, Consumers, &c, but what is the usual Consequence of large Vend, and constant Attendance at Market. . . . The said Lightermen, tho' they have acquired a great Share of Trade, yet have not been guilty of any Thing tending to a Monopoly." The charge that they gained unfair advantage by acting as crimps for their own ships they answered as follows: "And the said Lightermen apprehend the Shipping is in no danger of suffering by their acting as Crimps or Factors to such Ships as they themselves are Part-owners in, and from which 'tis very reasonable they should expect a Profit, especially since it is always in the Power of the Master to change his Crimp as often as he thinks fit." *The Case of the Watermen* (1730).

20. A pamphleteer in 1730 asserted much the same: "As by this Act several Persons who used to act as Crimps or Factors of Coals, will be prohibited from so doing for the future, notwithstanding the Masters and Owners might think it for their Advantage so to employ them; this is apprehended to be done only with intent to bring the Sale of all Coals in the Port of London into the hands of a few Factors, by which means they will be able more easily to combine and impose an exhorbitant Price to the Prejudice of the Publick." *The Case of the Coal Trade* (1730).

21. John (1965).

22. It was during this period that Parliamentary policy switched from an emphasis on influencing the structural form of the trade to direct price control. The government of the city of London at no time exhibited a preference for this policy initiative. See Hausman (1976, pp. 80–92).

REFERENCES

Ashton, T. S. (1959), *Economic Fluctuations in England 1700–1800*. Oxford: Clarendon Press.

The Case of the Coal Trade (1730), London.

The Case of Many Persons Keeping Wharfs, and Others, Dealing in Coals, in the Cities of London and Westminster (1729), London.

The Case of the Watermen and Lightermen Working on the River of Thames (1730), London.

Dendy, F. W., ed. (1901), *Extracts from the Records of the Company of Hostmen of Newcastle-upon-Tyne,* vol. 105. Durham: Surtees Society.

The Frauds and Abuses of the Coal-Dealers Detected and Exposed; in a Letter to an Alderman of London (1744). London: M. Cooper.

Hausman, William J. (1976), *Public Policy and the Supply of Coal to London, 1700–1770*. Unpublished Ph.D. dissertation, University of Illinois.

Historical Manuscripts Commission (1910), *Manuscripts of the House of Lords 1702–1704,* n.s. vol. 5. London: H.M.S.O.

Hughes, Edward (1952), *North Country Life in the Eighteenth Century: The Northeast, 1700–1750*. London: Oxford University Press.

John, A. H. (1965), "Agricultural Productivity and Economic Growth in England, 1700–1760." *The Journal of Economic History* 25 (March):19–34.

Journals of the House of Commons (1803), Reported by order of the House of Commons.

A Letter to Sir William Strickland, Bart. (1730), London: J. Wilford.

London (1694–1775), *Collector's Returns of the Orphans Duty of 4d. and 10d./ch.*, 25 vols., Corporation of London Record Office.

London, *Journals of the Court of Aldermen and the Court of Common Council,* Corporation of London Record Office.

London (1710), *Minutes of the Committee to Examine the Combination amongst Coal Traders,* Corporation of London Record Office.

London, *Repertories of the Court of Aldermen of the City of London,* Corporation of London Record Office.

Nixon, George (1739), *An Enquiry into the Reasons of the Advance of the Price of Coals, within Seven Years Past.* London: E. Comyrus.

Philalethes (1729), *A Free and Impartial Enquiry into the Reasons of the Present Extravagant Price of Coals.* London: T. Cox.

Povey, Charles (1700), *A Discovery of Indirect Practices in the Coal Trade.* London: H. Hills and A. Baldwin.

Rogers, J. E. T. (1902), *A History of Agriculture and Prices in England,* 7 vols. Oxford: Clarendon Press.

Smith, Raymond (1961), *Sea-Coal for London: History of the Coal Factors in the London Market.* London: Longmans, Green & Co.

Sweezy, Paul (1938), *Monopoly and Competition in the English Coal Trade 1550–1850.* Cambridge, Mass.: Harvard University Press.

Webb, Sidney and Beatrice Webb (1908), *English Local Government from the Revolution to the Municipal Incorporation Act: The Manor and the Borough,* vol. 3, part 2. London: Longmans, Green & Co.

Willan, T. S. (1967), *The English Coasting Trade 1600–1750.* Manchester: Manchester University Press.

REGULATION WITHOUT HISTORICAL JUSTIFICATION:

THE CASE OF HOUSEHOLD MOVING

Dana C. Hewins

The depression years of the 1930s spawned a considerable amount of legislation which either created new regulatory agencies or expanded the powers of existing agencies. One such piece of legislation was the Motor Carrier Act of 1935, which brought most interstate motor carriers under the control of the Interstate Commerce Commission (ICC). Whatever justification there may have been for regulating other interstate motor carriers in 1935, there was little or no justification for regulating interstate carriers of household goods. These moving companies, which numbered more than four thousand, should never have been regulated.

Variations in Business and Economic History:
Essays in Honor of Donald L. Kemmerer
Research in Economic History, Suppl. 2, pages 71–92.

ISBN: 0-89232-262-4

I. RUINOUS COMPETITION AND THE NEED FOR TRUCKING REGULATION

The literature on the origins of federal motor-carrier regulation is extensive.[1] However, the bulk of this literature argues that "ruinous" (or "destructive," "cutthroat," or "excessive") competition, both among truckers (intramodal) and between truckers and the railroads (intermodal), was the principal form of market failure which warranted the regulation of interstate trucking in 1935.

Competition among motor carriers became intense during the 1930s because of a general decrease in demand for transportation services and the large-scale entry of unemployed men with trucks ("fly-by-nighters") into the industry. The absence of entry barriers and the lack of alternative job opportunities made this industry exceptionally attractive.[2]

As was to be expected, increased supply in the face of decreased demand generated excess capacity and severe downward pressure on rates, the result being, according to the Federal Coordinator of Transportation, that rates were often "demoralized by operators with little or no knowledge of costs, or by those who have been driven by sheer financial necessity to quote rates which they know to be unremunerative" (United States Congress, 1934:14).

According to Fair and Williams, price discrimination also became rampant during the 1930s, and the quality of service deteriorated:

> There was no rate structure, variations in individual rates were wide, rates were constantly changing, charges to various shippers using the same carrier were often different, and the service was neither stable nor reliable. Shippers found it increasingly difficult to do business with motor carriers because of the unreliability of service and the financial irresponsibility of many of the carriers, and they were distressed at fluctuating rates and differential treatment. (Fair and Williams, 1959:488)

Hudson and Constantin have noted that, as the number of carriers increased during the depression, "competition became more intense and resulted in rate wars, extensive evasion of state regulations, and widespread destructive practices of various kinds" (Hudson and Constantin, 1958:475). According to Elmer Smead, bankruptcies were frequent but "newcomers were entering the industry as fast as the failures dropped out" (Smead, 1969:256). Hudson and Constantin ultimately concluded that, because of these chaotic conditions, "the whole structure of the industry was weakened" (Hudson and Constantin, 1958:475).

Competition between unregulated motor carriers and regulated railroads was also intense during the 1930s, and trucks began making serious inroads into many railroad markets. The proportion of domestic traffic carried by trucks more than doubled between 1928 and 1935, and much of this newly gained truck traffic consisted of high-value commodities which had formerly traveled at higher-class railroad rates (Cunningham, 1934:47–48). Consequently, the railroads' plight was more acute than the percentages indicate, since the traffic lost tended to be the most profitable portion of their business.

The plight of the railroads quickly became the focal point in the debate over trucking regulation in the 1930s. A 1932 ICC report (Interstate Commerce Commission, 1932), the 1934 report of the Federal Coordinator of Transportation (United States Congress, 1934), and virtually every Congressional hearing on the subject of transportation in the 1930s were almost completely dominated by the problem of railroad–motor carrier competition. Concern became widespread not only for the financial solvency of the railroads, but also for the financial solvency of the railroads' creditors. As Shepherd and Wilcox have commented:

> The Great Depression hit the railroads hard. Car loadings fell off; from 1929 to 1932 gross revenues were cut in half. If the railroads had been less highly levered financially, they would have been in a better position to sustain this loss. But 56 percent of their capitalization in 1932 was in bonds, bearing an average interest charge of 4.6 percent. In many cases, though operating costs were covered, interest could not be paid. By 1938, 111 railroads, with more than 30 percent of the country's mileage, had become insolvent and were in receivership. Railway bonds had been conservative investments, held by institutional investors. The railway problem became, not that of protecting the shippers against the railroads, but that of protecting the holders of railroad securities against financial loss. (Shepherd and Wilcox, 1979:382)

Nelson and Greiner have persuasively argued that Congress was also keenly interested in maintaining the discriminatory railroad rate structure which had historically subsidized the transportation of certain commodities, especially raw materials and foodstuffs:

> . . . it is clear that if, by the act of 1935, Congress sought to help the railroads, it was not solely out of concern for their employees and owners. Help for the railroads meant preservation of the rail pricing system and retention of depressed rates on some commodities. Truck competition clearly threatened the viability of that price structure and, if allowed to persist, would have necessitated the increase of some rail rates. Control of truck competition through regulation may have held out the prospect of helping the railroads, and no doubt railroad lobbying aided in the passage of the Motor Carrier Act but, nevertheless, chief among the confluence of interests which brought about passage of the act was pressure from certain shippers and representatives of certain regions to retain the benefits of value-of-service rates. (Nelson and Greiner, 1965:364)

Whatever Congress's motives, there appears to be a consensus of opinion that "increasingly intensive competition between motor carriers and rail carriers, more than any other single factor, was responsible for the enactment of Motor Carrier Act'' (Hudson and Constantin, 1958: 475). Hence, as has been often noted, the primary objective of the 1935 legislation was ''transport coordination,'' the euphemistic equivalent for minimizing intermodal competition between railroads and interstate truckers. Secondary objectives, formulated mainly in response to excessive intramodal competition, were allegedly to ensure reasonable and stable rates, promote financial responsibility and stability, guarantee dependable service, and prevent discrimination in the interstate trucking industry.[3] To achieve these ends the ICC was given jurisdiction over interstate motor-carrier rates, entry, mergers, security issues, bonding, and the adequacy of service.

II. RUINOUS COMPETITION AND THE REGULATION OF HOUSEHOLD MOVING

Careful study of the moving industry's experience before and during the 1930s suggests that these carriers should not have been swept up in the tide to regulate interstate truckers. Competition was not in any meaningful sense ''ruinous'' at either the intramodal or the intermodal level, nor was there any extenuating circumstance which might, on other grounds, have warranted federal regulation. Put simply, Congress apparently regulated the moving industry because it fell victim to the historically pernicious tendency of agglomerating all motor carriers into a single industry; Congress simply failed to appreciate the heterogeneous nature of motor carriage in general, and the uniqueness of the moving industry in particular.

The moving industry has always been unique. Compared to other segments of American trucking, the moving industry has always been quite distinct in its history, clientele, structure, costs, operational procedures, equipment, skill requirements, return-haul situation, and peak-load problems. For purposes of the present study, the industry's history prior to 1935, especially as it relates to intermodal and intramodal competition, is particularly revelant.[4] Since the history of the moving industry is not well known, a conscious effort will be made to present the arguments relevant to ruinous competition in a historical context.

The American household-moving industry is probably about two centuries old, dating back to shortly before the Revolutionary War when a newly formed express company began carrying household goods on the Eastern seaboard (Alexander, 1970:2–3). Since that time, the moving industry has gone through several periods of marked transition.

The first important transitionary period occurred during the latter half of the nineteenth century when the nature of medium and long-distance moving was radically altered by the advent of a nationwide network of railroads. Prior to the railway age, most moves were effected by horse and wagon, by boat, or by a combination of the two. The coming of the railroad had little impact on local and short-distance moving, but it had pronounced effects on moves of longer distances. As the nineteenth century progressed, it became increasingly common for migrating families to hire a local moving company to crate and transport their possessions to a railroad car which would, in turn, carry the goods across the country and deliver them into the hands of another mover who would transport them by horse and wagon to their ultimate destination. Hence, by the end of the nineteenth century a close relationship had developed between movers and the railroads, a relationship based on cooperation, not competition.

Following 1900 an accelerating trend away from the horse and wagon and toward the motor truck signaled the start of another period of revolutionary transition. This critical era of change was both difficult and long, lasting more than two decades.

The first moving vans appeared at about the turn of the century. They were makeshift vehicles, often just open-rack cattle trucks with tarpaulin covers. Prior to 1920, the principal impact of these trucks was on the local and short-distance moving markets. Many moving concerns, including the Bekins Moving and Storage Company, had completely replaced horses with trucks by 1920, but the limitations of these trucks and the generally poor quality of the roads limited their effective range to about forty to fifty miles (Hess, 1973:27–28); consequently, as Stanley Alexander has observed, "long distance moving at the time [prior to 1920] was almost entirely a matter of crating household goods for shipment by rail" (Alexander, 1970:230).

Enclosed vans designed and built specifically to carry uncrated household goods probably began appearing shortly before 1920. Ward Hiner, founder of the Red Ball Transit Company and a pioneer in the long-distance moving industry, was instrumental in the development of early moving vans. His first specially constructed moving vans had eighteen-foot bodies, but by 1920 semitrailers that were twenty to twenty-four feet long began appearing.

In 1920, Hiner decided that the time had come to begin shipping household goods for long distances by motor truck. In that year, Hiner's Red Ball Transit Company sent a caravan of nine vans loaded with household goods from Indianapolis to New York. Only 56 miles of the 729-mile route traveled by Hiner's trucks were paved, and the trip took two weeks. When Hiner's vans reached Times Square, newspaper photographers and Pathé newsreel cameramen excitedly recorded the arrival of "the first through shipments from the midwest" (Alexander, 1970:231).

The era of cooperation between movers and the railroads was coming to an end.

III. RAILROADS AND THE MOVING INDUSTRY: THE ERA OF COMPETITION

The relationship between railroads and the moving industry changed following 1920 as movers began increasingly to compete rather than cooperate with railroads on long-distance hauls. The contest quickly proved to be one-sided; the inherent advantages of trucks in transporting household goods were simply too great. As Charles Taff has written:

> Prior to the advent of the motor van, the transporting of the contents of a household to a new location was performed by rail. This involved cartage of household effects to a warehouse, packing and crating, transportation by the rail carrier, carting to the residence, and unpacking there. The development of household goods motor carriers made possible transportation from a household to the new location without the extensive crating and packing, rehandling, and longer time in transit. (Taff, 1969:145)

As Table 1 indicates, the total tonnage of "household goods and secondhand furniture" transported by the nation's Class I steam railways decreased sharply between 1920 and 1927. Data for the years 1928 and 1929 are not available due to a change in ICC cargo classifications, but it seems quite certain that trucks had effectively squeezed the railroads out of the moving business by 1930.

Table 1. Tonnage of Household Goods and Secondhand Furniture Originating on Class I Steam Railways, 1920–1927

Year	*Tons of Household Goods and Secondhand Furniture*	*Household Goods and Secondhand Furniture as a Percent of Total Class I Railway Tonnage*
1920	1,850,590	0.15
1921	886,880	0.09
1922	677,458	0.07
1923	684,900	0.05
1924	595,833	0.05
1925	511,478	0.04
1926	443,727	0.03
1927	364,608	0.03

Source: Interstate Commerce Commission, *Annual Report of the Interstate Commerce Commission,* for the years 1921 through 1928. The data are contained in appendixes entitled "Statistical Summaries."

Following 1930, an interesting change occurred. The depression years wrought changes in the basic economics of moving which spawned a desire in many movers to reverse the evolutionary process and give traffic back to the railroads.

As the depression unfolded, the number of movers increased while the volume of traffic decreased (Hess, 1973, chap. 3), and in some areas moving rates were substantially reduced. Booking return hauls became more difficult, and many movers came to view long-distance moving as a losing proposition. Early in 1932, several speakers to the annual convention of the National Furniture Warehouseman's Association (NFWA) argued that movers generally lost money on shipments of more than three hundred miles (Bateman, 1932). In that same year, a detailed statistical study was published in *The Furniture Warehouseman* which appeared to confirm the suspicions of many movers that cartage, the actual transporting of household goods, was in general a losing proposition; the profitable portions of the moving business, according to this study (which used fully allocated costs), were storage and packing and crating (*The Furniture Warehouseman,* August 1932:434–35).[5]

By 1932 it was also quite clear that there existed an ever-present danger that the railroads would soon establish their own moving companies—many railroads had already bought trucks to haul other commodities—to crate and carry household goods to their railroad cars. This had already happened on a large scale in England, and evidences of its happening in the United States were surfacing (Aspinwall, 1932:563; Ferguson, 1932:577). Movers were aware of this danger, and since they already faced an abundance of competitors, the prospect of even more companies' entering the moving industry must have appeared foreboding. F. L. Bateman appears to have echoed the sentiments of many of the participants at the 1932 NFWA convention when he stated:

> Right here is where the furniture warehouseman will preserve his business if we watch our step. Right here is where we will work into cooperative arrangements for a coordinated rail and truck service. We will not make the mistake which our English friends made in fostering rail competition by arbitrarily trying to hold household removals entirely to the highways. (Bateman, 1932:229)

Combining the apparent unprofitability of cartage, especially long-distance cartage, with the danger that railroads would enter the moving business on a large scale, it seems evident that movers were confronted with considerable inducements to revert to the old system of cooperation with railroads. If railroads did enter the moving business, existing members of the moving industry would lose packing and crating revenue they would otherwise have earned; by cooperating with railroads, movers lost cartage revenues, but such revenues, especially those accruing on long hauls, were believed insufficient to cover cartage costs anyway, so they were considered well lost. In short, it must have appeared to many movers that, by reverting back to the rail method of shipping household goods, they not only could forestall the entry of railroads into the moving business, thereby protecting packing and crating revenues, but also rid themselves of long-distance cartage, apparently the biggest drain on their profits. Small wonder that many movers sought a return to the rail method during the depression.

Additional impetus toward the rail method was supplied by the tremendous drop in furniture prices which occurred during the early 1930s. In 1932, it was estimated that a small apartment could be comfortably furnished for $200 to $300.[6] With the price of furniture this low, movers had to keep rates as low as possible, especially on the more expensive long-distance moves, or else stand idly by as prospective customers decided it was cheaper to sell their household goods at the point of origin and buy new furniture at the point of destination. The best way of keeping long-distance rates down was by shipping via the rail method; for despite the many inconveniences and delays associated with moving by rail, it was often cheaper than moving long-distance by motor truck (see, for example, Bateman, 1932:229; Holt, 1932:16).

In light of these several inducements, it is not surprising to discover that movers actively sought a return to the rail method. Henry Reimers, executive secretary of the NFWA, testified before the ICC on March 10, 1931, that there was an urgent need for increased coordination of movers and railroads (Reimers, 1931:231–32). Late in 1932, the NFWA openly appealed to the nation's railroads, with some success,[7] to lower rates on household goods in an obvious attempt to stimulate long-distance moving by rail (*The Furniture Warehouseman,* January 1933:14–17).

This latter action, more than any other single event, underscores the fundamental difference between household movers and other segments of the trucking industry. Other truckers often opposed efforts aimed at equalizing rail-truck rates, whether it was by lowering rail rates, raising truck rates, or a combination of the two. The reason was simple: these truckers were competing with railroads, trying to wrest away rail business in what must have appeared to be a zero-sum struggle. Movers, on the other hand, found it to be in their best interest once again to cooperate, not compete, with the railroads. To movers lower rail rates were a blessing; to other truckers they were anathema.

Unfortunately, data limitations render it impossible to determine to what extent movers succeeded in their efforts to revert to the rail method of transporting household goods. Problems of determining liability for damage, of coping with the relatively high cost and poor quality of existing containers, and of establishing mutually satisfactory through rates impeded but did not stop the movement to return long-distance moving, which in many instances was synonymous with interstate moving, to the rails.

In any event, the following conclusions appear to be warranted. Household goods and secondhand furniture accounted for only three-hundredths of one percent of Class I railway tonnage in 1927, and probably even less than this in 1929. Even if movers had sought and succeeded in wresting all remaining household-goods traffic from the railroads during the 1930s, railroad finances and rate structures could not have been significantly affected. As it was, many movers sought instead to give traffic back to the railroads rather than take it away. Accordingly, one must ultimately conclude, on the basis of evidence now available, that federal regulation of the interestate moving industry in 1935, in possibly sharp contrast to the regulation of other interstate truckers, cannot be justified on grounds that it was needed to eliminate cutthroat competition between movers and the railroads.

IV. COMPETITION AMONG MOVERS: 1900 to 1930

If federal regulation of the moving industry in 1935 cannot be justified on grounds of saving railroads from the movers, perhaps it can be justified on grounds of saving movers from themselves; expressed differently, perhaps regulation was needed to eliminate ruinous competition within the moving industry. The need for federal regulation to eliminate ruinous competition in the trucking industry has long been a favorite in some quarters, including the ICC, where it is asserted that innate characteristics of the trucking industry, such as low entry barriers and the joint-product nature of the service (i.e., the inevitability of return hauls), render the industry extraordinarily vulnerable to ruinous competition; the depression, so the argument goes, merely demonstrated this vulnerability in exaggerated form.

All available evidence indicates that exceptionally intense competition apparently was a problem in the moving industry during the period of transition from horse and wagon to motor trucks (Hess, 1973, chap. 2). Indeed, all things considered, it would have been remarkable if conditions in the moving industry (and in the rest of American trucking) had been anything but chaotic during the years between 1900 and 1930. These were years in which an infant industry, caught in the throes of technological revolution, sought desperately to grow up. Most moving companies during this period were small and owned but a single piece of equipment; most were also family owned and operated, run by men long on strength but short in business acumen, men strong in the desire to own their own businesses but weak in the knowledge of how to operate a moving company profitably (Hess, 1973, chap. 2).

In addition, since movers were increasingly willing and able to carry household goods for longer distances, the ever-present problem posed by the empty backhaul was seriously aggravated, since, as a general rule, it was (and still is) more difficult to book a return load from more distant locations and more costly to return home empty. It has been estimated that between 1924 and 1927 the nation's moving companies were, on average, only about 20 percent full on return loads (Hess, 1973:25). In view of this, it is most probable that movers frequently resorted to pricing at or below (due to ignorance) short-run marginal cost in procuring return hauls.

Industry experts recognized clearly that the problems of booking return loads and ignorance, especially about costs and costing methods, were the principal sources of instability in the moving business, and during the 1920s concerted efforts were made to alleviate both of these problems.

The most significant attempt at solving the return-loads problem during the 1920s involved the formation of mover groups whose primary function was to minimize light-loaded mileage. As John Hess has commented:

> It took no crystal ball for hard-headed businessmen to see that the lack of return loads for their intercity vans was definitely hurting business. They felt that they were not capitalizing on business that should be there and on the efficient utilization of equipment that was both expensive and heavy. So, these people tried to secure such return loads as they could by forming cooperative return-load ventures. (Hess, 1973:21)

The two most notable of these early cooperative ventures were the Intercity Return Load Bureau (founded by the NFWA) and the Return Loads Service, Incorporated; Allied Van Lines, now the nation's largest moving company, was spawned by the former in 1928, and the United Van Lines, currently the nation's fourth largest mover, was established by the latter also in 1928. Both of these van lines have always had as their principal objective the minimization of light-loaded mileage through member-agent coordination and cooperation.

The establishment of statewide trade associations appears to have been the industry's first organized attempt to combat ignorance, particularly in the areas of cost and rate setting. The principal aim of these trade associations during the early 1900s was apparently to convince movers, through both speech and written word, that rate cutting was a senseless and malicious practice. Typical of these efforts was the address delivered by Charles S. Morris to the Illinois Furniture Warehouseman's Association in June of 1914:

> The public has the erroneous idea that price agreement is a conspiracy against the consumer. Exactly the contrary is true. Price chaos eventually injures the consumer—prevents the honest businessman from rendering his best and encourages the cheat. (Morris, 1933:159)

Toward the end of his speech, Morris waxed passionate and spewed forth the following purpled invective:

> In our mercantile life the parallel (to a social anarchist) is the price-cutter, that venomous destroyer of organized effort, that cheat who defrauds the public of the best we are able to give—an assassin that kills honest competition and fosters in its stead bitter rate competition, rather than rate computation. This is the analogy—the business anarchist—aiming to destroy the structure reared on a foundation of service. (Morris, 1933:259)

Morris's plea for restraint was echoed numerous times during the following two decades as more trade associations were established, including, in 1920, the National Furniture Warehousemen's Association.

During the 1920s attention was increasingly focused on costs and costing methods, as an ever-growing number of movers began to recognize the linkage between ignorance about costs and excessive rate competition. In 1925, C. B. Carruth, actuary for the American Warehousemen's Association, delivered a major address in which he convincingly identified ignorance about costs as the primary cause of rate wars and the single greatest evil then facing the moving industry (Carruth, 1925:599–600). The industry's trade associations fought this evil during the 1920s by sponsoring speakers and printing articles on the subject of costs, by developing and disseminating cost-accounting manuals, and, in some instances, by employing specialists to answer the specific question of members on the subject of costs (Carruth, 1925:599–600).

Although it seems clear that the 1900 to 1930 period, viewed as a whole, was a most difficult one for the moving and storage industry, it also seems clear that the latter stages of this period must have witnessed at least the planting of seeds of increased stability due primarily to the dissemination of more and better information, the incipient trend toward cooperative return-load ventures, and the industry's increased familiarity with the intricacies of motor-truck operations.[8]

V. COMPETITION AMONG MOVERS: THE DEPRESSION YEARS

These seeds of stability were destined to germinate during a most difficult period—the depression years of the 1930s—a period in which the volume of moving business, particularly interstate moving business, dropped in most areas as fewer people moved and more of those who did change residences either moved themselves, sold their furniture before moving, or placed their household goods in storage before moving in with relatives. Add to this declining volume of business an influx of the much-maligned "fly-by-nighters"—essentially unemployed men with trucks, often secondhand, newly acquired vehicles—and one has all the ingredients necessary for marked instability. More movers—many of them uneducated, uninitiated, even unprincipled—fighting for a shrinking volume of business in an industry historically plagued by a backhaul problem and excess capacity; how could anything but ruinous competition and chaos have been the result? But ruinous competition was not the result, at least not in view of the evidence now available; instead, the moving industry apparently fared remarkably well compared with the rest of the economy.

Before attempting to defend this assertion about competition in the moving industry during the depression, a brief digression on the meaning of "ruinous" or "excessive" competition is necessary. Richard Posner has argued that, "When businessmen complain about excessive competition, what they usually mean is that they would be happier if their prices were higher than their marginal costs" (Posner, 1972:153). Meyer, Peck, Stenason, and Zwick have, in contrast, explained the economist's view:

> Excessive competition, if it is to be other than a term to cloak a self-serving dislike of competition, must mean a competitive situation producing prices persistently below costs, so that consumer choices are not guided by relative costs but rather are subsidized by the producer. Such subsidization, in addition to distorting the allocation of resources, produces low returns for investors, thus adversely affecting the long-run flow of capital into the industry. (Meyer et al., 1959:215–16)

Obviously, any decisive test for the absence or presence of excessive competition should ideally involve the careful examination of rate and cost data. Unfortunately, such data are simply not available with respect to the moving industry during the depression years. However, an abundant quantity of other types of evidence are available which do strongly suggest that intramodal competition was in no meaningful sense ruinous during the early 1930s.

Consider, for example, the years 1931 and 1932, certainly two of the worst years of the depression. During these two years, industry experts almost tripped over one another in their eagerness to point out how fortunate the moving and storage trade was in comparison with other industries. This theme was repeated in many places, including a March 1931 editorial by the editors of *The Furniture Warehouseman* (*The Fur-*

niture Warehouseman, March 1931:158), a September 1931 report by Harvey B. Lyon, vice-president of the Western Division of the NFWA (Lyon, 1931:596), and a March 1932 speech by E. B. Gould, a past president of the NFWA (Gould, 1932:163). Perhaps the most unequivocal and forceful statement of this viewpoint was delivered in a speech to the annual NFWA convention in 1932 by William I. Ford, a past president of the NFWA and a man intimately acquainted with the moving and storage industry. In the course of this address, Ford proclaimed:

> It is but natural . . . that we should take a sort of personal account; and I want to say to you gentlemen, each and every one of you, that we are the luckiest bunch in the United States. There is not a business which has stood the tests of the last two years like the household goods industry. (Ford, 1932:165)

If one assumes, as seems reasonable, that the experiences of the NFWA's more than seven hundred members were indicative of industry conditions in general, then there is considerable evidence to support the view that the moving and storage trade did fare comparatively well during the depression. In an unofficial search conducted by Harvey B. Lyon in 1932, movers in only five cities were found to have reduced prices significantly during the depression (Lyon, 1932:24). A more detailed 1932 survey indicated that 45 percent of all NFWA members had not cut rates at all, and another 14 percent had cut rates by less than 15 percent (Warren, 1932:208).

Compared with rates in other industries, moving rates were apparently well behaved in general, and do not appear to have taken the catastrophic plunge toward unremunerative levels which personifies ruinous competition. Instead, a two-tier system of rates evolved with the newcomers charging rates which remained on average about 25 percent lower than the rates of established firms (Warren, 1932:208). This two-tier rate structure proved remarkably stable since experience in several key areas had clearly demonstrated the futility of trying to match the rates of newcomers.[9]

Moreover, many established movers felt there was no need to match rates with newcomers; established companies believed they provided a higher-quality service and, as one industry expert put it in 1933, "the public has always been willing to pay for service and always will be" (Theibault, 1933:141). As this statement indicates, moving was considered a differentiated service; established companies offered the public better equipment, more highly skilled personnel, and more experience in the business of moving. Consequently, many established movers apparently felt it was unnecessary to match rates with the lower-priced competition.

Comparative rate stability in turn bred reasonably good profit performance during the early 1930s. C. F. B. Tippet, chairman of the NFWA

Statistical Committee, conducted detailed statistical studies of member operations for the years 1931 and 1932. Fortunately, the results of these studies were later published for the benefit of the NFWA membership (Tippet, 1932, 1933). Both of these studies were based upon information supplied by NFWA members; the two studies differ mainly in that, for summary purposes, Tippet's 1931 study used averages and the 1932 study used medians.

These two studies, both of which employed ratio analysis and used fully allocated costs for comparing the profitability of different services, indicate that the average NFWA company in 1931 and the median company in 1932 both earned a net profit.[10] In contrast, all American industries combined, and, more narrowly, all service industries combined both sustained net losses (United States Department of Commerce, 1960:581, 184).

Information about the year 1933 is scarce, and information about 1934 and early 1935 is tainted by the passage, in April 1934, of the Code of Fair Competition for the Household Goods Storage and Moving Trade which was adopted under the NRA. The main provisions of this code involved rules governing maximum hours, minimum wages, and the filing of tariffs which were to be compensatory on a fully allocated cost basis.

It is impossible to determine to what extent this code influenced industry performance. Technical matters and differences of opinion between the industry and the NRA Commission combined to obstruct enforcement of the code for many months after its passage (Dunn, 1935). Nevertheless, the mere presence of the code does make it difficult to interpret data concerning 1934 and 1935. In early 1935, for example, moving rates apparently rose nationwide by 10 to 20 percent, but the unknown impact of the code makes it impossible to infer much from this information (Warren, 1935:141).

In spite of this, it is still possible to draw some reasonable conclusions, based on the evidence that is now available, about the nature of competition in the moving industry during the depression years. The most important conclusion is that branding that competition as ruinous or excessive is apparently wrong. Conditions in the moving industry were not generally chaotic, and, in a relative sense, the industry was in many ways quite fortunate. Reasons for the industry's relatively good fortune were manifold and have been extensively discussed elsewhere (Hewins, 1975, chap. 2). These reasons include the vigorous and sustained efforts of trade associations, the dissemination of more and better information, the proliferation of cooperative return-haul ventures, the differentiated nature of the service, a trend toward increased diversification, the preparation and distribution of a comprehensive and clearly written study of moving operations by the General Motors Truck Company, and the relative stability of storage revenues.

In his history of the moving and storage industry, John Hess, in the course of describing the depression years, noted that it had been difficult for him to find "a complete and candid description of the way things really were in those 'difficult days'" (Hess, 1973:47). Hess's problem appears to have been twofold. First, his principal source of information was a series of interviews with senior moving men who had experienced the depression years firsthand. Second, he apparently had accepted in advance the premise that competition must have been excessive and conditions chaotic. When Hess was unable to elicit a satisfying description of the chaos and ruination which presumably should have characterized these years, he rationalized by observing that, "Now that the pain is far behind, people simply don't want to talk about those times" (Hess, 1973:47).

The evidence provided in the present study obviously suggests an alternative explanation for Hess's dilemma, and it further suggests that federal regulation of the moving industry in 1935 cannot be convincingly defended on grounds it was needed to rescue an industry which teetered on the brink of ruination due to excessive intramodal competition.

VI. THREE OTHER POSSIBLE REASONS FOR REGULATION

The possibility exists that federal regulation of the moving industry was historically justified for reasons other than the need to eliminate excessive intermodal and/or intramodal competition. The legislative history of the Motor Carrier Act of 1935 suggests three possible alternative justifications (see especially Wagner, 1935).

First, federal regulation may have been needed to make state regulation effective. Beginning with Pennsylvania in 1914, many states had decided to regulate intrastate trucking prior to 1935 in order to protect highways, ensure the public's safety, and curb an alleged tendency toward excessive competition which seemed to characterize the infant trucking industry. Many studies indicate that it was primarily the desire to ameliorate excessive competition among motor carriers and between motor carriers and the railroads which ultimately led most legislatures to adopt economic regulations, especially rate and entry controls (Harper, 1959). Most states—Kentucky, New Hampshire, and North Carolina were notable exceptions—included household-goods carriers under their newly opened regulatory umbrellas.

Prior to 1925 the states had generally assumed that their laws legally encompassed motor carriers operating in interstate commerce. This belief was shattered, however, by a series of landmark Supreme Court decisions in 1925.[11] As a result of these and subsequent decisions, the states could no longer compel interstate carriers to show that public convenience and necessity required their operation, nor could they regulate the rates of interstate carriers. The states were even stripped of the power to require interstate operators to carry liability insurance or indemnity bonds for the satisfaction of legal liabilities to passengers and shippers. Deeply disturbed by this turn of events, many state regulatory bodies banded together in forming the National Association of Railroads and Utilities Commissioners; it was this association that in 1925 sponsored the first bill in Congress aimed at federal regulation of motor carriers.

In 1928 the Interstate Commerce Commission, of its own initiative, conducted an extensive study into the need for federal motor-carrier regulation. The commission claimed that it undertook the study in response to the problems caused by the 1925 court decisions, and also because of the growing problems posed to regulated railroads by unregulated truckers.

During the course of its investigation, the ICC held hearings in thirteen U.S. cities and accumulated more than five thousand pages of testimony from the more than four hundred witnesses who appeared before it. These witnesses included shippers, farmers, manufacturers, truckers (including at least several household goods carriers), and representatives from local governments, trade associations, highway commissions, state regulatory bodies, the automotive industry, and the railroads.

The principal fruit of the ICC's efforts, a 1928 report entitled *Motor Bus and Motor Truck Operation,* has never been afforded the attention it deserves. Perhaps the most interesting feature of this sixty-five-page report is the almost complete absence of any mention of ruinous or excessive intramodal competition. This omission seems extraordinary in light of the commission's statement that it was "unnecessary and wasteful competition in the trucking industry which provided the primary impetus for most state regulation" (Interstate Commerce Commission, 1928:737). Perhaps ruinous competition among truckers was omitted as a possible reason for federal regulation because there was, by the late 1920s, "already much evidence of increasing stability, even under conditions of competition" (Peterson, 1929:618).

The commission went on to acknowledge openly that the quality of trucking services appeared to be generally high, noting that "few complaints were registered against the service rendered by either contract-carrier or common-carrier trucks" (Interstate Commerce Commission, 1928:708). Ultimately, the picture that emerged from this exhaustive study was encouraging: the nation's motor carriers, including carriers of household goods, were apparently providing an abundant quantity of high-quality services at reasonable rates.

Confronted with such a picture, the commission explicitly rejected the suggestion that the problems posed to the states by the 1925 court decisions were sufficient to warrant federal regulation; indeed, the commission concluded that there was no reason whatever to adopt federal regulation of trucking in 1928:

> While experience may show that the interstate transportation of property by motor vehicles operating as common carriers on public highways should be regulated, there does not appear to be at this time public need therefor. (Interstate Commerce Commission, 1928:746)

In view of this report and the relatively good performance of the moving industry even during the depression, it is difficult to accept the view that federal regulation was needed to make state regulation effective; indeed, it is tempting to conclude that the economic regulation of moving by the states was itself an anachronism by 1935, and that efforts should have been directed at exempting movers from the state statutes rather than subjecting them to a federal statute.

Second, federal regulation may have been warranted in 1935 in order to combat price discrimination. There can be no doubt that price discrimination did occur in the moving industry prior to 1935, but this was not necessarily evil. Under certain conditions, unregulated price discrimination can improve resource allocation, beneficially stimulate rate competition, and lead to lower average rates than would have prevailed in the absence of discrimination (see, for example, Scherer, 1980, chap. 10).

The issue becomes even more complicated when one recognizes that it is generally only "unjust" discrimination that most people want regulation to stop. Unfortunately, reasonable people can have markedly different ideas about what is just and what is unjust. Price discrimination does tend to redistribute income toward the discriminator and away from his customers; however, in the absence of some highly subjective value judgments or some necessarily imprecise interpersonal utility comparisons, it is impossible to say whether such a redistribution is just or unjust. To illustrate, is it unjust if price discrimination results in a redistribution of income from large industrial corporations to small moving companies? Reasonable people might give different answers to such a question. Reverse the situation so that income is being redistributed from small corporations to large moving companies, and the answers might again be quite different.

Income distribution aside, some people feel it is simply unjust on equity grounds for some persons, institutions, or groups to pay lower prices (without cost justification) for equivalent services than others. However, suppose those who receive the lower prices tend also to be in a lower income group: is discrimination under these circumstances unjust or otherwise socially undesirable?

Arthur Thompson has aptly observed, "Whether price discrimination is good or bad hinges upon subjective evaluations over which reasonable men may disagree. Value judgments inevitably creep into the picture" (Thompson, 1977:436). In view of this, it is perhaps best not to rely too heavily on price discrimination as an argument either for or against federal regulation of moving. Instead, it will simply be noted in closing that price discrimination in the moving industry, to the extent that it was objectionable, could, in the absence of regulation, have been challenged before, after, and during most of the depression under Section 2 of the Clayton Act, which was originally passed in 1914 and later amended in 1936. Regulation by independent commission was not the only or even necessarily the best method of combatting the evil of price discrimination, if in fact it was evil.

Finally, federal regulation of moving might have been warranted in 1935 in order to protect the public from irresponsible operators and ensure the qualitative adequacy of service. Although conclusive data are lacking, the fragmentary evidence which is available does suggest that during the depression years there was a significant number of moving and storage companies, mostly newcomers to the industry, which neither provided good service nor were able to pay legitimate claims filed against them.

However, the mere existence of such operators and the attendant problems created by them probably did not justify the imposition of economic regulation. The problem of financial irresponsibility could easily have been solved by compulsory bonding and did not require extensive economic controls.

The quality-of-service issue is not so readily dismissed, but, following two rather distinct lines of reasoning, it can be argued that economic regulation was not the proper response to poor service. One line of reasoning that leads to this conclusion begins by noting that throughout the depression the public was continually warned by the press, Better Business Bureaus, established movers, and mover groups that hiring a "fly-by-night" mover was a risky proposition.[12] Consumers must have realized, or at least suspected, that hiring a newcomer was more risky than dealing with established firms; those who ultimately chose to hire newcomers must have decided that, on balance, the higher risk was more than offset by the lower price. It is an essential part of individual freedom, the argument continues, that consumers, having been properly informed, be allowed to make such decisions. Therefore, federal intervention in 1935 was not warranted, at least not according to this free-market type of reasoning.

The same conclusion can be reached by a very different line of reasoning. According to this latter line of reasoning, government intervention was warranted to protect consumers in 1935; however, the method of intervention actually chosen was not appropriate. If inferior service was the major problem, then mandatory training programs, occupational licensure, and compulsory arbitration of claims would appear to have been the most appropriate forms of intervention, not the imposition of rate, entry, and merger controls.

VII. CONCLUSIONS

Federal regulation of the moving industry in 1935 is an example of regulation without any apparent rationale. Based on the evidence now available, such regulation cannot be convincingly defended on the traditional grounds of ruinous intermodal or intramodal competition, nor were there any other conditions or circumstances which might have warranted regulation on other grounds. This industry simply did not need to be regulated in 1935.

The implications of such a finding are not trivial. The moving industry, which currently grosses more than $2 billion a year in revenues, has long been a leading contender for the distinction, if that is the word, of being the most highly regulated industry in the United States, and the benefits of regulation have apparently been small in comparison to the costs (Breen, 1975; Hewins, 1975). It is, of course, senseless to fret over the past, but not to be concerned about the future. Serious and immediate consideration should now be given to deregulating the moving industry.[13] In so doing, this industry must be analyzed separately from other segments of American trucking, especially since the most popular argument advanced against the complete deregulation of trucking—namely, that such deregulation would foster a return to the ruinous conditions of the 1930s—is, in the case of household moving, singularly unfrightening.

NOTES

1. Good summaries of this literature are provided in Smead (1969), chap. 13, and Locklin (1972), chap. 29. See also Nelson and Greiner (1965).

2. For a more detailed description of the influx of newcomers and the condition of entry during the Depression, see United States Congress, *Regulation of Transportation Agencies* (1934), especially p. 14.

3. For further discussion of these other objectives, see Locklin, 1972, pp. 671–73.

4. A note concerning source materials is necessary at this juncture. There are currently only two books available on the subject of moving industry history: John Hess, *The Mobile Society: A History of the Moving and Storage Industry* (1973), and Stanley Alexander, *History of the Moving and Storage Industry in the United States* (1970). Both of these books are "popular" histories which contain no notes or references at all. Since such histories are not definitive, they cannot be relied upon to establish important or controversial points. Consequently, it will be necessary in establishing such points to rely heavily

upon information obtained from *The Furniture Warehouseman (TFW)*, the only major alternative source available.

TFW is a monthly publication of the National Furniture Warehouseman's Association, a national trade association of the moving and storage industry which had a membership of more than 700 companies nationwide during the depression. *TFW*, first published in 1920, is a veritable gold mine of information relevant to the historical issues of regulation. Since the NFWA was at the forefront of the movement to regulate interstate trucking, especially during the depression, the information contained in *TFW*, to the extent that it is biased, should be biased in favor of supporting the need for federal regulation of the moving industry.

5. References made directly to *The Furniture Warehouseman* rather than to a specific author are intended to indicate that the reference in question was the unsigned work of the editors of that periodical.

6. This estimate was provided in Barrett, 1932, p. 557. According to a price index constructed by the Bureau of Labor Statistics (1967 = 100), the price of household furnishings descended steadily between 1920 and 1932, falling from 82.7 to 42.9 during this period (United States Department of Commerce, 1975, pp. 210–11).

7. The Baltimore and Ohio Railroad and the Pennsylvania Railroad were prominent among those railroads which chose to significantly reduce rates on household goods during the depression (*The Furniture Warehouseman*, January 1933, p. 14).

8. There is some fragmentary support for this conjecture. See, for instance, "Competition Shows Improvement," an editorial in *The Furniture Warehouseman*, May 1927, p. 373.

9. On the futility of trying to match rates with newcomers, see Lyon, 1932, p. 24, and Woodside, 1931, p. 738. On the durability of the pricing structure, compare Warren's reports on the pricing situation in Warren, 1932, 1934, and 1935.

10. To illustrate, in 1931, the "average player's score," to borrow Tippet's own jargon, showed ratios of fully allocated costs to revenues of 1.02 for the cartage department, .83 for storage, and .96 for packing. Tippet also reported that 45 percent of the "average player's" total sales revenues came from cartage, 40 percent from storage, 8 percent from packing, and 7 percent from miscellaneous sources. Even though a cost/revenue ratio was not supplied for the miscellaneous category, these ratios and weights make it virtually inconceivable for the average player to have sustained net losses in 1931. For 1932, Tippet's study indicated that the median company earned net profits equal to about 2.6 percent of sales.

11. *Michigan Public Utilities Commission* v. *Duke*, 266 U.S. 573 (1925); *Buck* v. *Kuykendall*, 267 U.S. 307 (1925); *George W. Bush & Sons* v. *Malory*, 267 U.S. 317 (1925).

12. The Better Business Bureaus in many cities were especially active in this respect during the depression. See "Better Business Bureaus Cooperate with Storage Men," *The Furniture Warehouseman*, January 1932, pp. 25–26.

13. Congress recently reduced the degree of ICC control over trucking by passing the Motor Carrier Act of 1980. Such modifications must be considered a promising first step on the road to deregulation.

REFERENCES

Alexander, S. (1970), History of the Moving and Storage Industry in the United States. Garden Grove, Calif.: A-1 Printing.

Aspinwall, C. (1932), "Railroads as Competitors of the Furniture Packer and Mover." *The Furniture Warehouseman* 13(November):563 –64.

Barrett, J. (1932), "Containers as a Supplementary Service." *The Furniture Warehouseman* 13(November):577–78.

Bateman, F. (1932), "Report of the Container Service Committee." *The Furniture Warehouseman* 13(March):228–30.

Breen, D. (1975), *The Economic Effects of Regulation: The Case of Motor Carriers of Household Goods.* Unpublished Ph.D. dissertation, Ohio State University.

Carruth, C. (1925), "Our Industry's Greatest Evil." *The Furniture Warehouseman* 6(August):559–60.

Cunningham, W. (1934), "Correlation of Rail and Highway Transport." *American Economic Review* 24(March):47–56.

Dunn, J. (1935), "Conditions Will Be Improved through Organized Effort." *The Furniture Warehouseman* 16(June):224–25.

Fair, M. and E. Williams (1959), *Economics of Transportation.* New York: Harper.

Ferguson, R. (1932), "Railroad Competition in Household Goods." *The Furniture Warehouseman* 13(November):576–77.

Ford, W. (1932), "Address by Mr. William I. Ford." *The Furniture Warehouseman* 13(March):165–66.

Gould, E. (1932), "Address by Mr. E. B. Gould." *The Furniture Warehouseman* 13(March):163–64.

Harper, D. (1959), *Economic Regulation of the Motor Trucking Industry by the States.* Urbana, Ill.: University of Illinois Press.

Hess, J. (1973), *The Mobile Society: A History of the Moving and Storage Industry.* New York: McGraw-Hill.

Hewins, D. (1975), *Public Control of the American Moving Industry.* Unpublished Ph.D. dissertation, University of Illinois.

Holt, H. (1932), "The Future of the Container in the Transportation of Household Goods." *The Furniture Warehouseman* 13(January):16–18.

Hudson, W. and J. Constantin (1958), *Motor Transportation.* New York: Ronald Press.

Interstate Commerce Commission (1928), *Motor Bus and Motor Truck Transportation,* 140ICC685.

Interstate Commerce Commission (1932), *Coordination of Motor Transportation,* 182ICC263.

Locklin, D. (1972), *Economics of Transportation.* Homewood, Ill.: R. D. Irwin.

Lyon, H. (1931), "Report of Vice-President: Western Division." *The Furniture Warehouseman* 12(September):595–97.

Lyon, H. (1932), "Cartage Price Reduction: Is It Profitable?" *The Furniture Warehouseman* 13(January):24–25.

Meyer, J., M. Peck, J. Stenason, and C. Zwick (1959), *Competition in the Transportation Industries.* Cambridge, Mass.: Harvard University Press.

Morris, C. (1933), "The Business Anarchist." *The Furniture Warehouseman* 14(May):259–61.

Nelson, R. and W. Greiner (1965), "The Relevance of the Common Carrier under Modern Economic Conditions." In National Bureau of Economic Research, *Transportation Economics.* New York: Columbia University Press.

Peterson, S. (1929), "Motor Carrier Regulation and Its Economic Bases." *Quarterly Journal of Economics* 43(August):604–47.

Posner, R. (1972), *Economic Analysis of Law.* Boston: Little, Brown and Company.

Reimers, H. (1931), "Statement to ICC Creates Interest." *The Furniture Warehouseman* 12:231–32.

Scherer, F. (1980), *Industrial Market Structure and Economic Performance.* Chicago: Rand McNally.

Shepherd, W. and C. Wilcox (1979), *Public Policies toward Business.* Homewood, Ill.: R. D. Irwin.

Smead, E. (1969), *Governmental Promotion and Regulation of Business*. New York: Appleton-Century-Crofts.

Taff, C. (1969), *Commercial Motor Transportation*. Homewood, Ill.: R. D. Irwin.

Theibault, W. (1933), "Report of the Sales Promotion Committee." *The Furniture Warehouseman* 14(March):141–42.

Thompson, A. (1977), *Economics of the Firm*. Englewood Cliffs, N.J.: Prentice-Hall.

Tippet, C. (1932), "What Is Your Handicap." *The Furniture Warehouseman* 13(August):434–36.

——— (1933), "Tippet Makes New Statistical Study." *The Furniture Warehouseman* 14(December):530–33.

United States Congress, Senate (1934), *Regulation of Transportation Agencies,* 73rd Congress, Second Session, Senate Document No. 152.

United States Department of Commerce, Bureau of the Census, (1960), *Historical Statistics of the United States: Colonial Times to 1957*. Washington, D.C.: United States Government Printing Office.

Wagner, W. (1935), *A Legislative History of the Motor Carrier Act, 1935*. Denton, Md.: Rue Publishing Company.

Warren, W. (1932), "Report of the Local Moving Department Committee." *The Furniture Warehouseman* 13(March):208.

——— (1934), "Report of the Local Moving Department Committee." *The Furniture Warehouseman* 15(August):165–166.

——— (1935), "Report of the Local Moving Department Committee." *The Furniture Warehouseman* 16(April):141–42.

Woodside, J. (1931), "Maintain Service—Do Not Reduce Prices." *The Furniture Warehouseman* 12(November):738–40.

LABOR ABSORPTION:
CONVENTIONAL WISDOM AND ADDITIONAL DATA FOR LATIN AMERICA

John M. Hunter

Considerable attention has been given to the matter of the failure of industry in developing countries to absorb employment either in some absolute sense *or* as fast as the labor force grows *or* as fast as urbanization occurs.

Gerald M. Meier, in a general discussion of the subject, notes that

> industrial employment has lagged behind growth in industrial output, behind growth of the urban population, and even behind the general growth rate of population. . . . Whereas for all LDC's, industrial output grew at approximately 7.5 per cent per annum over the period 1948–61, employment in industry expanded at less than one-half that rate—by only 3.5 per cent per annum.[1]

Variations in Business and Economic History:
Essays in Honor of Donald L. Kemmerer
Research in Economic History, Suppl. 2, pages 93–99.

ISBN: 0-89232-262-4

Raúl Prebisch compares cumulative annual growth rates for "industrial product" and "industrial employment" for thirteen Latin American countries and Central America for the period 1950–68. In each case (except for Bolivia and the Dominican Republic), industrial product grew more rapidly than industrial employment. Hence, product per worker was also growing; the implication is that industry was doing less than its share with respect to absorption.[2]

The ECLA devotes considerable attention to the matter of labor absorption including the concept of "optimum capital intensity" but without careful definition and without statistical evidence.[3]

Jeannine Swift utilizes data to approach the point in a more recent publication.

Manufacturing as a Percentage of GDP and Employment in Manufacturing, 1970

	Percent of GDP	*Percent Total Employment*
Argentina	35.7	26.7
Brazil	25.8	8.2
Chile	29.2	17.0
Mexico	26.7	17.5
Peru	20.7	12.4

She concludes:

> In these four [*sic*] countries the discrepancy between the percentage of GDP from the manufacturing sector and the percentage of the labor force in that sector is very large. The data do not necessarily prove that the capital-labor ratio is excessive or inconsistent with the factors of production available in the country. . . . Nevertheless the data does [*sic*] show that, even with a very high proportion of GDP being generated by manufacturing, a much lower percentage of the labor force is absorbed.[4]

For a final example, the IDB, in a recent discussion of unemployment, notes:

> . . . combined with this is the fact that most import substitution investment in the industrial sector is usually relatively capital intensive and thus even in an expanding economy job opportunities are not increasing *sufficiently*.[5]

These citations reflect a familiar theme and give some flavor to the differences in formulation and the nature of the statistical evidence used in support. New data permit a reexamination of the general proposition, suggest what has occurred in recent years, and also permit greater precision in definition of the phenomenon.

The World Bank in its *World Development Report, 1979*[6] provides a great deal of information on 125 countries which permits comparison of changes between 1960 and 1977 in the sectoral origin of GDP and the sectoral distribution of employment. Table 1 reports these data for seventeen Latin American countries and the simple computations for examining what occurred. Some countries were omitted because data were not available.

Basically, the table compares the change in the distribution of the GDP with the change in the distribution of the labor force. For the former and for Honduras, as an illustration, the percentage of GDP derived from industry was 1.42 times greater in 1977 than it was in 1960. Similarly, the percentage of the labor force in industry grew from 11 to 15 percent, so that it was, in 1977, 1.36 times the 1960 datum. Comparison of these two figures describes what was happening to the relative growth of the share of GDP from industry and to the share of industrial employment. That is, a 1.00 in the column (a)/(b) indicates that the change in the share of GDP was the same as the change in the share of industrial employment. This is at least one measure of industry's labor absorption. If the industrial share of GDP increased 10 percent and industrial labor expanded from 20 percent of the labor force to 22 percent of the labor force (i.e., 10 percent), then in some sense the industrial sector absorbed its "share" of employment as it expanded. There is at least implicit in the capital-intensive argument the expectation that industrial expansion does not result in a like expansion in industrial employment.

The final column simply notes for each country whether or not the results are inconsistent with the expectation that expansion of the share of GDP occurred without a similar expansion of the share of industrial employment. In five cases, with the indicator close to 1, I used the characterization "doubtful," but it could be argued that any result close to 1 does not meet the expectation and suggests that the hypothesis is not valid.

It is useful to highlight the results for the more important countries covered.

Colombia	1.00	Doubtful
Mexico	.99	Doubtful
Chile	.84	Inconsistent[7]
Brazil	.80	Inconsistent
Argentina	1.46	Consistent
Venezuela	.62	Inconsistent

Parenthetically, the seventeen countries are listed in order of per capita GNP. Cursory examination by scatter diagram suggests no relationship at all between per capita income level and the (a)/(b) indicator.

Table 1. Relative Distribution of GDP and Labor in Seventeen Countries: 1960, 1977

	Distribution of GDP (%) Industry			*Distribution of Labor Force (%) Industry*				
Country	*1960*	*1977*	*(a) 1960/1977*	*1960*	*1977*	*(b) 1960/1977*	*(a)/(b)*	*Consistency with Hypothesis***
Honduras	19	27	1.42	11	15	1.36	1.04	D
El Salvador	19	21	1.11	13	15	1.15	.97	D
Bolivia	25	29	1.16	18	23	1.28	.91	I
Colombia	24	29	1.21	19	23	1.21	1.00	D
Paraguay	20	22*	1.10	19	19	1.00	1.10	C
Ecuador	19	36	1.90	19	24	1.26	1.51	C
Nicaragua	21	26	1.24	16	14	.86	1.44	C
Dominican Republic	23	21	.91	12	16	1.33	.68	I
Peru	29	31*	1.07	20	20	1.00	1.07	D
Mexico	29	36	1.24	20	25	1.25	.99	D
Jamaica	36	37	1.03	25	27	1.08	.95	D
Chile	38	29	.76	30	27	.90	.84	I
Costa Rica	19	25*	1.31	18	29	1.61	.81	I
Brazil	35	37	1.06	15	20	1.33	.80	I
Uruguay	28	36	1.29	29	32	1.10	1.17	C
Argentina	38	45	1.18	36	29	.81	1.46	C
Venezuela	22	17	.77	22	27	1.23	.62	I

Notes:
* 1976 rather than 1977.
** *D* = Doubtful; *C* = Consistent; *I* = Inconsistent.
Source: World Bank, *World Development Report, 1979,* Tables 3, 19. Calculations are mine.

What conclusions may be drawn from these results? Whatever they are, considerable care needs to be exercised in their interpretation.

1. One worries first of all about whether the data are good enough to be relied upon for these sorts of indications. There are many ambiguities in sectoral definitions, areas in which the grossest estimations have been made, with limited personnel to do the work. Certainly small changes through time are not likely to be significant.[8]
2. Assuming some statistical reliability, the data suggest that industrial expansion has not in recent years led to an expansion of GDP at a greater rate than it has led to expansion of the industrial labor force. In some countries, it has; in others, it has not. In others, the growth in each has been about the same. *Accepting a priori the proposition that expanding industrialization has not or will not lead to a proportionate expansion of the industrial labor force no longer seems acceptable*—at least for Latin America.
3. These data do not speak to the point of whether industrializing increased employment either as much as it "could have" or as much as it "should have"—in short, whether it was more capital-intensive than it "might have been." Because we have no standard of what "should have been," there is no statistical performance measurement. If this is to be approached at all, it will be through some other route, e.g., study of comparative wage rates and entry barriers of nonindustrial labor into industrial activities.
4. The data do not specifically address "manufacturing" performance, which for World Bank purposes is "industry less mining; less construction; less electricity, gas, and water." Reference in the literature usually is to "industry," but one suspects that authors had "manufacturing" in mind. Only construction, however, of the three seems likely to expand in a more labor-intensive fashion than "industry" in general, with at least the probability that expanded mining and utilities would probably be more capital-intensive. Thus, it is uncertain whether consideration of *manufacturing* alone would reinforce the conclusions or weaken them.
5. Nor do the data cast light on the proposition that foreign capitalized industry is a particular offender. One might expect it to be so: some products require great capital; capital is more plentiful abroad than domestically; therefore foreign capital might well find its way into capital-using industrialization. Even so, the policy conclusions are not evident. Prohibit foreign participation, capital-intensive production? Require foreign firms to utilize less capital-intensive techniques than is their wont? Tax all (foreign?) production of

greater than average capital-intensity to provide a research fund for developing less capital-intensive technologies? If one assumes at the outset that some production is more capital-intensive than others, it is really not offensive that capital-rich providers tend to steer investment into capital-using lines. But, I repeat, this says nothing about the issue of whether the degree of capital-intensity has been appropriate.

The major results of perusing these data are reported above. Several by-products are, however, worth considering.

1. Data for the percentages of the labor force in *manufacturing* are not available for the two relevant dates, so it was not possible to examine relative growth in manufacturing GDP and manufacturing labor, which would have been useful. It was possible to compare the rates of growth in the *product shares* of *industry* and of *manufacturing,* however, with the results from Table 1. There was no discernible pattern; that is, whether the industrial share grew more or less than the manufacturing share seemed to have no relation to the (a)/(b) indicator or to the qualitative conclusions drawn therefrom. This suggests that "industry" and "manufacturing" are not vastly different in capital-intensity. If they were, "consistencies" and "inconsistencies" might have been explained by the differences in share growth differences.
2. Comparison of these results with earlier and similar computations proved useful. Prebisch provides data for the same countries comparing cumulative annual rates of growth in industrial product and industrial employment in 1958–68.[9] Dividing the former by the latter is a measure of how much faster the industrial product was growing relative to industrial employment (not of "shares," as with the World Bank data).

Prebisch's ratios indicate that, with the exceptions of Bolivia and the Dominican Republic, industrial output increased by considerably more than industrial employment and for the area as a whole 2.14 times more. In comparing the two, the World Bank ratios are smaller in all cases except those of Bolivia and Uruguay, and in the latter case the difference is small. If the data are reliable, the conclusion is clear (with most differences being substantial): the apparent tendency in 1950–68 of industrial product growing more rapidly than industrial employment has been reversed. In 1960–77, the computations show a great deal more ambiguity with respect to indicating any sort of general behavior, and ratios are systematically smaller enough to suggest a significant change in the nature of the relationship from the first to the second period.

	Prebisch		World Bank*
Argentina	2.05		1.46
Bolivia	.50		.91
Brazil	3.32		.80
Central America	2.52	Costa Rica	.81
		El Salvador	.97
		Honduras	1.04
		Nicaragua	1.44
Chile	2.09		.84
Colombia	2.58		1.00
Dominican Republic	.91		.68
Ecuador	2.43		1.51
Mexico	1.43		.99
Panama	4.59		
Paraguay	1.21		1.10
Peru	2.29		1.07
Uruguay	1.12		1.17
Venezuela	2.52		.62
Latin America	2.14		

Note:

* Column $\frac{(a)}{(b)}$, Table 1.

NOTES

1. *Leading Issues in Economic Development: Studies in International Poverty,* 2d ed. (Oxford: Oxford University Press, 1970), p. 431. He cites principally United Nations, *The Growth of World Industry: International Analysis and Tables, 1938–61.*
2. *Change and Development—Latin America's Great Task* (New York: Praeger Publishers, 1971), pp. 44–45. See also the further discussion of these issues on pp. 42–47.
3. ECLA, *Development Problems in Latin America* (Austin: Institute of Latin American Studies, University of Texas, 1970), pp. 35–41.
4. *Economic Development in Latin America* (New York: St. Martin's Press, 1978), pp. 90–91.
5. Emphasis mine. *Economic and Social Progress in Latin America, 1977 Report* (Washington: IDB, 1978), p. 130.
6. Washington, 1979, Tables 3, 19.
7. Data for Chile suggest that careful examination of circumstances of each country may be important. The fall from 38 percent to 29 percent in the share of GDP (services went from 51 to 61 percent) is, to say the least, interesting. Is this the result of nationalization without great change in actual production?
8. Labor-force data are at least in part population-based projections of ILO 1970 estimates, which suggests they may be somewhat less reliable than the 1970 estimates.
9. *Op cit.,* Table 12, p. 45.

AFRICAN ENTREPRENEURS: A CASE STUDY OF NIGERIAN INDUSTRIALISTS, 1964–65

E. Wayne Nafziger

I am honored to contribute to a *Festschrift* for Professor Donald L. Kemmerer, who helped me so much when I was a graduate student. The initial inspiration for my subsequent work on entrepreneurship in less-developed countries arose from a conference on U.S. business history in the spring of 1964 at Indiana University that Professor Kemmerer arranged for several University of Illinois graduate students to attend. Furthermore, Professor Kemmerer was instrumental in helping me acquire a fellowship for research in Nigeria in 1964–65.

I. OVERVIEW OF THE STUDY

The accumulation of empirical evidence has recently undermined economic development theories based on the single factor of capital. These

Variations in Business and Economic History:
Essays in Honor of Donald L. Kemmerer
Research in Economic History, Suppl. 2, pages 101–120.

ISBN: 0-89232-262-4

studies are consistent with the contention that much of economic growth stems from improvements in the combination, organization, and coordination of inputs, attributable by many definitions to the entrepreneur, rather than to growth in the quantity of inputs. The exact contribution of the entrepreneur cannot, however, be gauged, given problems of measurement and conceptualization, but its undoubted importance makes it worthy of study.

The entrepreneur can be viewed in at least three ways: (1) as the coordinator of other resources of production, such as land, labor, and capital (Walras, 1954); (2) as the innovator (Schumpeter, 1939, vol. 1); and (3) as the decision maker (Knight, 1921). For this study, I am using Frank Knight's concept of the entrepreneur as the ultimate decision maker in the enterprise, the one who commits the capital and bears the risk. Each firm has one entrepreneur, the person with the largest capital share.

The study focuses on Nigerian entrepreneurs in footwear manufacturing, 1964–65. An industry approach to the study was taken in order to facilitate the making of comparisons among entrepreneurs and their firms. The footwear industry was chosen because of its great diversity in firm size and because of the author's access to firm records and independent sources of information. Generally, there is no reason to believe that determinants of entrepreneurship in footwear manufacturing differ significantly from those in manufacturing as a whole in Nigeria.

The statistical universe consists of the forty-one indigenous footwear manufacturing firms, with an average 1964 employment of eight or more, which were listed in the ten 1964–65 federal and regional directories. Most of the analysis is based upon the sample of twenty-five firms from which the author obtained reasonably reliable data.

In some cases, to facilitate analysis, the firms are divided into two size categories. The boundary between the categories is meant to correspond, by and large, to a separation between the firm characterized by a modern shoe factory with advanced, more capital-intensive techniques, a routinized production line, a specialized division of labor and machine tasks, a hired labor force, and a complex entrepreneurial and management structure, on the one hand, and an enterprise with a less-modern shoemaker's workshop, a simple, more labor-intensive technology, not more than a few simple machines, and a labor force predominantly consisting of apprentices, journeymen, and family workers who learn most of the operation in making a shoe from face-to-face supervision by a proprietor. Thus, the firms are divided into large firms—those with a 1964 net worth of £N20,000 or more, and small firms—those with a 1964 average net worth of less than £N20,000. Entrepreneurs in small and large firms are known as small and large entrepreneurs respectively.

There was no sample bias among the five large footwear firms, since all firms were in the sample. Nafziger (1977:262–64) indicates that, when distribution of firms by employment size is considered, small firms in the sample were fairly representative both of footwear firms in the statistical universe and of all small indigenous urban footwear firms in Nigeria.

Most of the studies on entrepreneurship in less-developed countries lack the data essential to the consideration of those factors related to entrepreneurial quantity and success. The determinants of the quantity of entrepreneurs are found in this study by comparing the data on the characteristics of entrepreneurs and the population as a whole. Factors related to entrepreneurial success are found by correlating education, training, work experience, occupational background, and paternal economic status of the entrepreneurs to 1965 value of output and 1964 rate of profit. In addition, the sources of capital for the firm are discussed. Limitations on space rule out a consideration of the market for entrepreneurs, the role of political power in business success, the relationship between communal origin and entrepreneurial success, labor relations and utilization, the interregional structure of entrepreneurship, and policies for the development of industrial entrepreneurship. Furthermore, statistical relationships, the evidence of which is reported in detail in Nafziger (1977), are mentioned only when significant at the 5 percent level.

II. THE NIGERIAN ECONOMY

Nigeria's population of about 50 million in 1965 and about 80 million in 1980 was the highest of all African countries. Official figures indicate that gross domestic product (GDP) in the fiscal year 1964–65 was £N1,457.0 million, or about £N29 (or $81) per capita. In 1965, Nigeria ranked among the bottom one-fifth of the countries of the world in GDP per capita. Growth in real GDP from 1958–59 to 1965–66 was 6.0 percent per annum, and growth in real GDP per capita probably in excess of 3 percent per annum. The mining and manufacturing sectors were the most rapidly growing sectors in Nigeria in the 1960s, even though in 1964–65 only 5 percent of GDP originated in manufacturing and 3 percent in mining, compared to 59 percent in agriculture.

During the colonial period between the beginning of the twentieth century and independence in 1960, Nigeria's modern sector was highly dependent upon Britain for trade, aid, investment, and loans. Although the colonial nexus declined in the 1960s, it remained fairly strong. One indicator of this is that as late as 1965, 38 percent of Nigeria's exports and 31 percent of imports were with Britain.

In Nigeria, the amount of indigenous manufacturing, especially in the private sector, was small. In 1965, foreign private ownership comprised 62 percent of total ownership and 85 percent of total private ownership in manufacturing establishments with ten or more employed. Foreign dominance of the manufacturing sector was accompanied by high rates of industrial concentration. Total value added of the largest four establishments in manufacturing industries as a percentage of the total value added was 69.0 percent in Nigeria in comparison to 3.7 percent for the same industries in the United States (Nafziger, 1977).

III. EDUCATION

Most studies indicate a higher level of education among entrepreneurs than among the population as a whole, and a direct relationship between the education and success of the entrepreneur. Persons with more education would have more knowledge to make decisions. In addition, the verbal skills of the better-educated person would assist him in acquiring new ideas and methods, corresponding and conversing in business relationships, and understanding instruction manuals and other routine written information. Finally, the quantitative ability of the educated entrepreneur should facilitate computation and record keeping.

A. Education and Entrepreneurial Quantity

An indication of the relationship between education and entrepreneurial quantity can be found by observing differences between the backgrounds of the entrepreneurs and the rest of the population. The educational level of sample entrepreneurs, which averaged 7.1 years (more than one year beyond primary school), was far above the educational level of the general population in Nigeria. In 1964–65, 88 percent of the entrepreneurs, but less than 25 percent of the population (seven years or older), had a minimum of four years of schooling. However, if the more than ten thousand entrepreneurs from firms with less than eight employed (mostly one-man enterprises) had been included in the sample, the educational level of Nigerian footwear entrepreneurs might not have been greater than the population as a whole.

B. Education and Firm Output

There was a positive relationship between entrepreneurial education and the value of output of the firm. Entrepreneurs in firms with a value of output of £N20,000 or more had an average level of education of 10.5 years, those with £N5,000–£N19,999 an average of 7.9, and those with £4,999 or less 6.0. Entrepreneurs in large, complex firms need the ability to communicate in writing within and outside the firm, the possibilities of obtaining access to new ideas and developments through reading and other forms of communication, and the ability to make computations for management control and firm analysis. Large, complex firms usually acquired entrepreneurs with some secondary education; firms with entrepreneurs lacking in education were limited in the growth of complexity of the firm.

C. Education and Profit Rate of the Firm

There was a significant negative relationship between entrepreneurial education and profit rate among the eighteen sample firms for which data on profit rates were available. Entrepreneurs with a profit rate of 13 percent or more had an average level of education of 6.0 years, those with 0–12 percent profit 8.0 years, and those with losses 9.7 years.

There is no evidence for the contention that primary education in Nigeria, by increasing job aspirations without significantly increasing labor proficiency, may have had a negative effect on the development of skilled manpower, including entrepreneurs. Other explanations for the negative relationship between education and profit rates are more plausible.

First, time and money spent in obtaining a formal education, particularly secondary academic education, often meant forgoing technical or vocational training, such as an apprenticeship. This training was a virtual necessity for success in a small footwear enterprise, as is shown below. Furthermore, the level of education was inversely related to the number of years of experience in footwear manufacturing, and the number of years of entrepreneurial and management experience, which were both positively correlated with the success of the entrepreneur.

Second, the remuneration of entrepreneurial pursuits divided by the remuneration in alternative endeavors was inversely related to the educational level of the person. Assume that in each educational class there was a positive relationship between the individual's competence and his remuneration. Thus, whereas in low educational classes entrepreneurs were more likely to be among the more competent, in high educational classes entrepreneurs were more likely to be among the less competent.

Consider the market for manpower in high educational classes. Because of high salaries, attractive fringe benefits, and favorable working conditions, foreign enterprises and government attracted most of the highly competent university and secondary graduates. Graduates unable to obtain the more lucrative positions with foreign firms or government were more likely to become entrepreneurs. A disproportionately large number of highly educated persons who became entrepreneurs of small firms either failed in other occupations or had low alternative wages.

IV. EXPERIENCE AND TRAINING

An important determinant of the rate of industrial growth is the rate at which the techniques available to developed industrial areas and entrepreneurs are transferred and dispersed to prospective industrial areas and entrepreneurs. Some of the ways these technical skills become embodied in prospective entrepreneurs are through work experience, training, and education.

A. Large Firms

In the five large firms, the entrepreneur's lack of technical and managerial experience stood out as a major barrier to success. There was a significant positive relationship between the management experience of the entrepreneur prior to establishing the firm and the rate of profit of the five firms.

Since the control of industrial technology has been concentrated in the developed economies of North America, Western Europe, and Japan, it is not surprising that countries like Nigeria that wish to industrialize have attempted to borrow this technology from abroad. Because of the barriers to dispersion of technology from foreign to indigenous firms, there is much merit in prospective entrepreneurs' and managers' trying to acquire this technology by training and employment in factories overseas. For example, Samuel Slater and Francis Lowell, separately instrumental in launching the two first ventures in the New England (U.S.) cotton textile manufacturing industry around the turn of the nineteenth century, cracked the British monopoly on textile techniques by acquiring information on machine design, installation, and operation while working in English textile mills (Kemmerer and Jones, 1959:158–59). The only businessmen from large sample firms with foreign experience included Messrs. M. E. Akitoye and M. W. Ejor, pseudonyms for the entrepreneurs of the firms with the highest profit rates. Mr. Akitoye held a submanagement position in a plastic-footwear-manufacturing firm for twelve months in England in 1959–60, operated a West African agency of this firm for ten months in 1960, and was the highest-ranking Nigerian manager (and third highest altogether) in an English plastic-shoe-manufacturing enterprise in Lagos for nine months in 1961. Mr. Ejor has fourteen years' experience in management positions with a foreign rubber-footwear-manufacturing firm, including four years studying business administration in Europe. In early stages of industrialization, it is difficult, especially for large entrepreneurs, to acquire experience at home as valuable as that acquired abroad in firms at the forefront of generating new industrial knowledge and techniques. Furthermore, since there was a shortage of skilled indigenous engineers and production managers, both entrepreneurs hired personnel from abroad to complement their own management skills.

The three entrepreneurs of firms with losses in excess of 50 percent of net worth in 1964 had no previous management experience in manufacturing. They also lacked a network of relationships with business-oriented friends and relatives to obtain access to trustworthy management personnel or even to acquire a reliable evaluation of the ability and integrity of prospective managers.

The chief example of entrepreneurial failure was that of Alhaji N. R. Shetima and his collaborators in the Northern Leather Works, Kano. From independent sources, it is clear that the initial entrepreneurs were not aware of the intricate planning and timing involved in bringing together managers, supervisors, laborers, materials, and machines to manufacture a commodity. They had little notion of minimal qualifications for management officials. The three top management and technical personnel were hired on the basis of recommendations by machinery suppliers and a manager of a foreign retail shop in Nigeria. The general manager had no experience or training related to an initial venture in manufacturing, the chief engineer had never held a managerial, supervisory, or engineering position, and the production manager could not communicate in either of the two major languages in the North, English and Hausa. Also, the entrepreneurs did not comprehend the market research, sales effort, and organization demanded in order to sell even 25 percent of the estimated capacity output of one thousand pairs of leather shoes per day. It was not until a backlog of unsold footwear had accumulated that the firm attempted to organize a network of salesmen, agencies, and supply depots. Furthermore, records of cost and revenue were meager. An audit in July 1964 revealed that operating cost had exceeded revenue by over £N1 for each pair of shoes produced, at a time when the management believed that revenue exceeded operating costs. The other losing firms also made serious management errors, attributable in part to a lack of experience.

B. Small Firms

In Nigeria, between the early 1940s and 1965, the number of indigenous footwear firms increased from less than one thousand to about fifteen thousand. In that year, all except sixty of these enterprises had less than ten workers, and most were directed by a single proprietor. Production was usually based on labor-using techniques, face-to-face supervision and instruction by the proprietor, a lack of division of labor or a routinized production line, and simple tools, such as a cutting knife, hammer, pliers, anvil, small workbench, wooden lasts, rags, and paper patterns.

Although the technology was widespread within Nigeria, it was not simple to master; small shoemakers spent years in apprenticeship. Under this system, a youth, usually fourteen to eighteen years old, enrolled for a two- to five-year course with a proprietor of a small firm. Over a period of a few years, the youth learned the craft on the job.

As indicated below, most entrepreneurs of small firms began their business lives as apprentices. The success of small entrepreneurs was closely related to the business success and teaching skill of the master-proprietor. No other type of work experience was correlated with entrepreneurial success, at least among small shoemakers.

C. Medium Firms

Although all the small firms in the sample had a net worth of £N3,000 or less in 1964 and 1965, some small entrepreneurs wished to expand. For purposes of discussion here, medium firms are defined as those with a net worth of £N3,001–19,999. This boundary between categories is meant to correspond roughly to a distinction between entrepreneurs of small firms, where apprentice training was necessary and probably sufficient training, and those of medium firms, where an upgrading of technical and entrepreneurial skills beyond that acquired in the apprentice course was required. Whereas small firms were relatively labor-intensive, the greater size and complexity of medium firms demanded that they be more management and technical-skill-intensive.

If the entrepreneur planning the expansion chose a labor-intensive technology, he could no longer rely on supervising the production process on an ad hoc basis. The organization of the firm needed to be more complex than before, with a greater necessity for delegation of responsibility, advanced planning of work tasks, and a system of communication. The entrepreneur with a more capital-intensive technology required further technical skill or the ability to supervise it, in addition to the obvious need for more skill to organize and coordinate increased and more-specialized capital and labor. The emphasis of the apprenticeship on designing skills and craftsmanship did not prepare the entrepreneur for such managenent and organizational problems.

Although other resources of production tend to be substitutable for each other, entrepreneurship is a complementary factor. The more capital, labor, and natural resources a firm has, the more entrepreneurship is needed to combine these productive factors. Frequently, especially where there was a discontinuity in its production firm, a medium firm reached a point in its growth where it was unable to absorb additional capital efficiently without a substantial increase in the input of entrepreneurial skills. In many cases, expansion was not feasible without training of the entrepreneur beyond apprenticeship. As discussed elsewhere (Nafziger, 1977:217–22), it was important that loan agencies coordinate their operations closely with industrial extension centers engaged in upgrading the entrepreneur's capabilities. However, as more entrepreneurs received advanced training, the apprentice training offered by entrepreneurs also became more advanced.

V. OCCUPATIONAL BACKGROUND

Many studies of industrial entrepreneurs in developing countries indicate trade as the major prior occupation (Sayigh, 1962; Alexander, 1960; Alexander, 1964; Kilby, 1965; Harris, 1967; Berna, 1960; Nafziger, 1978; Papanek, 1962; Carroll, 1965). A background in trade gives the entrepreneur a familiarity with the market, some general management and commercial experience, sales outlets and contacts, and some capital. The entrepreneurs in the two large firms with the highest profits both conceived the idea for their footwear-manufacturing firms while traders or agents in an earlier business endeavor. Mr. M. J. Ejor, the founder of the Midwestern Manufacturing Company, entered rubber manufacturing both because he saw increased opportunities for profits in industry relative to trade and because of the linkages with his existing rubber-processing and rubber wholesale enterprises. The major catalyst for the enhanced attractiveness of industry was deliberate government policy after independence encouraging import substitution in manufacturing through higher tariffs (e.g., on footwear).

As implied above, the major prior experience of entrepreneurs of small firms was apprentice training. Fourteen of the nineteen small entrepreneurs in the sample with apprentice training had not been engaged in any other occupation before they began their entrepreneurial activities in their present firms. Even more noteworthy, five of the six entrepreneurs in the highest profit-rate category had not been engaged in any other occupation prior to their entrance into entrepreneurial positions in their present firm.

VI. SOCIOECONOMIC CLASS AND MOBILITY

Many of the studies on entrepreneurship and economic development extol the achievements of the entrepreneur without examining class origins and monopoly advantage. To Joseph A. Schumpeter (1961:78–79, 93–94), entrepreneurs, with varied class origins and the dream and will to found a private kingdom, to conquer adversity, to achieve success for its own sake, and to experience the joy of creation, are heroic figures.

Recent empirical studies of the socioeconomic mobility of the entrepreneur have reinforced this conception of the heroic entrepreneur. Orvis F. Collins, David G. Moore, and Darab B. Unwalla (1964:238) found that most of the entrepreneurs in medium manufacturing firms in Michigan "clearly moved a long way from the somewhat impoverished economic levels of their childhoods." Both Nigerian and Greek industrialists were considered highly upwardly mobile by John R. Harris (1971) and Alec P. Alexander (1964:80–95), respectively. However, as suggested below, it is the particular way in which the authors asked the question in these empirical studies that led to their conclusions of substantial upward socioeconomic mobility. The data can be interpreted as corroborating the low degree of vertical mobility found in my sample of Nigerian entrepreneurs.

A period of rapid industrial growth and economic modernization, as in the post–World War II period in Nigeria, did not remove the advantages of ascribed status, even in entrepreneurial activity in manufacturing. The traditional Nigerian upper classes—chiefs, emirs, and administrators—whose strength was a legacy of the feudal and colonial periods, have allied, and in some cases overlapped, with the capitalist, political, and bureaucratic elites, most of whom originated from high-income families to control much of the access to key business positions. Families and clans with wealth and position used the monopoly advantage resulting from ready access to capital, greater information and mobility, superior education and training, and privileged access to concessions from government to become industrial entrepreneurs in disproportional numbers.

Here data on the distribution of entrepreneurs by class (paternal economic status) are compared with information on the population at large. The median personal income of entrepreneurs (profits, returns to capital, and wages to management in the footwear enterprise plus income from other economic endeavors) was £N450 per annum in fiscal year 1964–65, which, divided by the median number of persons dependent upon the entrepreneur's income, 6.5 (substantially higher than the median number of dependents of income earners in Nigeria), gives a median per capita income of £N69, much above the 1964–65 all-Nigerian average per capita GNP of £N29 (itself higher than the median figure). The paternal economic status of the entrepreneurs (especially those from large firms) was high compared to that of the population of Nigeria as a whole. The fathers of the five large entrepreneurs consisted of two members of the traditional aristocracy (a traditional title holder in a Northern emirate and a Southern chief), two high-ranking civil servants, and one large trader. Furthermore, one entrepreneur, whose father was a civil servant, was a member of a ruling family in the West, and the great-grandson of an oba (chief). Major occupations of the fathers of the small entrepreneurs were government service for three, trading for three, shoemaking for three, large farming for eight, small subsistence farming for two, and unknown for one. The high status is reinforced by the fact that 58 percent (14 of 24) of the fathers were in the nonagricultural sector (with a much higher income per capita than the agricultural sector), compared to 21 percent of Nigerian males.

Harris, who studied the sawmilling, furniture, printing, rubber-processing, and garment-making industries in Nigeria, does not have the information to compare the socioeconomic class background of entrepreneurs to the general population. Furthermore, he does not discuss the data available on the highly contrasting socioeconomic class between entrepreneurs and the general population. However, the fact that 56 percent (147 of 262) of the fathers of entrepreneurs in the Harris sample were in the nonagricultural sector augments my position that the socioeconomic class of Nigerian industrial entrepreneurs was far above that of the population at large (chi-square = 193.512, $p. < 0.001$).

The economic status of fathers was classified by the author on the basis of information about their occupation and income. Fathers who were subsistence farmers (where more than 50 percent of farm output was for the family or clan), farm workers, or unskilled workers were considered of low economic status. These three groups comprised about 75 percent of the male working population in 1952–53. The fact that only two sample fathers (8 percent of the total)—both subsistence farmers—were of low economic rank provides further evidence for the contention that class status of the entrepreneurs was substantially higher than the general population. High-status fathers included two members of the ruling aristocracy, three of the five civil servants, and two plantation owners. All others were classified in the medium category.

There was a close relationship between economic status of the father and certain measures of entrepreneurial success. Entrepreneurs with a higher paternal economic status tended to be associated with firms with a higher value of output, a greater net worth, a greater employment, and a higher rate of profit. A high economic status of the father assists the prospective entrepreneur in obtaining the appropriate business experience and acquiring resources for investment in education, training, and plant and equipment. In addition, businessmen with a greater paternal economic status, because of better education, a more extensive network of influential acquaintances, and more resources available to acquire information, were more likely to be successful in receiving government assistance.

Entrepreneurs with a high socioeconomic status were more highly represented and more successful than other entrepreneurs, not only in Nigeria but, contrary to a widely held viewpoint, also in most of the rest of the nonsocialist world, at least if evidence is based upon empirical studies of entrepreneurs. The proportion of fathers of Filipino manufacturing entrepreneurs from an upper socioeconomic position was thirty-six times that of the population. Opportunities for industrial enterprise were available chiefly to those who were already well established financially (Carroll, 1965:100, 126). A highly disproportionate number of the fathers of manufacturing entrepreneurs in Pakistan were from high-caste business communities, while a low percentage of fathers were in wage employment or agriculture. This pattern would suggest, contrary to Gustav Papanek's interpretation (1962), that the socioeconomic class status of entrepreneurs was high when compared to the population. My study of southern Indian entrepreneurs indicated that a disproportional number of entrepreneurs (especially successful ones) were from twice-born (high) castes and from families with a high economic status (Nafziger, 1978). Similarly, the analysis above of the data from the Harris sample, and the fact that in Alexander's study of Greek industrialists, 54 percent (282 of 522) of their fathers were large merchants, industrialists, professional men, or business executives compared to 2 percent of the working population support the contention that the socioeconomic class of the entrepreneurs was far above that of the population at large.

Many students of development identify a "rigid" social structure with Third World economies and a fluid social structure with developed economies in the United States and Western Europe (Smelser and Lipset, 1966; Alexander, 1964:80). However, innovators during the English Industrial Revolution were primarily sons of men in comfortable circumstances (Hagen, 1962). Furthermore, even though a dominant American folk hero has been the man who goes from rags to riches through business operations, this path, exemplified by Andrew Carnegie and depicted by the late-nineteenth-century stories of Horatio Alger, was very untypical of the U.S. business elite. Scholarship since World War II shows that the successful industrial leader in the late nineteenth and early twentieth centuries was usually American by birth, English in national origin, urban in early environment, educated through high school, and born and bred in an atmosphere in which business and a relatively high social status were intimately associated with his family life (Miller, 1962).

It is true that two-thirds of the sample entrepreneurs in Michigan studied by Collins, Moore, and Unwalla described their early family life as "poor" or "underprivileged." But the only other choices were "affluent" or "well off." Given the lack of any choice corresponding to a middle-level category, respondents may have avoided designations implying higher income. Furthermore, entrepreneurs may have evaluated parental family income in terms of contemporary standards (the 1960s) and in comparison with their own high level of economic well-being. The vast underrepresentation of Michigan sample fathers in unskilled, semiskilled, clerical, sales, and kindred work (24 percent from the sample and 61 percent from the general labor force), together with the disproportional representation of fathers in business, executive, managerial, official, and professional work (57 percent compared to 26 percent), points to median incomes substantially above the corresponding population of their period.

Entrepreneurs in Nigeria, Greece, and Michigan underwent, in the aggregate, an intergenerational upward movement (i.e., from father to son) in occupational status and material level of living. However, the fact that the socioeconomic status of the entrepreneurs was higher than that of their fathers does not conflict with the evidence that the paternal economic status of entrepreneurs was higher than that of the population as a whole. (Details are in Nafziger, 1977:174–81).

The foregoing discussion should make clear that the heroic model of the entrepreneur presented by previous empirical studies resulted from the types of questions posed. Although the data indicating the upward social and economic mobility of industrialists compared to their fathers are useful, this exclusive focus detracts from the considerable contrast between the socioeconomic class background of entrepreneurs and that of the general population. This suggests that industrial business activity, rather than being a path for substantial upward socioeconomic mobility, has been a way of maintaining or defending privileged status, and enhancing or consolidating the high economic position of the family.

VII. SOURCES OF CAPITAL

This section discusses how the entrepreneur acquired capital. Particular emphasis is placed upon the role of the extended family in hampering or facilitating the acquisition of capital.

A. Large Firms

1. *Initial Capital*

The major source of initial capital in large firms was loan capital. In two cases, the source of loan capital was a bank; in one case, a government loan organization; and, in another case, a private individual. The second major source of original capital was equity capital from individuals other than the initial entrepreneur. The personal savings of the entrepreneur was the major source in only one of the five firms.

2. *Additional Capital*

Retained earnings were the most important source of additional capital for the two firms that made a profit. Despite their losses, two of the other firms, with politically influential entrepreneurs, received loans from official agencies. (See Nafziger, 1977:132–36, 185–86.)

B. Small Firms and the Extended Family

Security against economic loss resulting from sickness, accidents, death, old age, poverty, and unemployment is valued highly by most societies. Social security, provident funds, old-age pensions, life insurance, unemployment insurance, accident insurance, medical insurance, and welfare programs instituted by government (and business) provide much of this security in economically advanced countries; in contrast, in many less-developed countries such as Nigeria, this function is assumed by the extended family. This family consists of two or more nuclear families in which the resources and its members are pooled for consumption.

Development economists generally contend that the institution of the extended family is a major barrier to entrepreneurial activity. The joint family is thought to dampen incentives to achieve, deter risk taking, and impede the mobilization of capital. For example, Wolf (1955) writes:

> The joint or extended family system provides another example of institutions deterring economic growth. . . . Where an individual member of the group contemplates a wealth-increasing activity, e.g., through investment in a productive asset that will yield future returns, he must bear all of the costs associated therewith. . . . However the fruits or returns from his investment are subject to sharing among the other members of the extended family. Because of the differentiation between responsible and benefitting economic units, what may appear objectively to be strong incentives to invest are not subjectively so regarded by the potential entrepreneur.

Here I plan to examine the effects of the extended family on capital formation and entrepreneurial activity in small footwear firms in Nigeria.

1. Apprentice Training for Prospective Entrepreneurs

Most entrepreneurs of small firms are trained in the indigenous apprentice system. The supply of entrepreneurs of new small firms is basically a function of the supply of apprentice-course graduates. It is very rare for a small firm to survive for more than three years if the entrepreneur lacks apprentice training. For example, all the initial entrepreneurs of the twenty sample small firms more than three years old (on January 1, 1966) had been trained in the apprentice system. As Callaway (1964) indicates, "Almost all the proprietors of the few Nigerian-owned and managed modern small [industrial firms] . . . began their business lives [as apprentices]."

As a result of the scarcity of capital and highly skilled manpower in Nigeria, small firms can compete in a number of industries by using very intensively the abundant factor, labor—especially unskilled apprentice labor, where the receipts from apprentice fees may exceed wages. However, these labor-intensive techniques demand designing skills and craftsmanship on the part of the prospective supervisor-entrepreneur that can only be acquired from a long period of training, supervision, observation, and practice.

Consider the expenditures required for apprentice training for prospective entrepreneurs of small firms. Total apprentice fees for a two- to four-year course usually ranged from about £N17 to £N40 in 1965. In addition, subsistence costs in Onitsha, for example, amounted to about £N25–£N30 a year. Since individual youths could rarely obtain access to credit or raise the funds themselves, the resources of the extended family were usually required.

Callaway's study of apprentices in 5,135 Nigerian firms found that 96 percent of the apprentice sponsors were members of the extended family. In addition, family members provided or financed the apprentice's room and board.

Moreover, the prospective apprentice was likely to be dependent upon the extended family for initial contacts with capable apprentice instructors.

In rare cases, the extended family may prevent a youth from obtaining apprentice training. The person who might otherwise be able to afford apprentice training may have to forgo it as a result of the demands on his income by the extended family.

2. *The Establishment of the Firm*

Raising the initial capital of the firm is one of its major problems. The outlay needed for the establishment of even a small firm was £N25 at a minimum, and perhaps more than £N150. Most prospective small entrepreneurs in Nigeria did not have access to funds from organized financial institutions.

The extended family, because of its age composition and size, may have been able to mobilize funds that the prospective entrepreneur would not have had available, especially if he were young. When asked for the sources of initial capital for the firm, fourteen of the twenty small entrepreneurs in the sample indicated that at least part was raised from other members of the extended family. Even though the median initial investment was no more than £N200, only five of the twenty entrepreneurs obtained all the intitial capital from their own resources.

On the basis of evidence from our sample and studies by Callaway and Harris, it seems reasonable to conclude that small Nigerian industrial entrepreneurs were very dependent upon the extended family for their initial capital.

Usually the entrepreneur had no formal obligation to repay family members the money expended on his training and the establishment of his firm. The lack of formal repayments was likely to be very advantageous to the enterprise in its early years when liquid funds were frequently scarce. However, as funds permitted, the businessman was expected to contribute to the subsistence, education, training, and establishment of firms of other family members.

The extended family may have reduced the entrepreneur's initial outlays in other ways. Family members often provided room and board, building space, or tools needed for the enterprise.

The family also sometimes helped the initial entrepreneur to obtain access to suppliers, merchants, creditors, market authorities, local officials, and persons with economic power and influence. For example, suppliers tended to extend credit to the entrepreneur only if a member of the extended family guaranteed payment.

In a few cases, however, the extended family may have impeded the establishment of a firm. Income which a person might have otherwise used for investment in training or in the establishment of an enterprise might have been allotted by the family for other purposes, such as consumption expenditures. On the other hand, the family may have allotted the funds for investment in the training, education, or enterprise of another family member whose investment project was expected to yield higher returns. This transfer of funds to other family members by prospective entrepreneurs occurred only rarely, however, since most of them were young and unlikely to have income and wealth to divert.

Finally, the associations of the extended family in the home village affected the businessman's acquisition of labor and apprentices. Most small firms obtained more than half of their labor force from the entrepreneur's home city or village, even when the firm was located in a different city.

It is not surprising that a large percentage of the labor force of the firm was drawn from the entrepreneur's home district. Over a period of years the extended family of the entrepreneur had incurred a number of (social) claims and obligations which could be satisfied in part when selecting a labor force. In some instances, the entrepreneur was pressed to hire a laborer or train an apprentice from some family to whom his family was obligated. On the other hand, it may have been difficult for the entrepreneur to find persons to evaluate applicants outside his home village.

Frequently workers from the village took their positions for granted and did not work as hard. However, it was sometimes easier to instill a high esprit de corps in the work force if the entrepreneur and most of the laborers were from the same district. Thus, on balance, the entrepreneur probably benefited at least as much as he lost from the fact that a large percentage of his labor force was drawn from his home district.

3. *The Growth of the Firm*

Entrepreneurs from eleven of the fifteen firms acquiring additional capital raised at least 50 percent of the funds from profits retained in the enterprise. Part of the expansion of two other firms was financed through profits. In no case did the entrepreneurs report that new capital had been received from members of the extended family.

In fact, the demands of the extended family curtailed the use of profits for the expansion of sample firms. As the income of the entrepreneur increased, the number of dependents he was required to support also increased. Among thirteen sample firms on which reliable data on profit were available, there is a strong positive relationship between the profit of the firm and the number of dependents of the top entrepreneur.

It seems reasonable to believe, though, that the prestige and power afforded the successful entrepreneur by the extended family may have provided an important incentive for entrepreneurial activity which may at least have partially offset the disincentive effects of sharing income and wealth.

Finally, as indicated in the discussion of the establishment of the firm, the extended family can affect the acquisition of labor and apprentice supply and assist in obtaining useful contacts with businessmen and persons with economic power.

VIII. THE SHORTAGE OF CAPITAL

Most Nigerian businessmen mentioned lack of capital as one of their major problems. For example, most sample entrepreneurs indicated that the output and profit of the firm would increase if they could acquire more capital. Some indicated an interest in borrowing money from government loan agencies.

As Sayre P. Schatz (1964) indicates, the desire for additional capital by the entrepreneur does not necessarily represent an effective demand for it. A number of the entrepreneurs wishing to acquire additional capital were probably overoptimistic, as some were making losses and many had a low rate of capacity utilization. However, even if entrepreneurs with a desire for capital but a lack of effective demand are eliminated from the analysis, there may be an excess demand for capital resulting from government loan agencies' charging a rate of interest below the market rate.

IX. SUMMARY

Because time and money spent for formal education represented relinquished opportunities in training more closely related to entrepreneurial occupations, the education of the entrepreneur was negatively related to the profit rate of his firm. In addition, with the brisk demand for educated persons in foreign enterprises and the civil service, those with a university or secondary education were likely to have chosen an entrepreneurial pursuit because of failure in another occupation, or limited options. However, education and literacy of the entrepreneur did set a limit to the size and complexity of the firm.

The lack of previous entrepreneurial and managerial experience was a major barrier to success among large entrepreneurs. Apprentice training appeared to be virtually necessary for the success of small entrepreneurs.

Trade was a major prior occupation for large entrepreneurs. The major catalyst for becoming industrial entrepreneurs was government policy encouraging import substitution in manufacturing through higher tariffs.

The paternal economic status of entrepreneurs was substantially higher than that of the population as a whole. There was a close positive relationship between the economic status of the father and the entrepreneurial success of the son. These findings, together with comparative information from other countries, suggest that industrial business activity, rather than being a path for substantial upward socioeconomic mobility, is a way of maintaining and defending a relatively high class status.

For large firms, the major sources of initial capital were loans; of expansion capital, retained earnings. The extended family was instrumental in the acquisition of initial capital for small firms.

Almost all prospective entrepreneurs were students in an apprentice course, which in virtually all cases is sponsored by members of the extended family. Only rarely did a potential entrepreneur forgo the necessary apprentice training as a result of demands on his income by the extended family. Clearly the effect of the extended family was to augment the number of students taking apprentice courses, which increased the supply of entrepreneurs.

Small entrepreneurs were very dependent upon the extended family for capital to establish a firm. Only rarely was the income of a prospective entrepreneur diverted from the establishnent of a firm to consumption expenditures of other family members. Thus, in toto, the extended family increased the establishment of firms by entrepreneurs.

Entrepreneurs wishing to expand their firms lost more than they benefited from the institution of the extended family. Although entrepreneurs rarely received funds from the family for expansion of the firm, the family did require resources for current consumption which might otherwise have been reinvested in the business.

The extended family hindered the expansion of the firm by the entrepreneur, but facilitated the entrepreneur's training and establishment of a firm. Without further evidence, there is no longer reason to believe that the extended family has, on balance, a negative effect on entrepreneurial activity. It is conceivable that, in many cases, the positive contribution of the extended family to the training and firm establishment of the entrepreneur exceeds the negative effect on firm expansion, but this question requires further research.

ACKNOWLEDGMENTS

Portions of E. Wayne Nafziger, "African Entrepreneurs: A Case Study of Nigerian Industrialists, 1964–65," were reprinted from E. Wayne Nafziger, *African Capitalism,* with the permission of the publishers, Hoover Institution Press. E. Wayne Nafziger, "The Relationship Between Education and Entrepreneurship in Nigeria," *The Journal of Developing Areas* 4(April 1970):349–360; and E. Wayne Nafziger, "The Effect of the Nigerian Extended Family on Entrepreneurial Activity." Reprinted from *Economic Development and Cultural Change,* Vol. 18, No. 1, Part I.

REFERENCES

Alexander, A. P. (July 1960), "Industrial Entrepreneurship in Turkey: Origins and Growth." *Economic Development and Cultural Change* 8(4), pt. 1:349–65.

——— (1964), *Greek Industrialists: An Economic and Social Analysis.* Athens: Center of Planning and Economic Research.

Berna, J. J. (1960), *Industrial Entrepreneurship in Madras State.* London: Asia Publishing House.

Callaway, A. (July 1964), "Nigeria's Indigenous Education: The Apprentice System." *Odu: University of Ife Journal of African Studies* 1(1):1–18.

Carroll, J. J. (1965), *The Filipino Manufacturing Entrepreneur: Agent and Product of Change.* Ithaca, N.Y.: Cornell University Press.

Collins, O. F., D. G. Moore, and D. B. Unwalla (1964), *The Enterprising Man.* East Lansing, Mich.: MSU Business Studies.

Hagen, E. E. (1962), *On the Theory of Social Change.* Homewood, Ill.: Dorsey Press.

Harris, J. R. (1967), "Industrial Entrepreneurship in Nigeria." Unpublished Ph.D. dissertation, Northeastern University.

——— (1971), "Nigerian Entrepreneurship in Industry." In Peter Kirby (ed.), *Entrepreneurship and Economic Development.* New York: Free Press.

Kemmerer, D. L. and C. C. Jones (1959), *American Economic History*. New York: McGraw-Hill.

Kilby, P. (1965), *African Enterprise: The Nigerian Bread Industry*. Stanford: Hoover Institution.

Knight, F. (1921), *Risk, Uncertainty and Profit*. Boston: Houghton Mifflin Co.

Miller, W., ed. (1962), *Men in Business: Essays on the Historical Role of the Entrepreneur*. New York: Harper and Row.

Nafziger, E. W. (1977), *African Capitalism: A Case Study in Nigerian Entrepreneurship*. Stanford: Hoover Institution.

——— (1978), *Class, Caste, and Entrepreneurship: A Study of Indian Industrialists*, East-West Center Book. Honolulu: University Press of Hawaii.

——— (1969), "The Effect of the Nigerian Extended Family on Entrepreneurial Activity." *Economic Development and Cultural Change* 18(1), pt. 1:25–33.

——— (1977), "Entrepreneurship, Social Mobility, and Income Redistribution in South India." *American Economic Review* 67(1):76–80.

Papanek, G. F. (1962), "The Development of Entrepreneurship." *American Economic Review* 52(2):46–58.

Sayigh, Y. A. (1962), *Entrepreneurs of Lebanon: The Role of the Business Leader in a Developing Economy*. Cambridge: Harvard University Press.

Schatz, S. P. (1964), *Development Bank Lending in Nigeria*. London: Oxford University Press.

Schumpeter, J. A. (1939), *Business Cycles*, 2 vols. New York: McGraw-Hill.

——— (1961), *The Theory of Economic Development: An Inquiry into Profits, Capital, Credit, Interest, and the Business Cycle*. Translated by Redvers Opie. New York: Oxford University Press.

Smelser, N. J. and S. M. Lipset, eds. (1966), *Social Structure and Mobility in Econonic Development*. Chicago: Aldine.

Walras, L. (1954), *Elements of Pure Economics or the Theory of Social Wealth*. London: George Allen and Unwin.

Wolf, C. (1955), "Institutions and Economic Development." *American Economic Review*, 14(4):867–83.

THE CIVILIAN CONSERVATION CORPS: A WORKFARE SOLUTION

Robert F. Severson, Jr.

During my graduate studies, Donald Kemmerer encouraged my attempts to use quantitative information of a variety not generally considered manageable by most economic historians of that time. He was amused and interested in what I thought to be possible, given the stone-age data processing equipment we had at our disposal during the 1950s.

This encouragement and support led me to inquire into sources of information usually ignored because of the difficulties of processing. I felt that a service was there to be performed in both discovery and simplified presentation of such volumes of information, and Don must share the blame for this predilection on my part.

The following presentation regarding the Civilian Conservation Corps is a sample of the kind of things my experience with Don has encouraged.

Variations in Business and Economic History:
Essays in Honor of Donald L. Kemmerer
Research in Economic History, Suppl. 2, pages 121–126.

ISBN: 0-89232-262-4

While it is not something we have discussed, I do believe it is something over which we could have substantial, sustained, and lively discussion.

I. THE EXPERIMENT

On March 31, 1933, the Seventy-third Congress gave the president a-thority to spend $300 million on a civilian conservation corps.[1] On April 5, 1933, the president issued Executive Order Number 6101, which set up the Civilian Conservation Corps. On April 10, 1933, the first 25,000 men were enrolled in the program, and in August of the same year there were 300,000 men in CCC camps throughout the nation.[2]

The Seventy-fifth Congress restated the purpose of the corps, making formal through congressional action what had been done under the executive order. The corps continued to operate in a manner that would provide "employment, as well as vocational training, for youthful citizens of the United States who are unemployed and in need of employment."[3] The program provided for a limited number of "older" youths, authorized by Congress, all of whom were either war veterans or Indians. Most enrollees were, in accordance with the law, unmarried male citizens between the ages of seventeen and twenty-three. They could enroll for not less than six months and not more than two years. They were provided food, clothing, and shelter and were paid $30 per month, of which $25 was sent to their families or saved for them.[4]

The CCC experiment is a possible model upon which to base contemporary welfare programs. It is generally the case that the human investment results presumed to flow from such programs have not been examined on the basis of possible private and social returns received from such programs as the CCC. This pilot study was undertaken to examine methodological problems in discovery of the long-run effect of such investment in human resources. The specific design is to test the feasibility of a thorough, statistically reliable examination of the financial experience of a past group of lower-income Americans. The financial returns of the individuals who were enrolled in the CCC should give some direction in this case. It was hypothesized that a sample of former CCC members would have identifiable group financial characteristics different from the general male population of the same age group. An awareness of such characteristics or differences could be useful in determining, from at least one vantage point, the value of this type of social investment. Additional studies of such a group might give more thorough understanding of costs and returns—e.g., ratios of CCC to general population with respect to time spent in penal institutions. Such studies could also provide data for judging the efficacy of undertaking new social welfare programs.

With this in mind, a sample was taken from the original public records of CCC enrollments between 1933 and 1943 (the entire life of the program). There are approximately three million enrollees recorded, and for the purposes of this pilot study, a random sample of one hundred names (with birth dates, birthplaces, and fathers' names) was collected. This list was presented to the Social Security Administration, which searched its records for these persons and found eighty-one of them. It then provided the records of these eighty-one individuals in such a way as to give earnings information without giving identifying information on any one individual. These records show the amounts of income against which these individuals paid Social Security taxes both in total since 1937 and annually since 1951. The annual data for 1956 and 1957 were then consulted for the CCC group and compared to the general male population of the same age group as reported in the Social Security Administration handbook for 1957.[5] With these data the financial success of this group may be compared to that of the same age component of the total population some twenty years after enrollment in the CCC.

The Social Security Administration also provided an aggregate breakdown of ages within the eighty-one member group. However, there was no way to determine the ages of each of these eighty-one persons whose records were found by the SSA. If such information were provided, federal disclosure rules might be violated. This does not appear to be too serious a shortcoming, however, because the application of the age distribution of the CCC sample to the handbook sample includes a high percentage of the CCC enrollees.

The age groups compared then were thirty through forty-nine and sixty through seventy-one. There were no CCC enrollees in the sample between the ages of fifty and fifty-nine in the year 1957. All of them had to be at least thirty-three in 1957, the latest birth date in the pilot study being July 10, 1924. The inclusion of the age group sixty through seventy-one means that some of the subjects were in their forties during the time of the CCC program. These were undoubtedly some of the war veterans or Indians allowed for under the original CCC act. The earliest birth date in the sample is December 1, 1887. There were five subjects who fell within the sixty-through-seventy-one age group.

The data used for comparisons in the pilot are based on the years 1956 and 1957. These years were chosen because of the immediate availability of data as presented in the SSA handbook.[6] Comparable data were compiled on the CCC sample from the individual records provided by the SSA. In the Social Security publication, reports on the national sample are based on those persons who were enrolled in Social Security and were currently contributing to OASDI. Those not contributing, even though enrolled, were not included in the analysis. Therefore, the same modification was made on the CCC sample as determined from the individual records. There were fifty-three of the eighty-one former CCC members who contributed to OASDI in 1956, and fifty-nine of eighty-one in 1957.

II. FINDINGS

Initial examination of the data generated for this pilot study suggests that the former CCC members had higher average dollar earnings than those persons of the same age groups in the general male population. The data in Table 1 show that the average OASDI earnings credits of the national sample stood at $3,559.26 in 1956. However, the average OASDI earnings credits among the CCC sample stood at $3,943.40 in 1956. In 1957, these averages stood at $3,617.23 and $3,994.92 respectively. Furthermore, a larger percentage of the CCC sample paid OASDI taxes at the maximum income level than was the case in the national sample; i.e., the CCC sample was 58.5 percent in 1957 and 57.6 percent in 1957, while the national sample stood at 49.5 percent in 1956 and 51.6 percent in 1957. The maximum against which OASDI taxes were payable in these years was $4200.

If statistically significant, the data would support the hypothesis that former CCC members occupied the higher-income groups with greater frequency than members of the general population. To test this hypothesis, the data were subjected to a two-sample test for means[7] which produced the values of 1.69 for 1956 and 1.80 for 1957. Hence, the differences are significant at the .10 level.

Given these findings, it appears that on a micro basis, the human investment value of the CCC program was positive with regard to the income levels of CCC participants as compared to the total relevant population over a twenty-year time lag. If similar results were to be obtained on the basis of a much larger sample of CCC members, we could then restate our policy recommendations regarding this type of human capital investment. That is, we already know that the CCC youths were employed as a group building and refurbishing portions of our nation during a time of great unemployment. A welfare and a public-consumption function were combined in the CCC program. But, given the data of this pilot study, there is also reason to believe that on a macro basis, the economy might also have gained a long-run benefit in that the former CCC members, as a group, were earning higher incomes than average for their total age group after a twenty-year lag had passed. A compound-interest effect may ultimately be the most important achievement of such a program.

Table 1. Frequency Distribution of OASDI Earnings Credits, Males, Selected Age Groups, 1956 and 1957, According to Income Group, National Sample, and CCC Sample.

Income Groups		*National Sample*		*CCC Sample*	
Class ($)	*Midpoint ($)*	*N*	*OASDI Earnings Credits ($)*	*N*	*OASDI Earnings Credits ($)*
		1956			
1– 599	300	1,314,000	394,200	3	900
600–1199	900	1,313,000	1,181,700	1	900
1200–1799	1500	1,368,000	2,052,000	3	4,500
1800–2399	2100	1,232,000	2,587,200	3	6,300
2400–2999	2700	1,406,000	3,796,200	2	5,400
3000–3599	3300	1,502,000	4,956,600	5	16,500
3600–4199	3900	1,738,000	6,778,200	5	19,500
4200 & over	5000*	9,297,000	46,585,000	31	155,000
SUM		19,170,000	68,231,100	53	209,000
		1957			
1– 599	300	1,329,000	398,700	1	300
600–1199	900	1,295,000	1,165,500	1	900
1200–1799	1500	1,301,000	1,951,500	3	4,500
1800–2399	2100	1,186,000	2,490,600	5	10,500
2400–2999	2700	1,393,000	3,761,100	4	10,800
3000–3599	3300	1,485,000	4,900,500	7	23,100
3600–4199	3900	1,643,000	6,407,700	4	15,600
4200 & over	5000*	9,955,000	49,775,000	34	170,000
SUM		19,587,000	70,850,600	59	235,700

Note:
* The $5,000 "midpoint" was selected as an estimate. The national sample is so reported because $4,200 was the maximum on which OASDI taxes were collected in 1956 and 1957. It was judged that selection of the $5,000 figure would not bias results in an upward direction.

Source: U.S. Department of Health, Education, and Welfare, Social Security Administration, *Handbook of Old-Age, Survivors, and Disability Insurance Statistics,* 1957, Baltimore, 1965, Table A100, p. 19, provided data for the national sample. CCC sample data computed from blind individual reports on former CCC members as obtained from the Social Security Administration by this author.

NOTES

1. 73rd Congress, 1st Session, chapter 17 (S 598) (P 5), March 31, 1933.
2. J. H. H. Darling, "The C.C.C. Makes Good!" *The Christian Century*, October 25, 1933, pp. 133–35.
3. 75th Congress, 1st Session, chapter 383 (HR 6551) (P 163), June 30, 1937.
4. *Ibid.*

5. U.S. Department of Health, Education, and Welfare, Social Security Administration, *Handbook of Old-Age, Survivors, and Disability Insurance Statistics 1957*, Baltimore, 1965.

6. *Ibid.*

7. See M. Hamburg, *Statistical Analysis for Decision Making*, New York: Harcourt, Brace and World, 1970.

U.S. TEACHERS' ORGANIZATIONS AND THE SALARY ISSUE: 1900–1960

Robert J. Thornton

I. INTRODUCTION

One of the most important developments affecting public school teachers in the United States over the past two decades has been the spread of collective-bargaining activity. It is estimated that, as of the late 1970s, more than 72 percent of all public elementary and secondary teachers are now members of employee organizations which are engaged in some form of negotiations activity (U.S. Department of Commerce, 1978:1).

In the minds of many, the active participation of teachers in the salary-determination process can best be viewed as originating in the early 1960s. As Stephen Cole notes:

> At the beginning of the decade [the 1960s], it would have been difficult to find a more conservative and acquiescent group than school teachers; in terms of participating in an illegal strike, perhaps no less likely group existed. Today, all that has

Variations in Business and Economic History:
Essays in Honor of Donald L. Kemmerer
Research in Economic History, Suppl. 2, pages 127–143.

ISBN: 0-89232-262-4

> changed. In cities across the United States, teachers are demanding a voice in the determination of their salaries and working conditions; and when these demands are ignored, teachers are using militant tactics, including strikes, to force compliance by school boards. (Cole, 1969:3)

In marking the early 1960s as the watershed, most observers point to the success of the United Federation of Teachers (UFT) in winning a representation election and substantial salary gains for New York City teachers in 1962. The UFT victory, it is usually claimed, was the impetus which motivated teachers in other cities to organize and demand a greater voice in the salary-determination process.

It will be argued here, however, that such a view is somewhat distorted. While it is true that the rate of growth of teacher bargaining increased after the UFT success, the pre-1960 era also saw teachers engaging in concerted activities on a widespread scale in order to improve their economic welfare. Such activities included formal salary-consultation procedures between teachers' organizations and school boards—procedures which sometimes culminated in collective-bargaining agreements—and even occasional periods of teacher militancy.

It will be the purpose of this essay to discuss the pre-1960 history of organized teacher efforts to gain a voice in the salary-determination process. Much of this history has been either recently overlooked or previously undocumented. When analyzed in this light, it will be seen that the UFT victory and the growth of teacher bargaining which followed can better be viewed as a continuation of a trend which had been proceeding for several decades, rather than as a radical departure from the past.

II. TEACHERS AND THE SALARY ISSUE BEFORE WORLD WAR II

A. Teachers' Unions

The first permanent teachers' union at the local level in the United States was the Chicago Teachers Federation (CTF), which was founded in 1897. The CTF had grown out of the rather short-lived Chicago Teachers Club, a group which included not only teachers, but supervisors and administrators as well. The CTF was organized primarily among elementary school teachers, and the majority of its members were women.

From the start the demands of the group were of a "bread-and-butter" nature, its raison d'être being nearly twenty years of stationary salaries in the public school system of Chicago. Besides battling for better salaries, the CTF also fought for teacher rights and a pension law (Clarke,

1966). In its very first year the Chicago group succeeded in persuading the Board of Education to agree to salary hikes. Its methods were rather informal, consisting chiefly of the circulating of petitions and lobbying the Board of Education. Even with the raise, however, it was felt that salaries were still far from adequate. And so in 1901 the CTF succeeded in obtaining a court order forcing the city Board of Equalization to list for tax purposes twenty-three previously unlisted city corporations. The intention was to secure more tax revenue for the city, some of which would be channeled into higher salaries for teachers. At the end of 1902, the CTF decided to affiliate with organized labor and joined the ranks of the Chicago Federation of Labor.

Early concerted activity among teachers was not limited to the Chicago public schools, however. From 1897 to 1916 at least twenty-one other teacher groups in eleven states organized into labor-affiliated locals, among them San Antonio, Oklahoma City, New York City, and Washington, D.C. The important point to note is that in nearly every case early unions arose where teachers' salaries and school conditions in general were very poor. A few were organized, however, strictly on an ad hoc basis, soon lapsing into nonexistence after the crisis had passed. Others faded away owing to apathy or dissension among their members (Fordyce, 1955).

The American Federation of Teachers (AFT) came into existence in 1916 with charter locals in Chicago, Gary, New York City, Oklahoma, Scranton, and Washington, D.C. Almost immediately it affiliated with the American Federation of Labor. The following year, new locals in San Francisco, Sacramento, LaPorte (Indiana), and Kansas City joined, once again the reasons being poor salary conditions and/or repressive school board tactics.

The first few years of the AFT were ones of fairly rapid growth. In fact, by 1919 more than 10,000 teachers and 136 locals had joined its ranks (Clarke, 1966:147). A rapid decline then set in, however, as the AFT (as well as organized labor in general) fell subject to pervasive antiunion attacks during the 1920s. A general sentiment of hostility toward organized labor was sweeping the country at the time, and school boards did not hesitate to employ all the weapons traditionally used against private-sector unions. Blacklists were common, as were yellow-dog contracts. In Chicago, for example, the Loeb Rule (after Jacob Loeb, past president of the Chicago Board of Education) forbade teachers to join labor-affilitated organizations under the threat of immediate dismissal. Although a temporary restraining order secured from the courts at first prohibited its enforcement, it was later upheld by the Illinois Supreme Court as a valid exercise of board powers. Reluctantly, the CTF withdrew from the AFT. The upshot of this and other attacks on organized teacher activity was a rapid plummeting of AFT membership, which reached a low of 3,500 members in 1926. Thereafter, slow but steady growth again set in, a pace which gradually picked up during the depression thirties as the AFT revitalized its organizing efforts and the nation's antilabor sentiment softened. By 1944, the AFT included approximately 35,000 paid-up members (Fordyce, 1955:130).

It has already been mentioned that the earliest teachers' unions, including those forming the nucleus of the AFT, generally espoused as their foremost goal the improvement of inadequate salary levels and poor teaching conditions. In the process they eschewed the philosophy that the "professionalism" of teachers precluded their acting together for such purposes.

A brief look at some specific instances will illustrate the type of conditions which unions sought to eliminate. In St. Paul, Minnesota, a single publishing company had for years monopolized the selection of textbooks in the city's public school system. It had, moreover, exerted its influence to include the selection of administrators and teachers. Later in the same city a "loyalty club" was set up for the teachers by the administration—a type of company union much like those set up by antiunion employers in the private sector. Presumably, only "loyal" teachers were to be considered for pay increases (American Federation of Teachers, 1955:34).

In many school systems there was no such thing as a fixed salary schedule for the teaching staff. Rather, the individual teacher bargained alone with the administration for his or her salary. The result was often an illogical and grossly inequitable salary structure within some school systems, and it was frequently the case that teachers with identical amounts of training and experience received substantially different salaries.

In Gary, Indiana, during the first days of the depression, each teacher was required by the school superintendent to donate one day's pay to a fund being used to buy a building for a nearby corset company. The superintendent justified this requirement by claiming that the prosperity of the city would be thereby increased (American Federation of Teachers, 1955:71).

Instances such as these were evidently far from uncommon during the period of the beginnings of teacher unionism. In general, it can be said that most of these early teachers' unions banded together to raise teachers' salaries, to improve working conditions, and to eliminate autocratic administration practices. To secure these ends, the unions fought for more funds for salary purposes, fixed and equitable salary schedules, adequate tenure legislation, and sound personnel policies—goals not much different from those generally espoused by teachers' unions today.

On the other hand, noticeably absent from the repertory of early teacher-union tactics were the now commonly used methods of collective bargaining—i.e., the seeking of exclusive recognition, formalized negotiations procedures, and written collective agreements. Many teachers' groups considered themselves fortunate to be granted the simple privilege of making a salary proposal at a meeting of the school board. (Indeed, the union making such a proposal often claimed that it was actually "negotiating" with the board.) A perusal of the annual convention proceedings of the AFT also finds no statements even advocating that its locals seek collective bargaining rights until 1935, although before that time it had encouraged the formation of teachers' councils and joint participation in policymaking (Moskow, 1966:106–7).

What is more, the resort to the strike on the part of teachers was quite rare until the 1940s. One researcher (Oakes, 1958:558) estimates that only twenty-two such strikes took place from 1918 to 1940, and a good many of these occurred in small, rather isolated Pennsylvania mining towns. For that reason, they were usually unpublicized. From its inception the AFT had officially adhered to a no-strike policy in its constitution, one which was formally reaffirmed at its Boston convention in 1947.[1]

As a rule, the methods used by the pre–World War II teachers' unions in pushing for higher salaries were of three principal types: (1) direct appeals to the superintendent or the board of education, (2) affiliation with organized labor as a source of political strength, and (3) the use of propaganda to sway public opinion (Kochman, 1947:9–16). Yet there were several cases in which bona fide collective bargaining occurred during this period. What may have been the first teacher collective-bargaining contract in U.S. history was rediscovered a few years ago in Illinois. Signed in 1934 in Benld, a small mining town in the central part of the state, it was negotiated by Local One of the now-defunct Progressive Trades and Labor Unions of America and represented the teachers and administrators of the Benld public schools. The contract was brief (one page), but contained among other items a closed-shop provision, seniority rules, and a grievance procedure. However, its life span was cut short when it was nullified a year later by the Illinois attorney general (*American Teacher*, December 1967:8).

In 1938 the Proviso Council of the West Suburban Teachers Union (WSTU) near Chicago negotiated the first continuing collective-bargaining pact for teachers in the country, one which the council has renegotiated many times since then. Other councils of the multi-branched WSTU soon followed suit with agreements of their own—the Maywood Council in 1940 and the Cicero Council four years later (*American*

Teacher, November 1944:6–12). The Cicero contract was far ahead of its time in terms of comprehensiveness: as the agreement contained exclusive recognition for the union, a negotiated salary schedule, and such fringe benefits as sabbatical leave and military-duty pay. The Chicago Teachers Union also managed to secure recognition from Mayor Kelley and the Board of Education in 1939 as the bargaining agent for Chicago teachers (*American Teacher*, April 1939:27).

B. Teachers' Associations

Teachers' associations, by way of contrast with teachers' unions, are professionally oriented groups which maintain no affiliation with organized labor. The birth of teachers' associations in the United States precedes that of teachers' unions by a considerable period of time. These associations arose on three different levels—national, state, and local—quite independently of one another. Big-city organizations were the first to come into being, beginning with the New York City teachers in 1794. Later, New York also became the site of the first statewide teachers' group—the New York State Teachers Association, established in 1845. It was not until 1857 that the National Teachers Association (NTA), the forerunner of the modern-day National Education Association, became the first permanent association of teachers organized on a national level.

Unlike the teachers' unions, which usually originated because of low salaries and poor teaching conditions, these early associations were mainly "professional" in nature. The state and local associations directed their activities mainly toward the cultural and professional improvement of their members. They undertook the task of spreading proeducational propaganda and sponsored legislation for the upgrading of the public school systems. Later, the NTA also declared itself to be an organization whose concerns were primarily with professional matters of education. As the preamble from its constitution stated, the NTA was founded "to elevate the character and advance the interests of the teaching profession and to promote the causes of education throughout the country." Further indicative of the focus of its interests is the fact that from its inception the NTA included among its membership not only classroom teachers, but also administrators. In 1870 the National Association of School Superintendents and the American Normal School Association merged with the NTA to form the National Education Association (NEA).

During the latter half of the nineteenth century neither the NEA nor the state education associations concerned themselves to any great extent with the economic status of classroom teachers. This lack of interest was the direct result of the prevailing philosophy of the times, for predominating in the early history of the teaching occupation in the nineteenth century were two somewhat contradictory ideas concerning teacher welfare. The first was based on the theory that teaching was a professional public service and that, therefore, teachers could not expect to receive compensation on a par with that received in private-sector occupations. The second was that only by the teachers' own personal and professional improvement would the public recognize their merit and be willing to pay for it (Fordyce, 1955:19). A superintendent of schools from Chicago in 1907 epitomized this philosophy by declaring that the reason that teachers' salaries were low was the teachers' own incompetence. Only greater efficiency, brought on by professional growth, would automatically improve their welfare, or so it was claimed (Clarke, 1966). In other words, the implication of the two theories mentioned above was that the first order of business for teachers was their professional improvement, and that attention to matters such as salary, pensions, tenure, etc. was not only secondary, but even irrelevant.

This is not to say that the NEA and the state associations were completely oblivious to the economic plight of teachers during these times, as some have charged. For example, the NEA did issue statements, albeit infrequently, decrying low salaries. As early as 1863, NTA president J. D. Philbrick insisted that "the situation of a teacher must be made desirable by adequate compensation." Apparently in response to Philbrick's address, the association passed its first resolution on salaries during that year (Wesley, 1957:334). Later, during the Great Depression of the 1870s, the NEA formed a committee to protest depression-induced salary cuts (Alexander, 1910:49). On the whole, however, the resolutions were rather futile and the committees short-lived.

In sharp contrast to the lethargy of the national and state associations, however, stands the activity of the city associations. With the spread of urbanization in the late 1800s, city associations grew in number. Teachers had long occupied the lowest rungs of the professional-salary ladder, and the city associations became quite attentive to their concerns. The 1880s and 1890s marked the approximate beginnings of such local teacher activity. As an indication of their effectiveness, Paul H. Douglas (1925:201) notes in his *Real Wages in the United States* that teachers' salaries rose during these decades at a faster rate than did average salaries of all workers in the economy. However, rises in the cost of living ate up much of the gains that teachers were finally beginning to enjoy.

The types of activities undertaken by these city associations have been carefully analyzed by Carter Alexander in a survey undertaken in 1910. He credits the associations, which by this time had spread to include groups in nearly every U.S. city with a population of thirty thousand or more, with engaging in campaigns to improve salaries, hospitalization and burial benefits, pensions and annuities, insurance, and tenure. From information gained from over one hundred city associations responding to a questionnaire, he reports that in almost every case local associations had engaged in organized efforts to improve salaries. Besides making extensive use of campaigns to arouse public sympathy, the associations are described by Alexander as resorting to such procedures as engaging in concerted legal action. The previously noted campaign of the Chicago Teachers Federation to enforce municipal tax laws was apparently followed by similar association action in many other cities. Suits for the remittance of back pay were also filed, as in the case of the New Orleans teachers who missed many paydays from 1882 to 1887 because of the lack of district funds.

Alexander notes that in some cities at this time local associations were lobbying for legislation consistent with teachers' interests. Although slightly fewer than half of the one hundred associations surveyed were legislatively active, those that were so engaged were devoting almost exclusive attention to matters of salary, pensions, or tenure.

Finally, Alexander's survey points out that many city associations began to undertake formal investigations regarding the economic status of teachers about this time. A few associations—including those of Chicago, Philadelphia, and Minneapolis—even published periodic surveys of teachers' salaries.

It is important to point out that the evidence above not only refutes the thesis that early associations were lacking in concern for the betterment of teacher welfare, but also contradicts the concomitant thesis that teachers' unions sprang up as a *reaction* to association lethargy. Some observers (e.g., Clarke, 1966:37) have claimed, for example, that teachers gradually turned to labor for help because their own association leaders not only failed to help but actually stood in the way of teacher welfare. The examples presented above, as well as the observation that city associations and unions very often worked together in a cooperative fashion, serve as proof to the contrary.

Turning from the local associations to the National Education Association, it is interesting to note the observation of the centennial historian of the NEA, Edgar Wesley. As Wesley (1957:335) points out bluntly in his rather apologetic chapter on the NEA and teacher welfare, "The record of the Association for its first 48 years (in this area) was almost entirely . . . devoid of action." In 1905, however, there occurred a significant change of course as the association published its first major report on teachers' salaries—a document of 466 pages based on questionnaire returns from more than 400 cities and representative rural districts. According to Wesley (1957:335), "The 1905 salary study demonstrated the efficacy of facts as weapons in the campaign for convincing the public and the profession itself of the need for remedial action." Carter Alexander (1910:62) further credits the report with evoking similar studies by state and local associations with a view toward remedying deficiencies in specific localities. The rising demand of the NEA's membership for a more active role in the improvement of its economic status later led the NEA to establish a permanent research division in 1922, one which has issued biennial (later annual) salary surveys since that time.

Besides the aforementioned, there is other evidence of the NEA's gradual change of philosophy in regard to salary matters. In 1918, the Superintendent of Public Instruction in Pennsylvania complained to the NEA that far too many teachers' meetings were concerned with the discussion of salaries, tenure, retirement, etc. He proposed instead that the NEA "put first things first"—namely, the welfare of the pupil rather than that of the teacher (Fordyce, 1955:49). By 1920, according to Wesley, the NEA was quite vigorously demanding the payment of higher salaries and the enactment of tenure laws. It was, furthermore, setting up permanent committees to develop standards regarding these subjects. Shortly before the depression it was even beginning to take a stand in favor of joint participation in the process of salary determination by teachers and administrators (*NEA Journal*, October 1929:225). In a considerable number of school districts, teachers were beginning to be allowed the privilege of representation on school board committees engaged in salary decision making.[2]

III. TEACHERS' ORGANIZATIONS AND SALARIES: THE POSTWAR PERIOD

Summarizing briefly the pre-1945 history of the concern of teachers' unions and associations with the salary issue, it has been seen that considerable activity toward the improvement of teacher welfare took place during this time, particularly at the local level. Moreover, the AFT and, to a lesser extent, the NEA officially encouraged such efforts. The activity, however, was still of a rather mild nature. Strikes were rare, numbering on the average fewer than one per year and taking place in smaller, rural districts. Only a handful of unions were engaged in actual collective bargaining. Joint decision making in the salary determination process was expressed as a desirable goal by both the AFT and NEA, but it was still not a fact accepted by many boards of education.

The period beginning in approximately 1945 marked a noticeable turning point in two respects. In the first place, teachers grew increasingly militant in persuading school boards to meet their demands. Second, appeals on the part of both national teachers' organizations encouraging their locals to play a more active role in salary determination became more numerous and more persistent. We will examine both of these developments more closely.

A. Teachers' Strikes

War and postwar inflation took a heavy toll on teachers' salaries during the 1940s. Average annual wages and salaries for all U.S. workers rose from $1,300 in 1940 to $2,356 in 1946, an increase of 81 percent (see Table 1). The average salary for teachers, however, which was above the all-industry average wage in 1940, fell *below* the all-industry average in 1946, having increased only 38.9 percent. When the effect of rising prices is brought into consideration, the real earnings of teachers fell sharply during this period. Rising prices, of course, had the same effect on the incomes of groups other than teachers. But the earnings of most other groups increased rapidly enough to more than offset the fall in the value of the dollar (National Education Association, 1949:137).

This relative decline in the earnings position of teachers has usually been considered (Yabroff and David, 1953) the principal factor in the heavy outbreak of teachers' strikes during the decade of the 1940s. Significantly, the record shows that the years of the highest strike incidence (1946–48) coincide precisely with the time of the most rapid rises in the Consumer Price Index. In all, sixty-nine strikes occurred during the decade, fifty-seven of these after 1946. Most of the strikes were relatively brief, the average duration being about nine days, compared

Table 1. Average Annual Teachers' Salaries and Average Annual Wages and Salaries in All U.S. Industries, Selected Years: 1930–60

Year	*Average Teachers' Salaries*	*Average Wages and Salaries in All Industries*[1]	*Index of Teachers' Salaries Relative to All-Industry Average*
1930	$1,420	$1,368	104
1936	1,283	1,184	108
1940	1,441	1,300	111
1946	1,995	2,356	85
1950	4,010	3,008	100
1956	4,156	4,042	103
1960	5,174	4,707	110

Note:
[1] Per Full-time Equivalent Employee

Sources: Table constructed by the author from data appearing in the *U.S. Statistical Abstract, Survey of Current Business* (various years), and *Historial Statistics of the U.S., Colonial Times to 1957.*

to the average of seventeen days for strikes by employees in the private sector. However, a high percentage of teacher strikes took place in the larger cities of the nation and paralyzed school services for a considerable number of pupils. New York City, Buffalo, Providence, Minneapolis, and St. Paul were among the principal cities hit by walkouts while strikes were only narrowly averted in Chicago, Detroit, and Gary.

It should be noted that the decision to strike was not related to the local's affiliation with a national teachers' organization. Slightly over one-quarter of the locals engaging in strike activity were affiliated with the AFT. Another quarter were local professional associations, most of which were NEA affiliates. The remainder were called by independent groups or affiliates of the CIO. It will be remembered that both the AFT and the NEA at this time formally disavowed the use of the strike weapon. Interestingly, however, both organizations compromised their no-strike policies in a few instances. In the St. Paul strike of 1946, the AFT refused to contemplate disciplinary action against its local because the strike "was called to relieve intolerable conditions denying to the children of St. Paul adequate educational opportunity, and because it was supported by all of organized labor, the parent-teacher associations, community leaders, and civic organizations of St. Paul" (*American Teacher*, February 1947:5–6). The work stoppage by the Norwalk, Connecticut, Teachers Association (also in 1946) was held by the executive secretary of the NEA not to be in violation of the NEA code since the teachers had not signed new contracts at the time they decided to strike (*New York Times*, 1947:22).

With the eventual halting of the postwar inflation, the number of teacher strikes tailed off sharply. Still, it has been estimated that at least thirty-five such strikes took place during the decade of the 1950s. Most of the striking locals were either affiliates of the AFT or independent groups. No NEA affiliates struck again after 1951 until 1964 (Glass, 1967:43–46).

In most instances strike action produced salary increases and cost-of-living adjustments for teachers. It is difficult to determine whether these gains would have been forthcoming had the strikes not occurred. But one observer (Schiff, 1952:210–11) notes that maximum salaries in Minneapolis, St. Paul, Pawtucket, New York, Buffalo, and other cities involved in strike action afterwards exceeded the median of the maximum salaries (for similar cities) scheduled for 1950–51 as reported by the Research Division of the NEA. It should be noted further that in many cases teacher strikes precipitated action both on the state and local levels for increased taxation for school needs. And as Table 1 shows, the level of average teachers' salaries rose fast enough to again overtake the all-industry average wage and salary level by 1950.

One major consequence of the increased level of teacher militancy during this period was the subsequent proliferation of state antistrike legislation. Shortly following the Buffalo teachers' strike in February of 1947, the New York state legislature enacted into law the Condon-Wadlin Act, which outlawed all public employee strikes. There is little doubt that the quick passage of the bill resulted in large part from the Buffalo strike. Penalties for violating the law were extremely harsh; the Act (Section 5) provided that a striking public employee "shall thereby abandon and terminate his appointment or employment and shall no longer hold such position, or be entitled to any of the rights or emoluments thereof, except if appointed subject to the following provisions: (a) his compensation shall in no event exceed that received by him immediately prior to the time of such violation; (b) the compensation of such person shall not be increased until after the expiration of three years . . . and (c) such person shall be on probation for a period of five years following . . . during which period he shall serve without tenure."

The passage of the Condon-Wadlin Act precipitated legislation in other states also, some of the laws quite similar in wording and penalties to the New York law. By 1951 Ohio, Texas, Pennsylvania, Michigan, Missouri, Minnesota, and Nebraska followed suit with antistrike acts of their own. In each instance the legislation was strictly of a punitive nature, with very little in the way of attempts to examine or alleviate the conditions which led to the outbreak of strikes by teachers or by other public employee groups.

B. The AFT and Salaries in the Postwar Period

It was not until 1935 that the AFT first officially advocated that teachers make use of collective bargaining to achieve economic gains (Moskow, 1966:216). Beginning in the 1940s, AFT appeals to local to seek collective-bargaining rights became more numerous and more persistent. The 1944 annual convention, for example, passed a resolution to set up a special committee on collective bargaining. Significantly, the chairman was the head of the Illinois West Suburban Teachers Union, many of whose councils had already succeeded in negotiating collective agreements. The first paragraph of the convention resolution (*American Teacher*, February 1945:6) declared that "the AFT assumes leadership in forming, counseling with, and actively aiding the locals in gaining recognition in negotiating, and in securing written agreements." The Executive Council also voted that the committee on collective bargaining "should endeavor to secure the information required by . . . the resolution" and that "all locals which have had experience in negotiating definite agreements and contracts report their method of operation for the benefit of other locals." To carry out the latter provision, a further resolution was passed that "this material be published in a handbook of union techniques and cases." Soon afterwards, the AFT began to publish collective bargaining contracts negotiated by its locals in the *American Teacher*, the official newspaper of the AFT. Perusals of the annual convention proceedings and of the *American Teacher* also point to frequent pleas to local unions to secure collective-bargaining status.

It should be pointed out that the evidence presented above contradicts the claims sometimes made by other researchers that the AFT was not pursuing a collective-bargaining policy until after the victory in New York City in 1961. Michael Moskow (1966:107), for instance, states that "there is strong evidence . . . to indicate that it was not until the UFT victory . . . that the AFT actively began to encourage its locals to strive for collective bargaining rights." On the contrary, it appears that it may have been the reluctance of many of the local unions and not the lack of encouragement of the AFT that resulted in the small number of pre–New York City contracts. A survey of nearly 50 percent of the more than 300 AFT locals in existence in 1947 undertaken by Phillip Kochman (1947) reported that about 120 locals desired a greater role in the formulation of teacher welfare policies; but only 7 of these locals claimed that they desired to become the collective bargaining agent for the teachers in their districts.

It is difficult to say for certain how many collective-bargaining agreements were in existence before the New York City contract in 1962. The problem of accurate documentation is compounded by the fact that many districts at this time claimed to have been bargaining collectively with school district authorities when, by most definitions of collective bargaining, no such situation existed. Throughout the 1950s, for example, the *American Teacher* is replete with literally hundreds of accounts of teachers' groups claiming to have "negotiated" or "successfully bargained" with a school board for salary hikes or supplemental benefits. In most of the instances which could be checked, however, what the local termed "bargaining" could better be termed a process of informal petitioning or discussion with the authorities.

The author has discovered twelve instances in which comprehensive collective-bargaining pacts were negotiated by AFT locals before the UFT contract in 1961. Three of these (Proviso, Maywood, and Cicero) have already been mentioned, inasmuch as they were negotiated before the end of World War II. The other nine, in chronological order of appearance, were: Bremerton, Washington (1946); New Britain, Connecticut (1946); Pawtucket, Rhode Island (1946); Butte, Montana (1949);

Eau Claire, Wisconsin (1949); Anaconda, Montana (early 1950s); East St. Louis, Illinois (1956); Dearborn, Michigan (1959); and Cahokia, Illinois (1960). As might be surmised from the dates, several of these contracts were negotiated in the aftermath of postwar teacher strikes. Apparently all of them specified the union as the recognized collective-bargaining agent and set up some form of negotiations procedures. Most of them also contained other specific items agreed upon, particularly salary schedules. The Butte and Anaconda contracts were quite unique insofar as they were subsequently renegotiated in the 1950s to include union-shop clauses. These clauses were later declared invalid by the Supreme Court of Montana, however.

More numerous are the instances in which AFT locals secured recognition as collective-bargaining agents during these two decades. The AFT began a running "box score" of representation elections in the *American Teacher* in 1965. Although it listed only two pre–New York City elections (Proviso and East St. Louis), the present author has discovered many other instances where a union secured representation status via an election. More numerous still are instances where such status was granted by a school board without an election, although it has not proved possible to document and check all of these cases. Very little evidence exists that comprehensive collective-bargaining agreements were eventually concluded in these districts, however. In most cases the conferral of collective-bargaining status simply allowed the union the right to make proposals at board meetings.

C. The NEA and the Salary Issue in the Postwar Period

A survey of school boards undertaken by the Research Division of the NEA in the 1945–46 school year (National Education Association, 1946) reported that 26 percent of the boards surveyed never sought the advice of teacher representatives on matters of salary and other personnel matters. Only 13 percent claimed that they regularly consulted with teachers regarding such matters, while 61 percent said that they sometimes asked for teacher opinions.

Undoubtedly, it was this finding that many teachers possessed such a small voice in the determination of policies regarding their own economic welfare, as well as the rapid erosion of teachers' earnings through inflation, that caused the NEA in 1947 to speak out in favor of a definite program of joint action. In a policy statement that was termed "among the most important in the 90 year history of the NEA" (*NEA Journal*, February 1947:77–80) the Executive Committee urged teachers to employ "group action" to obtain professional salary scales and to be "bold and forthright" in their demands. This call to action was considered to be a part of the NEA's "Victory Action Program," among the other goals of which were to be the strengthening and unification of the teaching profession.

In seeking adequate salaries, the NEA urged each local to adopt the following program:

1. The election of a teacher-salary committee by the membership of the local education association with the authority to represent it and act for it;
2. The study by the committee of the local salary schedule and financial conditions within the school district;
3. The submission of a plan of action to the local association for approval;
4. The confirmation that the understanding reached by the teachers' group with the board of education be approved by the board and then entered in its entirety in the minutes of the board;
5. The exertion of influence on the part of the teacher organization during salary discussions to prevent unprofessional acceptance of appointments replacing teachers involved.

The program also insisted that agreement should be achieved through the "democratic cooperation of teachers, administrators, and board members." It was reasoned that the general administrator served as a "vital and friendly connecting link" between the board and the teaching staff and that teachers should avoid labor channels in resolving disputes.

William Givens, the executive secretary of the NEA at the time, labeled the above program one of "democratic persuasion" and not collective bargaining. A poll taken later in the year by *The Nation's Schools* magazine (1947:51), however, reported that only a slight majority of the teachers surveyed seemed to think the NEA program to be different from collective bargaining.

The resolution summarized above was the official NEA policy regarding joint decision making until 1961. It is difficult to ascertain the number of joint agreements which were actually concluded by local education associations according to NEA guidelines. This is so because of the fact that agreements reached were to be incorporated into the minutes of the school board meetings rather than drawn up separately in the form of collective contracts. Yet there is some evidence that the NEA policy was followed by a large number of state and local affiliates. For example, midway through the 1950s the Connecticut Education Association, the Connecticut Federation of Teachers, the Connecticut Association of School Boards, and the Superintendent of Public Instruction cooperatively drew up a report regarding board-staff relationships. The report spelled out in specific detail a "Recommended Plan for the Joint Consideration of Matters of Mutual Concern by Boards of Education and Teacher Organizations." It outlined a procedure for reaching agreement in cases of impasse, including the utilization of fact-finding committees established by the Connecticut State Commission of Education. According to one of the drafters of the plan (Barstow, 1961:63) a large number of Connecticut communities reached written agreements under the framework of the plan in the late 1950s.

As far as comprehensive collective-bargaining contracts are concerned, apparently only one local association succeeded in negotiating such an agreement before 1960. The agreement was drawn up in Norwalk, Connecticut, in 1946 following a strike by the teachers of that city. The ensuing settlement provided for recognition of the Norwalk Teachers Association as official bargaining agent, increased the salaries of the professional staff, and established a committee to study further the question of teacher salaries. The agreement was later renegotiated periodically, a formalized appeals procedure being added in 1959.

IV. CONCLUSION

As the previous sections on the pre-1960 history of teacher bargaining have indicated, there were many instances of local teacher organizations actively engaged in some form of collective negotiations during this period. It is, of course, true that the negotiations procedures were much less formalized than is the case today. Strikes, while not occurring with the frequency which was to be evidenced later on in the 1960s and 1970s, were also by no means uncommon, particularly in the larger cities of the nation. Furthermore, after 1945 both the AFT and NEA were actively encouraging local affiliates to seek a greater voice in the decision-making process where the economic welfare of teachers was concerned.

Viewed from this perspective, the success of the United Federation of Teachers in achieving a collective-bargaining contract for the teachers of New York City in 1962 does not appear to represent as sharp a break with past practices of teacher-salary determination as some have thought. Rather, the UFT success can better be viewed as a continuation of a trend which had already been in progress for several decades before 1962. The above conclusion should not be construed as minimizing the importance of the UFT victory in New York City, however. It was still to have enormous repercussions with respect to accelerating the demand for collective-bargaining rights on the part of many other local organizations of teachers throughout the nation. Furthermore, it was to help bring about in the next few years many changes in the negotiations philosophies and attitudes toward teacher militancy of both the AFT and the NEA.

NOTES

1. In fact, no AFT local had ever participated in strike activity until the 1940s.
2. As stated in the *NEA Journal*, May 1949, p. 353, "During the past quarter century salary schedules have improved largely as a result of the participation of school employees on local and state salary committees."

REFERENCES

Alexander, Carter (1910), *Some Aspects of the Work of Teachers' Voluntary Associations in the United States*. New York: Teachers College, Columbia University.

American Federation of Teachers (1955), *Organizing the Teaching Profession*. Glencoe, Ill.: The Free Press.

American Teacher (various issues, 1939–67).

Barstow, Robbins W. (1961), "Teachers and Boards of Education." *NEA Journal* 50(October):63.

Clarke, James E. (1966), "The American Federation of Teachers: Origins and History from 1870 to 1952." Ph.D. dissertation, Cornell University.

Cole, Stephen (1969), *The Unionization of Teachers: A Case Study of the UFT*. New York: Praeger Publishers.

Douglas, Paul (1925), *Real Wages in the United States, 1890–1925*. Boston: Houghton Mifflin Co.

Fordyce, Wellington (1955), "The Origin and Development of Teachers Unions in the United States." Ph.D. dissertation, Ohio State University.

Glass, Ronald (1967), "Work Stoppages and Teachers: History and Conflict." *Monthly Labor Review* 90(August):43–46.

"Group Action on Salaries." (February 1947), *The Nation's Schools* 41(February):51.

Kochman, Philip (1947), "The Developing Role of Teachers Unions." Ph.D. dissertation, Columbia University Teachers College.

Moskow, Michael (1966), *Teachers and Unions*. Philadelphia: Wharton School of Finance and Commerce.

National Education Association, Research Division (1949), *Salary and Salary Schedules of City School Employees, 1948–49*. Washington: National Education Association.

——— (1946), *Status and Practices of Boards of Education*. Washington, D.C.: National Education Association.

NEA Journal (various issues, 1929–61).

New York Times, January 2, 1947, p. 22.

Oakes, Russel (1958), "Public and Professional Reactions to Teachers' Strikes, 1918–54." Ph.D. dissertation, Columbia University Teachers College.

Schiff, Albert (1952), "A Study and Evaluation of Teacher Strikes in the U.S." Ph.D. dissertation, Wayne State University.

U.S. Department of Commerce, Bureau of the Census and U.S. Department of Labor (1978), *Labor-Management Relations in State and Local Governments: 1976*, State and Local Government Special Studies No. 88. Washington, D.C.: United States Government Printing Office.

Wesley, Edgar B. (1957), *The NEA: The First Hundred Years*. New York: Harper and Bros.

Yabroff, Bernard and Mary D. Lily (May 1953), "Collective Bargaining and Work Stoppages Involving Teachers." *Monthly Labor Review* 76(May):475–79.

A NEW LOOK AT THE GOLD STANDARD:

IS DONALD KEMMERER RIGHT?

Richard K. Vedder

Nearly two generations have passed since the United States and much of the rest of the world abandoned a monetary system centered around gold. To be sure, under the Bretton Woods system of international finance prevailing for twenty-five years after World War II, gold played some role in international payments, but at the most the system could be regarded as a pseudo-gold-exchange standard, a system in which gold assumed no meaningful role in the domestic monetary base and an increasingly nominal role in the determination of international monetary reserves, particularly given rules of the system permitting fairly frequent currency devaluations. Americans under the age of sixty-five or seventy cannot remember a world in which gold played an integral role in determining the size of the stock of money and therefore the level of prices.

Variations in Business and Economic History:
Essays in Honor of Donald L. Kemmerer
Research in Economic History, Suppl. 2, pages 145–156.

ISBN: 0-89232-262-4

During those two generations since 1934, economists have come to regard the gold standard as an historical anachronism, an archaic, crude monetary system with many defects, not the least of which is that it limits the ability of government policymakers to effectively utilize the macroeconomic policy prescriptions that followed from the new economic theory of Lord Keynes. Only a few economists, including Donald Kemmerer, clung to the notion that the gold standard was desirable. These economists were generally dismissed as cranks who maintained their views in spite of overwhelming empirical evidence that a non-gold monetary system could and would promote economic objectives far better than a gold standard.

This paper attempts to reassess the historical experience of the United States under the alternative monetary arrangements, namely the gold-coin standard prevailing (with intermittent interruptions) over much of the century prior to 1934 and the paper-money standard existing after that date. In this connection, some of the objections to the gold standard will be reassessed in light of both the evidence and new theoretical insights (or perhaps more accurately, a rediscovery of old theoretical insights).

I. THE OBJECTIVES OF MACROECONOMIC POLICY

It appears that three major concerns have dominated policy debates over the past century dealing the the performance of the whole economy. The first concern relates to price stability. Even a cursory investigation of the platforms of major political parties and the speeches of leading politicians suggests that the achievement of stable prices has been a continuing objective of the sources of political power. Political behavior in this regard may in part reflect popular opinion, as public-opinion polls on numerous occasions have shown that the American public perceives inflation as a problem.

Second, the dominant attention of policymakers for decades since the traumatic experience of the 1930s has been centered on the attainment of full employment. Indeed, the central message of Keynes was: "full employment will not normally be achieved through the market mechanism, but it can be achieved with appropriate government policy." Belief in the notion that full employment is attainable led to such legislative enactments as the Employment Act of the 1940s and the Humphrey-Hawkins bill of the 1970s.

Third, while Keynes in his *Tract on Monetary Reform* argued that "in the long run we are all dead," there has been considerable concern at various times about the long-run rate of economic growth of the American economy. In less-developed countries, the goal of a high rate of economic growth has an even higher priority. Within the past generation, concern about the U.S. growth rate was sufficiently strong for the issue to be a central theme in the 1960 presidential campaign, and more recently an increasing number of persons have decried the United States' sluggish growth rate and its probable proximate causes (e.g., insufficient capital formation).

Accordingly, the success of a monetary system might be evaluated by measuring the degree or extent to which the system helps promote the three major objectives previously stated. At the very minimum, a system of monetary payments must have demonstrated that it contributed to improved performance with respect to at least one of the objectives to be considered a success. It would seem appropriate, therefore, to look at the historical record with respect to these three objectives, looking at the two generations before and the two generations after the abandonment of gold.

A. The Record with Respect to Price Stability

Without any question, prices in the United States were far more stable in the period before 1934 (defined here as 1890–1933) than since. This is indicated in Table 1. In nearly one-half of the forty-four years prior to leaving the gold standard, prices in the United States were quite stable. Moreover, in years in which prices were not stable, inflation and deflation were nearly equally prevalent. Over longer time periods, prices were roughly stable. Wholesale prices at the end of the gold-standard era, for example, were not much different than in the early days of the

Table 1. Annual Changes in Prices before and after the Gold Standard

Price Change	*Gold-Standard Era, 1890–1933*[a]	*Post-Gold-Standard Era, 1934–1979*[a]
Deflation[b]	25%	4%
Stable Prices[c]	43	20
Inflation[d]	20	43
Severe Inflation[e]	11	33

Notes:

[a] Numbers refer to the percent of the years in the period in which a given type of price change occurred.

[b] Defined as a decrease in the consumer price index of more than one percent a year.

[c] Defined as a change in consumer prices between +1.0 and −1.0 percent a year.

[d] Defined as a change in consumer prices between 1.1 and 4.9 percent a year.

[e] An increase in consumer prices of 5 percent or more a year.

Source: Author's calculations from data in *Historical Statistics of the United States, Colonial Times to 1970* (Washington, D.C., 1975), 1978 *Statistical Abstract of the United States* (Washington, D.C., 1979).

Republic, well over a century earlier.[1] By contrast, prices doubled in the first generation after the abandonment of gold, and have more than doubled in the still-not-complete second generation since the end of the gold-coin standard.[2] Shorter-term price stability has likewise been absent in the post-gold-standard era. In more than three-fourths of the years since 1934, inflation has existed, and in many of those years it has been severe. Moreover, this comparison actually *understates* the price stability of the gold-standard era, because three of the years of severe inflation in the pre-1934 period—1917, 1918, and 1919—were years in which the United States abandoned internal convertibility into gold.

B. The Record with Respect to Unemployment

"The one area where the post-gold-standard performance is clearly superior to that of the gold-standard era is with respect to the attainment of full employment." True or false? The answer is *false*. The evidence, presented in Table 2, suggests that the historical record of the post-1933 era is nearly identical to that of the gold-standard era, in spite of a large increase in the emphasis going to the attainment of full employment in the past several decades. The median or "typical" unemployment rate since 1933 has been actually somewhat higher than in the gold-standard era. It is very difficult after looking at the actual performance of the economy to conclude that the Keynesian Revolution has improved the plight of the unemployed (Kemmerer, 1979). Moreover, at least one structural development in the American economy should have worked to lower unemployment, namely the significant shift in labor force composition away from manufacturing employment toward employment in the service industries. The fact that unemployment has not generally fallen is therefore all the more surprising.

Table 2. Unemployment before and after the Gold Standard

Unemployment Condition	*1890–1933*[a]	*1934–1979*[a]
Full Employment[b]	32%	28%
Moderate Unemployment[c]	32	39
High Unemployment[d]	36	33

Notes:

[a] Numbers refer to the percent of years in time period in which a given unemployment condition was achieved.

[b] An unemployment rate of 4.0 or less percent.

[c] An unemployment rate between 4.1 and 5.9 percent.

[d] An unemployment rate of 6.0 percent or more.

Source: Same as for Table 1.

C. The Record with Respect to Economic Growth

A quick glance at the evidence with respect to the long-term rate of economic growth suggests that economic growth has been significantly enhanced since the United States left the gold standard. Real per capita gross national product rose only 0.87 percent a year from 1890 to 1934, but 2.35 percent a year in the following forty-five years. Such a comparison, however, is patently misleading, since short-term business-cycle fluctuations distort the evidence significantly. To look at economic growth from 1890, a relatively prosperous year, to 1934, near the depths of the Great Depression, is quite inappropriate, as is looking at the growth from the highly depressed 1934 to the relatively more prosperous 1979.

If one compares economic growth in the period 1890–1929 with the period 1929–79 (predominantly post-gold-standard-era), the growth rate in the former period (1.79 percent a year) is greater than that in the latter era (1.52 percent). Unless one concludes that the existence and magnitude of the Great Depression were predominantly a consequence of the gold-coin standard, an argument that not even many Keynesians have made, it is incorrect to state that American economic growth has accelerated since the United States abandoned gold. Moreover, its growth rate *relative to other countries* has clearly declined in the post-gold-standard era.[3]

D. Summarizing the Record

On balance, the American performance has markedly worsened with respect to the goal of price stability since the end of the gold standard, and its performance with respect to economic growth is probably not as good as in the gold-standard era. Even with respect to the full-employment objectives so fervently sought since the United States abandoned gold, no meaningful improvement has been made, and by at least one important indicator the record shows that full employment has been more elusive since 1934 than before.

One must be cautious, however, in interpreting these statistics as "proof" that the gold-coin standard was the basis for better economic performance prior to 1934 than since. Many other things have changed over time that have a bearing on the magnitudes of inflation, unemployment, and economic growth. Government regulatory policies and price controls have added to costs and have tended to increase prices in the post-1934 period. Many studies have found that federal minimum-wage laws and expanded unemployment-compensation programs enacted after 1934 have served to increase the rate of unemployment (Feldstein, 1976;

Gramlich, 1976). Similarly, America's tax structure, which punishes returns to capital investment, and its post-1934 system of Social Security have both served to reduce the rate of private savings below that of virtually every major nation in the world, contributing to a reduction in capital formation and the rate of economic growth (Feldstein, 1974, 1977). In short, governmental actions unrelated to the monetary system have probably also contributed to our worsening economic performance.

Accordingly, it is probably best simply to state that "the historical evidence is not consistent with the view that the abandonment of the gold-coin standard was accompanied by an improvement in our performance with respect to the achievement of the goals of price stability, full employment, and a high rate of economic growth." It is probably too strong to state on the basis of the evidence presented that "the historical record demonstrates that the gold-coin standard brought about greater economic growth, fuller employment, and greater price stability," although that may in fact be the case. In this connection, the reader is reminded that Professor Kemmerer has written numerous articles demonstrating how the gold standard has aided not only the attainment of price stability but other objectives as well.

II. REEVALUATING SOME OBJECTIONS TO THE GOLD STANDARD

A fundamental objection to the gold standard is that reliance on rigidly fixed exchange rates and exogenously determined growth in the monetary base reduces the flexibility of policymakers in engaging in economic policies designed to achieve macroeconomic goals. The above analysis argues that any added flexibility given to policymakers since the abandonment of gold has not in reality led to a better achievement of economic objectives than before. That, however, may reflect institutional constraints on policymakers or their ineptitude. Can policymakers solve major macroeconomic problems even when they have few constraints and they act intelligently? A whole generation of Keynesian economists believed that the presumably primary goal of full employment could be achieved by stimulating aggregate demand, increasing prices in the process. Inflationary aggregate-demand policies would lower real wages (as inflation lowered the purchasing power of a given money wage) toward a market clearing the full-employment level.

According to Keynesian thinking as it had evolved into the "New Economics" of the sixties, policymakers simply had to decide where they wanted to operate on the Phillips curve depicting the trade-off between inflation and unemployment. A newer "rational-expectations" theory of the seventies, however, has denied the existence of the downward-sloping Phillips curve in the long run; certainly the experience of the seventies also questioned the notion that inflation could be used to reduce unemployment. To be sure, a statistical relationship between inflation and unemployment similar to that illustrated by Professor Phillips's curve can be observed over long time periods in many countries. Yet there have been many exceptions to the rule, including some very notable inflationary episodes such as the German hyperinflation of the 1920s as well as the American stagflation of the seventies.

The observed downward-sloping Phillips curve for some time periods that suggests that nations can buy their way to full employment by inflating the economy may well reflect the fact that in the short run people can be tricked into accepting relatively low wages in a real sense (adjusting for productivity) but, after they overcome their "money illusion," will modify their behavior in such a fashion as to increase real wages, thereby increasing unemployment. Inflating the economy to lower wages can work only in the short run. In the long run, labor unions and other forces will demand and get larger money wage increases than before, aggravating unemployment and creating in addition a wage-price inflationary spiral that gives rise to stagflation. Inflationary expectations will develop to the point where expansionary fiscal policy of the Keynesian variety is rendered impotent unless the policy becomes very much more inflationary than before, in which case hyperinflation begins. As Abraham Lincoln so wisely put it, "You can fool all the people some of the time and some of the people all of the time, but you cannot fool all the people all the time."

In other words, it would appear that little can be done in a capitalistic society to alter the long-run median rate of unemployment from its "natural rate" by government policy, other than removing labor-market imperfections, many of which (e.g., minimum-wage laws) are created by governments themselves. Given that reality, constraining the growth in the money stock by imposing a gold standard would not seem to have adverse effects on the achievement of full employment.

A second major objection to the gold-coin or even gold-exchange standard is that the stock of specie is not likely to grow enough over time to provide adequate liquidity. Even to maintain stable prices, the stock of money in the United States needs to grow 3–4 percent a year, the rate of growth in real GNP in past American history. The opponents of the gold standard argue that the stock of gold is growing very slowly, and that the gold standard will create a deflationary trend that is as undesirable as inflation. To be sure, a nation could maintain a growth in the stock of money of 3–4 percent per annum even with a slower growth in the stock of monetary gold which forms the monetary base. Suppose the gold stock were to grow 1 percent a year and the money stock were to grow at a 3.5 percent annual rate. Suppose further that initially the gold stock equaled 20 percent of the total stock of money. In twenty years, the gold-money ratio would fall to 12.3 percent. In the long run in such a situation, maintaining a money stock consistent with level prices is possible only by allowing the ratio of reserves in the form of gold to decline dangerously in relation to the stock of money (largely in bank demand deposits). The stability of the banking system would ultimately be threatened if the reserve-deposit ratio fell too low. Internationally, a fall in gold reserves relative to the volume of world trade would cause liquidity crises because there would be insufficient monetary assets to handle transactions needs, a problem only temporarily relieved by using paper currencies convertible into gold as "reserve currencies."

While the objection does have some validity, it can be overstated. To begin with, Professor Kemmerer has demonstrated that the stock of monetary gold grew around 2 percent a year during the heyday of the gold standard, not too far below an optimal growth rate of perhaps 3 percent.[4] Second, this supply of newly mined gold obviously varies directly with price, and a reestablishment of the gold standard would require a realistic gold price to be established, one which would allow the monetary value of gold to be a fairly large proportion of total monetary assets and would also stimulate production. That means a price more like current market prices (at this writing, in excess of $400 an ounce) than the official price of slightly over $42 per ounce.[5]

While the growth of the monetary base under a revived gold standard might be less than optimal, the relevant question is, "Would the growth in the money stock come closer to achieving the goal of stable prices than would a paper-currency standard controlled ultimately by the political process?" At the worst, the gold standard would promote a relatively mild "creeping deflation" with prices falling 1–2 percent a year, as in the 1880s, a period of generally unexcelled prosperity. Most important, it would be a relatively predictable deflation, not subject to sudden unanticipated gyrations as election time nears. Price instability is an evil *primarily because it is so often unanticipated,* and the effects on income distribution and growth are far less when inflation or deflation continues consistently at some relatively constant rate (interest rates, wage rates, prices, etc. all adjust accordingly).

The stability of gold production and the monetary base under a gold standard is far greater than the stability of the paper monetary base since 1934. It has been bad enough that the money stock in the past fifteen years has consistently grown far more than the 3–4 percent per annum optimum. Even worse, the rate of increase has changed frequently (in some years 5 percent, in others 10 percent, etc.), catching workers, investors, and others unaware. Aside from the sometimes tragic impact that this has had on the economic status of some groups of the population, it has reduced incentives to save by imposing added uncertainty and risk, thereby contributing to the current very real "capital shortage."

III. THE POLITICAL ECONOMY OF MONETARY EXPANSION

The creation of money has an economic impact that differs in the short run from that in the long run. Monetary expansion that is inflationary (and most is) can serve to reduce unemployment in the short run even though in the long run the employment-expanding effects of expansionary policies are offset by changing economic behavior on the part of persons hurt by inflation. Where there is no constraint in the form of reserve requirements in the form of gold, it is easier for politicians to use monetary policy for political gain. Specifically, they can attempt to temporarily lower unemployment, a move which wins votes.

To be sure, Congress attempted to protect against political tampering with monetary policy when the Federal Reserve Act was passed, and the Federal Reserve Board does maintain some degree of independence from the legislative and executive branches of government by not having to rely on governmental operating appropriations and by having board members with long (fourteen-year) terms of office. The board is aware, however, that it is a creature of the political process, and that what the politicians have created they can also destroy. With that in mind, the Federal Reserve accommodated massive deficit spending in World War II by buying government debt, thereby expanding the money supply. In more recent years it has likewise continued to buy bonds in the wake of continuing large deficits, fearing repercussions if it failed to accommodate the fiscal policies of the president and Congress.

A simple test is possible of the hypothesis that the money-creation process has to some extent become politicized. If politicians try to pressure the monetary authorities into creating more money in order to stimulate the level of economic activity, they presumably will do so especially in election years, and in particular in presidential-election years when the control of both the executive and legislative branches is at stake. If this hypothesis is valid, in the post-gold-standard era the average annual rate of monetary expansion should be greater in election years than in other years. In the pre-gold-standard era, however, that should not be the case for two reasons. First, relating monetary expansion to gold stocks limits the ability of politicians to engage in monetary expansion, and the operation of the specie-flow mechanism makes it unlikely that human action could sustain politically inspired increases in the money stock for long. Second, for much of the gold-standard era under investigation, there was no central bank, making it almost impossible for politicians to control the money stock.

Performing this simple test, Table 3 reveals that monetary expansion has tended to increase in presidential election years after 1933 from levels prevailing in nonelection years. Before that date, however, the money stock actually grew slightly less in election years. This evidence supports the notion that our paper-money-standard system is subject to manipulation by politicians seeking office. Again, the evidence is not conclusive, because other factors that might have changed over time are not taken into account. One could argue that the results reflect as much the increased role of central banking in the post-1933 period as the abandonment of gold. Nonetheless, the results are consistent with the notion that monetary stability today is being undermined by political considerations.

IV. CONCLUSIONS

The gold standard may not be perfect in terms of meeting the needs of a dynamic economy for monetary expansion. Paraphrasing Winston Churchill, however, one might say that "the gold standard is the worst monetary system except for all others." In a world with a perfect political process, it might be possible to achieve an optimal money-stock growth using the "monetary-rule" approach of Milton Friedman, which disallows discretionary monetary and fiscal policy. This author, however,

Table 3. Monetary Expansion in Presidential-Election and Nonelection Years, 1890–1933 and 1934–79

Period	*Mean Annual Growth in Money, Presidential-Election Years*[a]	*Mean Annual Growth in Money, Other Years*[a]	*Ratio, Money Stock Growth in Election Years to Money Stock Growth in Nonelection Years*
1890–1933	4.70%	5.42%	0.87[b]
1934–1979	8.89	7.44	1.19

Notes:

[a] The definition of money used is M2, which includes currency, demand, and time deposits of commercial banks. Data are not available for the entire period permitting the use of the M1 definition that excludes time deposits.

[b] The years 1917, 1918, 1919, and 1933 might logically be excluded since the gold-coin standard was not operative during part of all of these years. Excluding those years, the ratio falls to .85.

Source: Author's calculations from data in *Historical Statistics of the United States, Colonial Times to 1970,* the 1977 *Statistical Abstract of the United States,* and the *Federal Reserve Bulletin,* August, 1979; 1979 money-stock growth is partly estimated.

believes that the political economy of monetary expansion is such that the approach would not be allowed to exist for long. The short-term perspectives of politicians (never exceeding four years) probably would lead to a breakdown of such a "rules" approach. Therefore, the gold standard deserves very careful consideration in any reform of our current poorly working monetary system.

NOTES

1. Splicing together the Warren-Pearson and Bureau of Labor Statistics price indices, it appears that wholesale prices in 1933 were actually well over 20 percent lower than the levels prevailing in 1800 and about equal to levels prevailing in the early 1790s. See *Historical Statistics of the United States, Colonial Times to 1970* (Washington, D.C.: United States Government Printing Office), pp. 200–203.

2. The consumer price index of the U.S. Department of Labor in 1978 was almost precisely five times the level prevailing in 1933. Needless to say, prices have continued to rise after 1978.

3. At this writing, gross national product per capita expressed in U.S. dollars at prevailing exchange rates is lower in the United States than in several other nations, including Switzerland, West Germany, and Sweden. To be sure, this in part reflects the depressed value of the dollar relative to other currencies arising from a lack of confidence in Americans to control inflation in future time periods (a problem that would be substantially alleviated by a gold standard). Even isolating from exchange rate fluctuations, however, the rate of economic growth in the United States since World War II has been lower than most other industrialized nations (excepting Great Britain). Certainly, GNP per capita in Germany, Switzerland, and Sweden in 1933 was far below the level prevailing in the United States even in that depressed year.

4. Even in recent times the production of gold would have permitted a 3 percent growth in the stock of monetary gold. In the 1950s and 1960s, free-world production of gold typically was \$1.2 to \$1.4 billion a year (at \$35 per ounce), about 3 percent the stock of monetary gold (around \$41 billion) then prevailing. This ignores the production of gold in the Soviet Union, which may have been considerable. I am indebted to Professor Kemmerer for this information.

5. At this writing, the monetary gold of the United States valued at current market price would approximate \$100 billion, about 30 percent of the narrowly defined stock of money (M1) that includes both demand deposits and currency but not time deposits. It is doubtful that the market price of gold would be anywhere near \$400 in a noninflationary environment; a realistic valuation of gold under a gold standard might be \$300 an ounce, although that is nothing more than a guess.

REFERENCES

Feldstein, Martin S. (1974), "Social Security, Induced Retirement and Aggregate Captial Accumulation." *Journal of Political Economy* 82(September):905–926.

——— (1976), "Unemployment Compensation: Effect on Unemployment." *Monthly Labor Review* 99(March):39–41.

——— (1977), "Does the United States Save Too Little?" *American Economic Review* 67(February):116–121.

Gramlich, E. M. (1976), "Impact of Minimum Wages on Other Wages, Employment and Family Income." *Brookings Papers on Economic Activity* 2:409–451.

Kemmerer, D. L. (1979), *Why a Gold Standard and Why Still a Controversy?* Greenwich, Conn.: Committee for Monthly Research and Education.

U.S. Department of Commerce (1975), *Historical Statistics of the United States, Colonial Times to 1970*, Washington, D.C.: United States Government Printing Office.

SOME MONETARY-STANDARD-OF-VALUE CONCEPTS OF THE LATTER NINETEENTH CENTURY

Richard D. Winkelman

One of the more interesting topics to stir the human mind is money. What is it? What does it do? What is its material form? Over the period of human history these questions have been answered many times and in many ways. Of all the questions asked about money the most intriguing is, "What is or ought to be the monetary standard of value?" By the start of the modern period the metals gold and silver had emerged, singly or jointly, as the almost universally accepted standard of value for money. The acquisition of treasure was an avowed policy goal of European mercantilists, and the increasing abundance of the metals as a result of New World mines was financing a greater and greater level of international trade. The dawn of a rapidly expanding world economy was approaching, made possible, some might suggest, by the higher level of

Variations in Business and Economic History:
Essays in Honor of Donald L. Kemmerer
Research in Economic History, Suppl. 2, pages 157–189.

ISBN: 0-89232-262-4

liquidity which all of this new money provided the international traders.

Although metallism appeared to be well entrenched as the universal standard, human curiosity with respect to alternative standards was not completely satisfied. In colonial America of the late seventeenth century we observe an early utilization of paper money. In the early eighteenth century we observe the operations of John Law and the "Mississippi Bubble" and the continual utilization of paper money issued through a variety of bank schemes in colonial North America. While these early Americans might have preferred a more stable money, they clearly opted for acquiring imports with gold and silver rather than using them as money.

Upon the establishment of the United States under our Constitution, one of the first necessary tasks was to establish both a monetary standard of value and a system of money under that standard. This was accomplished with the Coinage Act of 1792, in which bimetallism was adopted as the monetary standard of value. Bimetallism remained the de jure standard until the Gold Standard Act of 1900. Over the course of the nineteenth century the de facto standard vacillated between gold and silver as Gresham's Law worked on any important difference between the mint ratio of value of gold to silver and the market ratio.

With the advent of the Civil War, the United States found itself on the "greenback standard." During this time, paper money issued by the Treasury was not convertible to either gold or silver at a fixed par. The policy decisions of the federal government to reestablish the de facto gold standard after the Civil War provided the impetus, through the deflation required to get back on gold, for a new look at the monetary-standard-of-value question. During this period of economic, political, social, and intellectual ferment over the last quarter of the nineteenth century, the gold, silver, and bimetallic standards all had their champions, but a variety of new ideas (sometimes old ideas in new clothing) as to what would best serve as the monetary standard of value were also promulgated. Some of these ideas have a distinctly modern ring, while others do not. It is to these other candidates for the standard of monetary value, which run the gamut from variations of metallic standards through a variety of nonmetallic standards and from the highly theoretical to those alleged to be very practical, that this paper is addressed.

I. OTHER METALLIC STANDARDS

The "other metallic standards" to which this section refers should not be construed to mean that metals other than gold and silver were brought into the monetary standard. The metallic standards under consideration were based on gold and silver. It was the way in which gold and silver were to be utilized which distinguished these metallic standards from the bimetallic, gold, and silver standards.

A. Bullionism

In the April 1893 issue of *The Forum* a New York businessman, Jose F. de Navarro, presented a plan which would, he alleged, arrest the fall in the price of silver and restore its value to a par (16 to 1) with gold in its monetary usages. Navarro's plan was simply to substitute, for the silver treasury certificates issued under the Sherman Silver Purchase Act and redeemable in gold, a government note which could only be redeemed in silver bullion at the gold or market price of silver on the day on which redemption was requested (Navarro, 1893:227). This idea was not unique with Navarro, but his publication of it brought it to the attention of John Rogers Commons. Commons recognized that Navarro's idea was very similar to one proposed by then Secretary of the Treasury William Windom in his report to Congress in 1889 (Department of the Treasury, 1889:lxxiv).

The general scheme, no matter what its source, impressed Commons. He evidently envisioned it as a means of ending the outflow of gold which was occurring in 1893. He said, "It would check at once the scare about the loss of our gold. In fact, with such a system of silver bullion currency, the United States could dispense with gold altogether" (Commons, 1893:299). In this respect, Commons was probably thinking in terms of a gold-exchange standard for the United States. By putting this concept into practice the United States, instead of keeping a monetary reserve of gold or pounds sterling to redeem its dollar obligations, would redeem its obligations with silver bullion at its pound sterling or gold price. This, in effect, would be the equivalent of gold redemption.

If this were the case, speculated Commons, there would be no reason the United States could not institute an elastic currency based scientifically on bullion notes. Such a plan, he noted, had been put forth by President Andrews of Brown University. Andrews's plan, however, was objected to because American prices were to have been based on depreciating silver. This was tantamount to going onto a silver standard. But if the currency consisted of bullion notes redeemable at the current gold price of silver, this particular objection would be met. "We," predicted Commons, "could become the great regulator of world-prices, and not with great loss, such as France incurred when she played the role under simple bimetallism, but with unexampled profit" (Commons, 1893:301). This statement implies that if this system were adopted by the United States, it would raise the price of silver. Thus many of the bullion notes issued at the inception of such a scheme would be redeemed for less silver than the amount for which they had been issued. Only in this manner could the United States profit.

Commons also believed that such a monetary scheme, if implemented by the United States, would put an end to any need for international monetary conferences or bimetallic treaties. He said, "An international money would be created which the nations of Europe would soon be driven to imitate" (Commons, 1893:301). If this monetary plan proposed by Secretary Windom and Mr. Navarro and advocated by Commons were put into effect, Commons expected the need for monetary gold to decline as other countries imitated the United States by utilizing silver bullion. This, it was probably expected, would lower the value of gold relative to silver and commodities in general. In other words, the price level would rise. If such a scheme were to be successfully introduced, however, it would have to be shown that the increase in prices would be imperceptibly slow, or gold-standard people would never accept it.

Unfortunately Commons fell into the same trap as the untrained monetary writers: the concept that the United States had the economic power at that time (1893) to sway world opinion away from gold. In the meantime, between the publication of Navarro's article in April and Commons's note in September, Congress had repealed the Sherman Silver Purchase Act. This was certainly not an opportune time to advocate any additional monetary usage for silver. That is probably why the silver bullion scheme was never seriously considered.

B. Globe Standard

Another metallic monetary scheme was that proposed by Congressman Michael Harter of Ohio (Fetter, 1895:606). Harter, in principle, advocated the gold standard. All prices in Harter's scheme were to be based on the legal value of the then existing gold dollar. Harter presented his plan to Congress as a bill, in which he proposed that the United States Mint be opened to the free coinage of both silver and gold on the same terms that existed prior to 1873. But none of the new silver and gold coins were to be legal tender. Instead of being denominated as dollars, the new coins were to be called "globes." Nothing in his bill, however, was to be construed as removing the legal-tender status of silver or gold coined previously.

Harter believed that these new "globes" would circulate at their bullion value alongside the legal-tender coins. This meant that the silver globes would be accepted only at their market value, not at some overpriced monetary value. He expected that, in time, the silver and gold "globes" would be utilized by all nations to settle their international balances. Since only their weight and fineness would be attested to, they would prove very handy for this purpose. He believed that "the trading world would draw its bills of exchange (partly because of the convenience of our decimal system) in 'globes' instead of pounds sterling" (Harter, 1894:606).

In short, under Harter's plan, each country would maintain its own monetary unit as the unit of account but would use "globes" of both silver and gold in its circulation and for international purposes. This scheme differed only in detail from that advocated by John Rogers Commons. Since Harter believed in the gold standard and wished to maintain gold values, this scheme may be viewed as one designed to prevent the free coinage of silver or any further erosion of the gold standard as exemplified by the Bland-Allison and Sherman Acts.

C. Joint Metallism

Another metallic standard proposed and discussed in the United States was joint metallism. Its principal advocate was Anson Phelps Stokes (Stokes, 1896:122). His plan was unique only in part. He proposed to increase the money supply by introducing the free coinage of silver in such a way that gold would not be driven out of circulation. Like the plans discussed above, joint metallism proposed that silver circulate at its market value instead of some arbitrarily defined monetary value.

Under joint metallism, suggested Stokes, both gold and silver would be admitted to free coinage. But they would have to be submitted for coinage in equal amounts by value. The government's ratio of value should be based on the current market ratio and should change with the market ratio. The gold coins were to retain their present gold content, whereas silver would be coined into standard units. The weight of these standard silver coins was to be determined by the "integral number of standard silver coins which, in the market value of the silver they contain, most nearly equals a standard gold coin of like weight" (Stokes, 1896:122). In other words, a ten-dollar gold piece contained 258 grains of gold nine-tenths fine. Ten dollars' worth of silver nine-tenths fine, assuming a market ratio of 20 to 1, would contain 5,160 grains. Thus the standard silver coin would weigh 258 grains and be worth fifty cents in gold. Twenty of them would equal the ten-dollar gold piece in value. However, silver coins of that low a denomination need not be coined. The silver could be coined in multiples of it.

Stokes thought that these new silver coins or the gold coins would not circulate because Americans were accustomed to, and desired the convenience of, paper currency. Therefore, on deposit of an equal value of gold and silver coins in the United States Treasury, the depositor would receive "Joint Legal-Tender Currency Certificates" redeemable, on demand, half in gold and the other half in the quantity of standard silver coins which were equal in value to the gold half of the redemption at the market ratio current on that day (Stokes, 1896:122). Since it was likely that only large amounts of silver and gold by value would be submitted for coinage, Stokes thought, "A silver coin as heavy as $5,000 in gold would be more suitable than silver dollars for deposit in the Treasury" (Stokes, 1896:123). Such a coin, if it could be minted, at the ratio of 20 to 1 would contain 129,000 grains of standard silver, be worth $250, and weigh over eighteen pounds! The gold value of such a silver coin would necessarily be less with a higher ratio and greater with a lower one.

The merits of joint metallism as seen by Stokes were many (Stokes, 1896:124–26). (1) It would conform to the Constitution in that both silver and gold would be legal tender. (2) It would promote the use of silver in the currency without impairing the obligation of contracts. (3) It would allow for easy adjustments in the mint ratio so that it would always equal the market ratio by altering the number of silver standards it took to equal a given gold coin. (4) It would permit the ultimate establishment of international gold and silver coins. (5) It would avoid the principal pitfalls of bimetallism: (a) impairment of contracts by depreciating the currency, and (b) a market ratio differing from the mint ratio. (6) It would recognize that honest money must be an equivalent of value as well as a measure of value. (7) It would make the measure of value more stable because it would be based on both precious metals jointly. (8) It would prevent speculators from cornering the metallic basis of money and would provide elasticity in the volume of currency because the production of silver could be increased by applying more labor. (9) Since the relative coinage value of gold to silver is not arbitrarily fixed, the chief cause of disturbance in trade and finance would be removed. This chief cause, according to Stokes, was the fact that the market ratio of gold to silver was subject to change but the mint ratio tended to remain the same. This would not be the case under joint metallism, since the ultimate mint ratio would not be legislated until the market ratio had achieved a long-run equilibrium position.

Stokes believed that the ratio which would result in a long-run equilibrium between the values of gold and silver could not be determined without first opening the mints of the world to the free coinage of silver at the market ratio. With the unlimited demand for silver from the mints of the world, or even from the United States Mint alone, the market ratio of gold to silver would decline until the true economic ratio was determined. The relative costs of production in the poorest silver mines and gold mines that could be worked at a profit would determine the true (long-run equilibrium) market ratio (Stokes, 1896:126–27). Once this true market ratio was established, it would seldom change, and the government ratio, once set, might never need to be changed. This, of course, depended upon the magnitude of fluctuations from equilibrium that the market ratio might undergo. Since the market price of each metal was based on both jointly, their relative fluctuations would be lessened. This was based on the bimetallic principle that a rise in the price of one metal will increase the demand for the cheaper, thus offsetting the price increase of the dearer. In addition, once the ratio was established no recoinage would be necessary. This implied that until the mint ratio became finalized the size of the silver standards would be subject to revision.

Joint metallism, thought Stokes, would provide a broad enough metallic basis for currency so that the "illegitimate" fall in prices would be checked. He defined the "illegitimate" fall in prices as that part of the decline which could not be attributed to reduced costs of production, but rather to the scarcity of money (Stokes, 1896:136). Since falling prices were responsible for the poor condition of the economy, prices must be prevented from falling further. Joint metallism proposed to do this. In fact, it would probably raise prices, because the long-run equilibrium ratio of gold to silver would be lower than the ratio then existing.

The most unique thing about Stokes's plan was that gold and silver were jointly legal tender. A debtor could pay his obligations in Stokes's new certificates, which could be redeemed half in gold and half in silver but all at the market ratio so that the creditor could not lose. In fact, Stokes's plan is very similar to that of symmetallism, proposed earlier by Alfred Marshall (Marshall, 1887:363–65).

Like other advocates of proposals to do something for silver in which the results would be less severe than free coinage at 16 to 1, Stokes had the misfortune to offer his plan at a time when free silverites were exerting maximum pressure for 16 to 1, while gold-standard people were making an all-out effort to preserve that standard from any encroachment by a greatly depreciated silver currency. Like many others who offered a plan as a panacea for the country's trouble, Stokes did not foresee what the real effects of his proposal would be. He merely stated what he wanted to happen if his plan were adopted and blithely assumed that things would happen as he wished.

II. NONMETALLIC STANDARDS OF PSEUDO-ECONOMISTS

The nonmetallic standards of this section are similar to the metallic standards in that they could all be placed in the general category of commodity standards. The significant difference is that the commodity backing the money supply in the nonmetallic standards was not in limited supply relative to gold or silver. There is more than a hint of "John Lawism" in these proposals.

A. Government Revenue Standard

One of the monetary standards discussed in the early 1890s evolved from the concept that the money supply should be based on government revenues and commodities in general.

1. *John Davis*

Congressman John Davis of Kansas was elected in 1892 as a candidate of the People's Party (Davis, 1892:553). As a Populist, Davis advocated fiat money, the value of which was determined by the ability of the government to remain intact and to continue its function of collecting and disbursing revenue. A money whose value is determined on this basis is, said Davis, "precisely as good as the issuing government—no better, no worse" (Davis, 1892:545).

Davis said the money supply must be maintained "in ample, even, and unfluctuating volume" (Davis, 1892:553). His precise meaning, however, was unclear. As a Populist he disliked falling prices. On this basis his statement could be interpreted to mean a money supply ample enough at all times to provide for even, unfluctuating prices. On the other hand, "ample, even, and unfluctuating volume" could also be interpreted to mean a fixed money supply which at the time established provided ample money given the transactions in the economy and the velocity of circulation of money. Over time, however, a fixed volume of money, if velocity remains constant, will lead to lower prices as transactions increase. He may have assumed an increasing velocity to offset the effect of increasing transactions on prices, but he did not indicate this.

The government's ability to perform this task of monetary regulation through its collection and disbursement of revenues was to be bolstered by a system of taxation whose burden rested heaviest on those with the greatest ability to pay: the large incomes, large legacies, and the large landed estates (Department of the Treasury, 1889:553). The unique element in Davis's scheme was that he did not stress the old greenback concept of direct loans to the people by the government. Thus he eliminated what to many was the most objectionable element in the Populists' monetary program. Government control of the money supply, however, would not be abandoned.

2. C. J. Buell

About fifteen months after Congressman Davis's article appeared in *The Arena,* another article was published in that same periodical along much the same lines. Its author was C. J. Buell (1893:196). Buell also believed that the government should issue money based on its taxing power.

His idea was that with the given tax structure the government could expect to obtain a certain amount of revenue. This revenue could be used for national purposes. Unlike John Davis, Buell was not concerned with any questions of equity in raising the revenue so long as the money issued by the government was based on expected revenues.

Buell proposed that the government buy its goods and services and pay for them with certificates which stated the dollar value of the goods and services received. These certificates would, in turn, be returned to the government in payment of taxes. Such certificates would circulate among the people because of the knowledge that they could be used to pay taxes. Their value would be maintained as long as they were issued only to pay for goods and services acquired by the government.

These certificates would not be the only medium of exchange or means of paying taxes available to the public. The other media available to the public would be the constant amount of greenbacks as fixed by legislation, the subsidiary coinage, and possibly, for Buell was not explicit on this point, gold and silver legal tender already in existence. In addition, Buell saw no objections to the issue of revenue certificates by the separate states based on their taxing power. He thought the latter much more desirable than the notes of private banks. Under Buell's scheme the amount of money would be steady and would increase over tihe as the revenues and expenditures of the government for public needs increased; therefore, there was no danger from inflation or contraction so long as the certificates issued by the federal and state governments did not exceed their revenue.

The quantity of money would be determined by government revenues, but the standard which would regulate the value of money in Buell's scheme was labor. Each of the certificates issued by the government "would show on its face the average amount of labor or material for which it was issued, and . . . that every bit of material purchased by government would have a value equal to the average amount of labor required to reproduce it; and we see that our proposed currency is based upon and measured by the very source of all value—human labor, expended under normal conditions in the production of useful things" (Buell, 1893:198). Buell believed that the value of labor was much more stable than that of any single commodity such as silver or gold.

There is much that is faulty in Buell's scheme. It is readily seen that the money supply as he envisioned it would behave in a procyclical manner. During a depression, or any cyclical downturn no matter how slight, revenue would decline, and thus government expenditures would also decline. In other words, he expected the budget to be balanced annually.

Buell's concept of allowing states to issue certificates in anticipation of revenue is not at all sound, although constitutional objections could be avoided by not making these state certificates legal tender. His labor theory of value is a throwback to a crude labor theory of value and completely ignores supply and demand as determinants of value. Buell was not an economist, but simply another of those individuals with simple solutions to complex problems with which the nation abounded in the 1890s.

B. John Lawism

The American contributors to the monetary-standard philosophy of John Law believed that the amount of money and its value should be determined by the output of the nation's farms. If the output of the gold mines could determine the money supply, why not the output of land, especially food?

1. Miles M. Dawson

Miles M. Dawson was an actuary who wrote extensively in insurance and statistics and some in mathematics. His interest in the monetary problems of the country probably stemmed from his career in the insurance profession.

Dawson wrote that the ideal basis for a currency is that which "represents absolute value or the 'prime utility'" (Dawson, 1892:86). Dawson believed that there was one commodity which men would prefer over all others if they could have only one. The commodity which men chose should have absolute value. This commodity should be a natural measure of value. It should be a commodity such that nothing else would be of value unless it could be obtained first. This particular commodity would possess prime utility. Therefore, wrote Dawson, "the surplus of the prime utility over the requirements of its owners balances all other commodities, and also, which is of the greatest importance, controls and limits the possibilities of production" (Dawson, 1892:86). That is to say, the production of any other good is determined by its value in the quantity of the prime utility good which must be forgone to accomplish its production.

Dawson termed all these other goods the latter utilities. Those latter utilities furthest removed from the prime utility are luxury items, which include gold and silver. In other words, there exists a definite rank order of goods for every individual and for society. The very fact that gold and silver are latter utilities is what makes their value fluctuate so much—so much that they are unsuited to serve as monetary standards.

What was Dawson's prime utility? He wrote, "The natural starting point of all exchanges is the farm; the increase of its products means an increased demand for currency. At some time during the year every dollar of real money exchanges for food products; for food is the prime utility, and the surplus food product the natural currency" (Dawson, 1892:88). Labor could not serve as the prime utility because labor was itself measured by the prime utility. The amount of labor available for the production of "latter utilities" was limited by the surplus of the prime utility over subsistence. If society, by exerting all of its labor, could only obtain the subsistence amount of the prime utility, nothing else could be produced.

Since all other commodities were produced at the sacrifice of food—the prime utility—it was only natural to value other products in terms of food. Only by the standard of food can the costs of production and prices of "latter utilities" be estimated. Dawson's system can be likened to a production-possibilities curve for an economy with food on one axis and all other goods represented on the other, the product mix of all other goods being determined by their rank in the order of latter utilities and by the surplus of the prime utility.

Much of Dawson's thought in this article was evidently supplied him by the Physiocrats. Production and the exchange of other goods depended solely upon the surplus of food. He said, "The rule admits of no exception for it is the rule of causation" (Dawson, 1892:91). In addition, food was especially suited to serve as a standard of value because it alone is of constant value. A bushel of wheat supports life for the same amount of time during feast or famine; "its intrinsic or absolute value is the same" (Dawson, 1892:91). The increased production of food or the ability to increase the production of food would mean an increased standard of living, for it would raise wages and stimulate the demand for other goods—that is, those goods with latter utilities.

The circulating currency under Dawson's scheme would be issued to farmers by the government in the form of warehouse receipts for the products they had deposited. These certificates would then be spent by farmers for other kinds of goods. Eventually these certificates would be redeemed by the government. The manner in which they would be redeemed or what they would be redeemed with was unclear. Evidently they would ultimately be redeemed in food equal to the amount and quality of the foods for which they had been issued. This, in effect, would make the government the food outlet for the nation, or at the very best, the food wholesaler for the nation.

The amount of currency under this scheme would always be exactly right, for it would represent the value of all production, other than agricultural production, that it would be possible for men to accomplish. "As in the creation of other industries," wrote Dawson, "the production of food must of necessity take the initiative, so the initial or starting point of currency should be not the mine but the farm" (Dawson, 1892:93).

Dawson's scheme was an interesting one, especially because of its apparent Physiocratic background. However, it had its shortcomings. A market society cannot always guarantee full employment, which was one of Dawson's implied objectives. Also, he did not take account of the fact that technology, which increased food production, would not extend necessarily to other types of production. The result of issuing extra certificates because of improved technology in agriculture would be inflation; that is, the prices of other goods in terms of food would be higher. The greatest fault, however, would come about as a result of poor harvests, which, in Dawson's scheme, would bring everything to a standstill. If there were no surplus of food, nothing else could be produced. Nonetheless, Dawson had followers with similar ideas, and there were others who arrived at similar concepts independently.

2. *Anson J. Webb*

One of Dawson's "disciples" was Anson J. Webb, who wrote for *The Arena* several years later. Webb extended their common principle on which currency was to be issued. He went further than Dawson by suggesting that the government issue currency certificates to an individual on any type of property, not just staples or food" (Webb, 1895:86). The problem with money, in Webb's view, was that it was always involved with the mechanics of supply and demand and with the dynamics of the production of precious metals.

Webb thought the monetary problem was an artifical one because the supply of money was always depressed below its demand. He wrote, *"Money must be studied from the standpoint of ethics, not the standpoint of mechanics. Money is an ethical fact"* (Webb, 1895:205). Money was neither a precious metal nor a commodity of any kind, nor was it fiat. Money was evidence. If an individual had money, it was only evidence that he had given up something of value for it. Money was the proof that the individual had an ethical right to regain his wealth or its equivalent.

Since money arose only from real transactions, its quantity was of no consequence. One truth—i.e., the exchange of a good for a claim (money) on it or its equivalent—could not reduce the value of another truth. A change in the quantity of money had no effect on prices. Therefore, the only essential quality of good money was that it arose from a real transaction. The only limit to the money supply, then, was the private property of society and the government's willingness to issue money on the basis of that property.

Webb addressed the question of the interest rate as a price by asserting his belief that the interest rate would be zero since an individual could always secure money by pledging property. Even though money had no value in terms of a rate of interest, it did have utility. Webb divorced utility from value with his belief that it was prior to value. He went on to write, "the true nature of money then becomes apparent in practice as well as in theory. It is clearly an ethical fact. Truth is its only test. The question of the volume of the currency has no import whatever" (Webb, 1895:208).

The principal failure of Webb's new philosophy of money was that he did not establish a standard by which the government could determine the value of any item of property offered for deposit in exchange for money. Furthermore, he did not explain the consequences of redemption when holders of the certificates demanded more of a particular commodity as an equivalent instead of the property their certificates actually represented. The result, of course, would be disequilibrium in which the supply of some goods held on deposit would exceed the demand. For other goods supply would be less than the demand. This would alter the structure of prices. On the other hand, his claim that money is bound up in ethics can hardly be denied. This, after all, was the crux of the entire silver controversy and the problem of falling prices. Is the payment of debt in terms of goods, of more than was borrowed, or the receipt of payment of less than what was borrowed justifiable on ethical grounds?

The individuals discussed above may all be called, and justifiably so, monetary "cranks." The ideas of some were novel, but those of all of them were naive. Yet all had a public hearing in a national periodical. They were read.

III. NONMETALLIC STANDARDS PROPOSED BY ECONOMISTS

The following theories of the monetary standard of value contrast sharply with those in the preceding section. These theories are both more rational and more complete. They represent three types of monetary standards. The first type is the utility standard. Ideas were offered with respect to both marginal utility and total utility as monetary standards. The second type is the labor-day standard, which recommended gold as the monetary metal. The third main type is the tabular standard, in which a price index is used to regulate the money supply.

A. Utility Standards

Marginal utility analysis was a relatively new trend in economics at the end of the nineteenth century that was gaining many followers. An American, J. B. Clark, is credited with being an independent codiscoverer of the margin. The works of the following American economists represent the first attempts by Americans to utilize the marginal concept in monetary-standard analysis.

1. Edward A. Ross

In 1892, Edward A. Ross, a Cornell University economist-sociologist, set out to examine the validity of the bimetallic and gold arguments then current in order to find what, if any, was a just standard of deferred payments. The arguments from both camps, as Ross saw them, involved two principal controversies. The first was over the ultimate standard of value; the second concerned who should receive the benefits of industrial progress (Ross, 1892:297).

With respect to the first controversy, Ross cited the bimetallist argument that justice was served when the creditor could buy the same amount of goods with the principal of a loan when it was repaid that he could have purchased with the principal at the time that he lent it. The argument of the gold-standard advocates as cited by Ross was that justice was served when the creditor received in payment the product of the same amount of labor as that which he had lent because the price of labor had not fallen. Both sides, said Ross, admitted that the question revolved around the concept of justice, and both agreed that economic justice consisted of the exchange of equal values.

Ross believed that the controversy over the ultimate standard of value evolved from the nature of value itself. It was opposing theories of value which clashed, not monetary standards. In effect, gold standardites and bimetallists were not even arguing on a common ground. The bimetallists postulated that equal quantities of consumer goods were of equal value even if separated by time. The monometallists postulated that the product of equal quantities of productive labor were of equal value even though separated by time. The controversy was not between gold and silver, said Ross, but "between the two great opposing theories of value—that of *labor-value* and that of *use-value*. The one derives value from production, the other from consumption. The one looks to cost, the other to utility'' (Ross, 1892:298). Which was correct? Ross leaned toward use value.

Basing value on labor sacrifice was wrong because the sacrifice was only a means to an end. The sacrifice was important or had value because it was a primary condition in production. The product which stood between labor sacrifice and human satisfaction was valuable not because it embodied past sacrifices but because it offered future satisfaction. The labor theory of value, in which prices were determined by cost of production, had merit in a perfectly competitive world, but in modern industrial society there are too many monopolized goods which have brought to light many cases where prices were not proportionate to cost. Marginal analysis, however, had changed economic theory and raised new hope for value theory. Ross sarcastically remarked, ''By furbishing up the obsolete and discredited labor-value theory in order to beat the bimetallists, the gold standard defenders have shown themselves [to be] the Bourbons of political economy'' (Ross, 1892:299). In society, concluded Ross, people do not barter equal quantities of labor time which are unequal in terms of the quantities of goods they represent. The bimetallists, he thought, had the best of the first controversy.

The second controversy was over the distribution of the benefits of industrial progress. There were three alternatives in this issue: (1) either the creditor received the entire benefit; or (2) the debtor received the entire benefit; or (3) the benefit was shared. The first alternative was unjust because factors other than capital contributed to industrial progress. Besides, the creditor was already receiving interest, which by itself allowed him more consumption than if he had not loaned his capital at interest (Ross, 1892:300–301). The second alternative, thought Ross, was just. The debtor's labor was utilizing the creditor's capital in a more efficient manner than the creditor himself could have. If this were not so, the creditor would have used the capital himself. The debtor, therefore, could not be expected to exchange his more efficient labor for the less efficient labor of the creditor on a one-for-one basis, although this was what the creditor desired (Ross, 1892:301–2). The third alternative was also just, depending upon the circumstances of the creditor. If he was a current producer as well as a past producer (represented by his capital lent to others), he would receive part of the benefits of industrial progress, but he was not entitled to those benefits simply on the basis of being a creditor.

The marginal utility of goods, it was argued, had decreased; therefore, the creditor should be compensated for the decline by receiving more goods. But this was false, declared Ross, because marginal utilities are values and a ''general decline in marginal utilities is as impossible as a general decline in values'' (Ross, 1892:304). Since Ross was speaking of a "general decline," perhaps he meant that the decline in the marginal utility of one good would be compensated for by an increase in the marginal utility of another, leaving the general level of marginal utility and value for all goods and services the same. However, this is only conjecture; Ross made no attempt to explain what he meant when he said that marginal utilities in general could not decline.

Ross then proceeded to his concept of objective utility, which could decline. On this basis the creditor's claim to a portion of the benefits of industrial progress was valid (Ross, 1892:304). Objective utility was dependent upon social esteem, which he defined as the ability and right of creditors to maintain their position on the social scale.

For example, at the time the creditor lent money to a debtor, the social distinction of his class might have been a ten-room house. If at the time the loan was repaid, the badge of distinction for his class was a twelve-room house (because ten-room houses had become so plentiful) the creditor should be able to enjoy the new social distinction of his class. "It would therefore seem but just," commented Ross, "that the creditor should participate in the benefits arising from general industrial progress sufficiently to compensate him for the depreciation of that portion of his wealth devoted to satisfying the needs of his social nature (Ross, 1892:305).

Ross concluded that the monometallist argument based on labor value was wholly unsound and that the bimetallist argument based on use value was not entirely right. The monetary standard should be based on objective utility. Therefore, some premium above the market rate of interest should be paid to creditors in order that they might maintain a given objective utility which, in terms of goods needed to satisfy it, probably increased over time. "The debtor," said Ross, "is not to return a value measured in *labor,* nor yet a value measured in *commodities,* but a value measured in *objective utility*. And with industrial progress this is secured by a slight excess of commodities" (Ross, 1892:305).

A just monetary standard, Ross continued, would permit alterations in the ratio between labor and goods to take the form of a rising price for labor rather than a falling price for goods. The money unit should depreciate in terms of goods. The money supply should be sufficient to maintain the level of retail prices. He intended real income to increase via higher money income, not by lower prices.

The article in which Ross put forth his objective-utility standard of deferred payments sparked a controversy. His antagonist was Lucius S. Merriam of the Johns Hopkins University.

2. Lucius S. Merriam

Merriam objected strenously to much that Ross had written. He maintained that Ross was advocating nothing more than a simple commodity standard in which the debtor merely returned the same amount of goods that he had borrowed. Ross contended that the debtor was returning equal value because the marginal utility of goods had not fallen. Merriam denied Ross's contention by arguing that, in fact, marginal utilities and values (prices) had fallen owing to the great increases in production and the greater ease with which human wants were satisfied (Merriam, 1893:484). Therefore, when equal quantities of goods were paid back by the debtor, the creditor was not receiving the same value that he had lent, because a lower marginal utility or price times the same quantity of goods yielded less total value than that same quantity of goods at a higher marginal utility or value.

Merriam went on to say that Ross had modified the commodity standard with his belief that creditors should receive a premium above the market rate of interest. This meant, in effect, that Ross recognized the injustice perpetrated on the creditor by the simple commodity standard. He merely veiled his recognition of that injustice by arguing that the relative social position of the creditor must be maintained. Had Ross's deviation from the simple commodity standard been greater, Merriam contended, he would have arrived at the right standard of value, that which returned value for value. The right standard was the marginal-utility standard, which would have returned more goods, but of the same value that had been borrowed (Merriam, 1893:500–501).

Merriam also criticized Ross for professing an allegiance to final or marginal utility as the determinant of value and then turning around and making use of a slightly modified commodity standard, with the result that he finally advocated a standard based on "objective utility." This, to Merriam, was unpardonable, for it was not possible for utility to be measured objectively. "All utility," said Merriam, "is relative to the mind of the individual or of society. All utility, therefore, is subjective either directly or indirectly" (Merriam, 1893:500).

Merriam advocated a monetary standard based on repaying equal values, which meant that as marginal utilities declined, prices declined, and with the repayment of debts the creditor should have command over more goods than he had originally. He objected to Ross's modified commodity standard and his assumption that marginal utility and value did not decline. Justice was served not by maintaining the social standard of the creditor but by making sure that he received payment, value for value on that which he had lent.

Merriam's objections, written in January 1893, had a significant effect in helping Ross clarify his own argument. Ross, now at Stanford University, did this in an article published in November 1893. In this latter article, Ross cleared up his own meanings of concepts to a considerable extent.

He began by identifying his concept of objective utility with total utility (Ross, 1893:427). Objective utility allowed the creditor to maintain a given social status. Total utility implied much the same thing. From the time the loan was made until it was repaid, the total utility of the creditor should not diminish. More significantly, Ross abandoned the idea that marginal utility or value could not decline. Then, with the aid of a simple diagram, he proceeded to demonstrate why he thought his monetary standard for deferred payments was superior to that offered by Merriam.

Dr. Merriam, Ross began, proposed the total-value or marginal-utility standard. This required that the volume of money should reflect changes in total value—for example, from *ABCE* to *AFHK* (see Figure 1). Price fell, with the decline in marginal utility, from *BC* to *FH*. The total-utility standard proposed by Ross required the volume of money to reflect changes in total utility, for example, from *ABCD* to *AFHD*. Prices would fall in the ratio of *ABCD*/*AB* to *AFHD*/*AF* (Ross, 1893:427).

The misuse of the total-value concept, wrote Ross, was the error of the marginal-utility standard. Marginal utility or value times the quantity of goods provides a measure of total value, but not a correct one. Mar-

Figure 1.

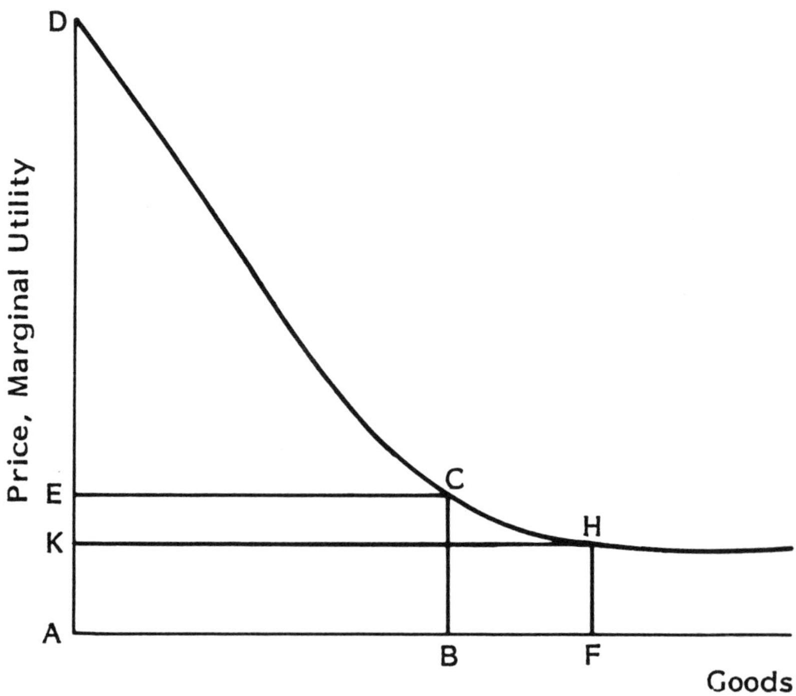

ginal utility or value can only be applied to those goods in or for the market, whereas total value purports that all goods are measured by the value of the marginal good (Ross, 1893:430). Total value, when measured in this manner, implied Ross, understates the real value (by real value, Ross meant total utility) of all goods, for when goods are finally in the possession of consumers, the basis for valuation has changed.

Valuation of goods was formerly external. But when goods were finally in the hands of consumers, valuation became internal and subjective. The price that currently rules the market does not accurately reflect the value or utility of a good to each individual. The attempt to measure total value by present market price was unscientific. Thus, to Ross, total utility was the summation of what goods were worth to individual consumers, not what they were worth in the market on the basis of price times quantity. For example, at price *FH,* total value under the marginal utility standard is *AFHK,* but total utility is *AFHD.* The difference between the two was Marshall's concept of consumers' surplus. The utility of goods to many people was greater than the price they had to pay.

If the production of goods had succeeded to the point where marginal utility and price had declined from *BC* to *FH,* the money supply would have to expand in the ratio *AFHD/ABCD* (Ross, 1893:438). Ross concluded that *"total utility, and not 'total value' based on marginal utility, is the scientific standard to which money should conform in order to do justice as a standard of deferred payments"* (Ross, 1893:440–41). The money supply under this standard would, of course, be regulated by the government. Such a standard would justify both a greater volume of money and a higher level of prices than would be justified by the marginal-utility standard.

Professor Merriam died before he could publish an answer to Ross's second article. However, he left some notes for an answer which he was preparing. John B. Clark took Merriam's notes and fashioned a posthumous reply to Ross for him (Clark, 1894:970).

Merriam objected to Ross's total-utility standard on the basis that the first increments of many goods have an importance beyond computation. General comparisons of articles consumed at one period of time with those same articles consumed at a later period are impossible because the figure which expresses the utility measure is, in both cases, infinity. In other words, if the good in question was formerly a luxury which only certain income groups could afford, the total utility of the first increment of the good consumed by that group was infinite. By the same token, if after the passage of time the good came into use by a lower income group, the total utility of the first increment consumed by that group would also be infinite. But, said Merriam, we can measure total value on the basis of marginal utility because value is social. "By reason of free exchanges there is an economic resultant from the action of many consumers and of many producers. An article has a final utility to society; and it is on the basis of this final social utility that articles are exchanged in the market" (Clark, 1894:971). Each man has his utility function, but no two are alike. Therefore, prices can only be determined through the interplay of social forces. Clark wrote:

> It is known that Dr. Merriam had in mind a statement of the relation that money bears to the different standards proposed for deferred payments. He would have shown that, as a tool of the market, money can express valuation, but never total utility. He would have offered a powerful argument in favor of the value standard for deferred payments, in contrast with the standard that requires the return by a borrower of the same kinds and quantities of goods that he has received, or again, one that requires the return of the same total utility that was borrowed. (Clark, 1894:972).

Merriam's death was unfortunate because it stopped a budding controversy at its virtual beginning. Several more exchanges between him and Ross might have brought a greater clarification by each and a more complete analysis by each of the total- and marginal-utility standards of deferred payments. As it was, only one other economist, aside from J. B. Clark, who made use of Merriam's notes, picked up the threads that each was developing and he did so only to refute the concepts of both as standards. That economist was Frank A. Fetter, then of Cornell University.

3. *Frank A. Fetter*

Fetter did not think it possible that debts could be repaid on the basis of total utility because there are a number of goods, the total utility of which, to many individuals, is infinite. If a debtor could repay the first increment of any one of these goods, his debt, in terms of utility, would be paid off. "But," said Fetter, "it is impossible under normal circumstances to pay total utilities" (Fetter, 1895:885). This, in effect, was the same argument used by Merriam in his dispute with Ross.

The marginal-utility standard as offered by Merriam was no better, in Fetter's view. What, asked Fetter, is to measure these marginal utilities? Is it the intensity of the creditor's desire which is satisfied? If this were the case, the debtor might be required to repay much more than he thought just. Merriam, however, had said that value was social, that society, acting through the marketplace, would determine marginal utility. Fetter implied, however, that not until utility could be measured cardinally so that the want-satisfying power of goods for different people at different times could be definitely known "could the marginal utility theory of value aid in the question of the standard of deferred payments" (Fetter, 1895:891). Armed with all the economic theories of value in the world, a standard which would bring about the return of equal value could not be invented.

Fetter did not believe that the question of a just monetary standard could obtain a final answer from pure economic theory. The best that could be hoped for was a standard which would provide the minimum of discouragement to both debtors and creditors and one which would "ensure that the benefits of industrial advance shall on the whole go to those classes in whose encouragement and economic growth society has the greatest interest" (Fetter, 1895:896).

B. Labor-Day Standard

Four months after Fetter had stated that the solution to the problem of the monetary standard did not lie in pure theory, J. B. Clark published an article in which he concurred, but only in part, for Clark believed a study of the true theoretical standard for deferred payments was necessary. What was that standard? Clark wrote, "This point may seem to lie in the region of pure theory. In reality it is the point of largest practical consequence" (Clark, 1895:394). He thought that the establishment of a theoretical standard, whether practical or not, would provide some kind of basis to determine whether the current monetary system of the United States, which was based on gold, was the best that could be practically attained.

Clark believed there was an ideal standard to which the value of money should conform. The value of the dollar should conform to the physical amount of goods which could be secured by a day of labor. This would be a just standard, for the benefits of industrial progress would be equally divided between creditor and debtor. Clark's day of labor did not consist of a fixed number of hours. Through technology the day of labor was getting shorter. Therefore the ideal dollar was one that would buy a decreasing number of hours of labor but an increasing quantity of goods. Clark wrote, *"Labor that diminishes in actual amount, as measured in hours, and that diminishes in sacrifice entailed,*—this affords a standard of payments by which debtor and creditor may share alike in the benefits or progress" (Clark, 1895:398).

Since the currency was on a metallic basis and since it seemed apparent that it would remain on a metallic basis, the metal used to define the dollar should be one which best follows the divergence between labor and commodities. The present metallic basis of gold seemed to be the best possible in this respect. An ounce of gold then commanded about the same number of average days of labor (keeping in mind that the number of hours in the average work day had declined) as it had in the past. At the same time it had gained in its purchasing power over commodities (Clark, 1895:400–401). Whether or not the gain in commodity-purchasing power of gold was offset by the loss in its power to purchase labor was an unsettled question.

C. Tabular Standard

Up to this point three different concepts of the ideal standard advocated by economists have been offered: the total-utility standard, the marginal-utility standard, and the labor-day standard. The next standard to be discussed is the tabular standard. It was not a new idea conceived by an American economist, but rather an old idea of which some American economists made excellent restatements. The English economist W. Stanley Jevons discussed the tabular standard briefly and traced it back as far as two English writers of the early nineteenth century (Jevons, 1875:325–33). The tabular standard was under discussion in Great Britain during the 1870s, as is shown by Walter Bagehot's criticism of it in 1875 (Bagehot, 1875). One of the earliest American writers to discuss the possibilities of the tabular standard was E. B. Andrews of Brown University. His knowledge of the concept was derived from Jevons's book.

1. E. Benjamin Andrews

Andrews believed firmly that the price level had to be stabilized for a country to prosper. He realized that the free-silver advocates were wrong in wishing to restore the Civil War price level. He believed the gold-standard advocates were wrong in thinking that prices should continue to fall. Andrews was classified previously as an international bimetallist. His stand with respect to the tabular standard takes nothing away from his bimetallism. Apparently he looked upon the tabular standard as a suitable alternative which would provide for the greater monetary usage of silver. This is a valid assumption in light of the fact that international bimetallism was no closer to reality in 1889 than it had been since the demonetization of silver in 1873. On the other hand, there would be many difficulties for the tabular standard to overcome to be established. The greatest difficulty arose from an *a priori* prejudice on the part of many people against the close control by the federal government which would be required to make such a monetary system operate smoothly (Andrews, 1889:439). But Andrews was impressed with the potential of the tabular standard to maintain a constant price level.

For the tabular standard to function, much work would be required to collect price data in order to construct a price index. However, once this was done, the government would maintain the price level by issuing or withdrawing legal-tender money from circulation depending upon whether prices had fallen or risen. Andrews thought the index should be derived from a group of commodities which would satisfy the following conditions. (1) Commodities entering the tabular standard should be taken from two classes of goods: (a) those subject to the law of diminishing returns, and (b) those not subject to the law of diminishing returns. (2) The commodities chosen must be those least subject to either artificial or accidental fluctuations in value. (3) The greater the number of commodities used to compute the index the better. (4) Prices used in computing the index must come from all the major markets in the nation—or, for an international good, from all the countries affected. (5) The index should be weighted so that each commodity influenced the index in proportion to the quantity of it consumed; it may be assumed that he meant by value as well as by quantity (Andrews, 1889:431–32).

Once the index was computed and a price level established, officials would check the index at proper time intervals to determine whether the general level of prices had risen or fallen. If the former, there was too much money in circulation and some would have to be withdrawn. If the latter, there was not enough in circulation and more would have to be issued. Andrews wrote, "In a word, inflate or contract, . . . so as to keep the footing of your great price list perpetually the same. . . . The very knowledge of an existing purpose thus to regulate would do much to regulate" (Andrews, 1889:433).

Andrews believed that a monetary scheme such as this would serve purposes beyond that of regulating the price level. One of these would be the final solution to the silver problem. He did not mean that silver would regain the free-coinage privilege but that it would come into a greater monetary use "no less distinguished than international bimetallism would assign to it" (Andrews, 1889:435). Gold would remain the only full-value money and would still be freely coined. Silver's role would be that of the legal-tender token money which would be coined at the government's discretion and then issued or withdrawn to regulate the price level. Andrews did not think paper money without metallic banking could serve this purpose because it simply was not safe.

An internationalist to the core, Andrews suggested that a possible condition for the attainment of a tabular standard would be international cooperation. He believed that cooperation for such a monetary system would be much easier to obtain than cooperation for bimetallism, because the sole purpose of the tabular standard was to stabilize prices. It did not call for the free coinage of silver or for the establishment of a mint ratio that might necessitate the recoinage of all existing coins.

Andrews knew that the French economist Leon Walras had also devised a monetary scheme in which the government expanded or contracted the money supply depending upon the movement of prices. Andrews pointed out the differences between the idea he proposed and that of Walras. First of all, he noted, Walras would inflate or contract the money supply on an *a priori* basis, whereas he would only do so on an *a posteriori* basis. He implied that he would be less presumptuous than Walras in determining the money needs of the economy. Second, said Andrews, Walras did not discuss how the money supply would be increased or decreased, whereas he, Andrews, had.

2. *James Allen Smith*

Andrews's treatment of the tabular standard was not complete. His administrative duties at Brown University might have been responsible for this. Be that as it may, it was seven years before any American economist made a complete statement of the tabular standard. The economist who did so was James Allen Smith of Marietta College in Ohio. Smith, however, chose to call his standard the multiple money standard (Smith, 1896:192). He implied that it was another step beyond a tabular standard of the type discussed by President Andrews.

The tabular standard was not much more than a simple composite standard. The only element which differentiated it from the simple composite standard was that more than two commodities entered into the price table. The simple composite standard was one in which the monetary unit was equal to x grains of gold plus y grains of silver. This will be recognized immediately as the joint metallism advocated by Anson Phelps Stokes, which was similar to the symmetallism of Alfred Marshall. Smith believed that the composite standard of gold and silver was not the best that could be achieved. The purpose of such a standard was to secure greater stability of value. The fluctuations in one metal were expected to be neutralized by opposite changes in the other so that the value of the standard remained stable in terms of commodities. But, said Smith, gold and silver were closely related commodities, and therefore their values were more likely to fluctuate in the same direction rather than to counterbalance one another. The direction in which their values changed was also likely to be different from that of all other commodities (Smith, 1896:196). This meant that as the values of gold and silver increased together, they would buy more and more commodities. The general price level would fall, defeating the purpose of the composite standard, which was to maintain stable prices.

The tabular standard would prove more stable than the composite standard because it would be made up of goods from distinct commodity categories. The fluctuations of values in one distinct group (agricultural products) was more likely to be compensated for by fluctuations in the opposite direction by another distinct group (the precious metals). If a large number of commodities were properly selected and weighted, they would form an almost invariable standard. That would be in direct contrast to the gold standard, which was steadily appreciating in terms of commodities. It meant that the dollars paid back to creditors would buy more than the dollars lent by the creditors.

Under the tabular standard, however, the number of dollars to be paid back to creditors sometime in the future would depend on the difference between the index of value of the tabular standard when the debt was contracted and when it was due. The creditor would receive in payment the same purchasing power he had lent. His payment for forgoing current consumption when he made the loan would be interest, not interest plus appreciation. The creditor, by the same token, was also freed from the risk of inflation. A similar idea, long-term mortgage loans with a flexible interest rate, reflects this same idea today.

The principal benefit of the tabular standard would be to keep alterations in the purchasing power of money from seriously disturbing debtor-creditor relations. At the same time it would promote greater industrial stability by providing a greater degree of certainty with respect to the value of debts. Smith wrote, "Long time contracts could be made in terms of money without danger of the obligation of the one being increased or the claim of the other being diminished" (Smith, 1896:197–98). Under this monetary system, a general rise or fall in the price level could take place, but it would not be followed with dire consequences.

Smith also saw some inconveniences in the tabular standard. The first was that the real standard (the group of commodities) could not be incorporated into the monetary system. The change in a commodity's price could be caused by a real factor, a change in the value of the commodity itself, or by a change in the value of the monetary unit itself. A change in price was only an effect; it did not indicate what the causal factor was. In order to determine why price had changed, both the commodity in question and the monetary unit had to be referred to the monetary standard. The cause of the change could be discovered by determining whether the value of the good in question had changed. The possibility existed that some change in each had contributed to the change in price. Both the good in question and the monetary unit had to be referred to the standard, a third party, to explain price changes. For this reason, Smith believed that the tabular standard lacked both simplicity and direction.

What Smith desired was to combine these two relationships: to incorporate the tabular standard into the monetary system so that the price of a good would not only indicate its relation to the monetary unit but also the monetary standard of value. The multiple money standard would serve as the monetary unit as well as the standard of value (Smith, 1896:199).

The number of commodities which comprised Smith's multiple standard need not be large, but they should comprise a significant portion of the nation's annual output. The commodities selected were to be represented in the standard in ratio to their importance. For example, since the annual value of the corn crop exceeded the value of the output of domestic gold, corn should be represented in the standard by the number of times its value exceeded that of gold. The same should hold true for all other commodities employed.

The legislation which would put the multiple money standard into operation need not try to fix the relative values of the commodities in the standard. All that would be required of the law was that it declare the aggregate value of the quantities selected for the standard to be $100,000, just as previous legislation had declared that 23.2 grains of fine gold constituted a dollar (Smith, 1896:200).

The price of each commodity as well as the aggregate value of each commodity within the standard was subject to change. The prices and values of each commodity could change relative to one another but the aggregate value of the standard would always be $100,000. The change in the price and value of one commodity would always be offset by changes in the opposite direction of one or more of the others. Smith's major assumption was that the prices of all the commodities which comprised the standard could not rise or fall at the same time. The aggregate value of the standard could only be changed by increasing or decreasing the quantity of one or more of the commodities which comprised it.

In order to demonstrate how the aggregate value of the standard would remain constant even though the relative prices and values of goods within the standard were changing, Smith assumed a decrease in the demand for one of the standard commodities. If the supply remained constant, the price would fall to a new market equilibrium. A lower price for any of the commodities could also come about by an increase in supply brought on by technological change. For example, new technology in agriculture would lower the prices of farm products in the standard relative to other goods. The effect of either cause would be to lower the value of that portion of the multiple standard which the commodity comprised.

But Smith wanted to avoid permanent declines in the price of one commodity relative to the others. He did so with the realization that a reduced price for one commodity was the same thing as an increase in real income. Thus with a change in one of the determinants of demand, the demand for one or more of the other commodities would increase. This would raise the prices of these goods to new market equilibria. After the new equilibrium prices for all commodities had been established, the value of the standard would still be $100,000.

The multiple money standard, said Smith, would reduce the price fluctuations of all the component commodities. Just as the price of gold (in terms of gold) is constant under the gold standard and just as the price of corn (in terms of corn) would be constant if corn were the standard, the price of the multiple standard would also be constant in terms of itself. But the price fluctuations of each commodity within the multiple standard would be minor. This would be so, said Smith, because "each commodity in the standard is compared with a unit of value of which it forms a part and to the extent that it enters into the standard, just to that extent are its fluctuations in price diminished" (Smith, 1896:101–2).

Smith's multiple money standard was not a static concept. The makeup of the standard would be subject to change. He realized that the relative importance of a given commodity to the economy could change over time. As a product's relative importance declined, the quantity of it in the standard would have to be reduced, while the quantities of those goods that had increased in production and importance would be increased. In addition to this, if some commodity not currently in the standard were to become relatively important, it was to be added, while any commodity that had become relatively unimportant should be dropped. This will be recognized as the process to which our current CPI basket of goods is subjected on a periodic basis. The only requirement not subject to change was that the aggregate value of the new standard should be equivalent to that of the old (Smith, 1896:204).

The effect of revising the standard either by revising the quantities of those goods already in it or by substituting new goods would be to give it even greater stability. After revision of the standard, the fluctuations of the prices of those goods which comprised it would be smaller than before. Since any revision of the standard would have no great influence on prices, it could not be followed by any serious economic consequences.

Unlike E. B. Andrews, Smith wanted to take the prices for the commodities in the standard from only one market, e.g., Chicago. If transportation costs between major market areas were assumed to be constant, actual prices of commodities in New York and Chicago would differ only by the cost of transport. Therefore, Chicago prices would have a fixed relation to prices in all other cities. On this basis, given the prices for Chicago, prices everywhere else could be readily determined. He admitted, however, that local supply-and-demand conditions could cause slight variations of prices in local markets that could not be accounted for by transport charges. He did not believe, however, that price variations from that cause would be disruptive.

After explaining the makeup of the multiple money standard and how it was subject to change, Smith proceeded to discuss the criteria by which the original multiple money standard would be established. The $100,000 value of the original multiple standard would be based on the gold prices of the commodities comprising the standard at the time when the multiple standard was made up. That is, the original standard for the multiple money standard would be gold at the mint price then current, approximately $20.67 per ounce. But since the price of gold would then be subject to change, the gold equivalent of the standard was also liable to change. The price of gold could not remain permanently at $20.67 per ounce. Therefore, the number of ounces of gold which would be equal to the multiple standard was also subject to change. The mint price of gold would have to be changed from time to time to correspond with changes in the market price of gold. However, as long as the mints of the world kept buying gold at fixed prices, they would exert such great influence on both demand and the market price that it was inconceivable to expect significant changes in the price of gold even if the United States itself did not have a perfectly elastic demand for gold at an established mint price.

When once established, the multiple money standard instead of gold would regulate both the money supply and the value of money with respect to its purchasing power. New circulating notes would be issued and given legal-tender status. For a period of time all previously existing legal tender of every kind could be exchanged, dollar for dollar, for the new notes. After that, old legal tender (referring solely to gold coins and silver dollars or the certificates by which they were represented) could be redeemed in terms of its bullion value only.

Evidently, in order to maintain some semblance of a metallic standard, the new multiple-standard notes could be redeemed in gold or silver, not at a fixed price but at the market price of one or the other of the metals. That is, $100,000 of multiple-standard notes would be redeemed with the number of ounces of gold or silver which those notes would buy at the market price on a given day. Since the value of the gold or silver in the domestic market would be no greater than the value of the notes themselves, there was no reason to expect that the notes, when depreciated because of rising prices, would be converted into gold or silver. Smith wrote, "The man who buys gold or silver with depreciated currency and sells it again when the currency has regained its normal value finds that he is no better off than he would have been if he had merely retained the depreciated notes. They would have appreciated as much in his hands as the gold or silver" (Smith, 1896:209).

The goal which Smith sought with his multiple money standard was the same that many of the other standards sought: a stable price level. Smith realized that a deterrent to stable prices was a continually fluctuating money supply. Greater control over this variable would do much to minimize possible price variations. Control of the money supply should rest with a central authority. In addition, control over the money supply would provide a useful tool in aiding the multiple standard to maintain its value. It would take time for the value of the standard to adjust itself either upward or downward to its real value of $100,000 after the price of one of the standard commodities had changed. During this transitional period the purchasing power of the monetary unit itself would undergo change. These changes in the purchasing power of the dollar would be reflected in the dollar amount by which the money value of the standard was above or below $100,000. The value of the dollar would have depreciated in the former case and appreciated in the latter. The time lag, during which the purchasing power of the monetary unit underwent change, could be shortened by judicious manipulation of the money supply.

Smith desired the currency to be elastic so that its volume could be decreased if the dollar had depreciated or increased if the dollar had appreciated. There were two ways in which the government could regulate the currency to achieve the desired results: by borrowing or lending as the situation required, and by selling or buying as the situation required. Smith rejected the first alternative because it would require the government to create and maintain elaborate machinery which would establish banking as a government function.

Smith favored the second alternative. Any needed addition to the currency could be supplied through government purchases of good securities—i.e., open-market operations by the Treasury. He thought these securities might include national, state, or municipal bonds, and "the bonds of such industrial corporations as are under government regulation and control" (Smith, 1896:212). This would primarily mean interstate railroads. An excess of money could be removed from the economy by reversing the above procedure. If the government did not possess enough securities to implement the necessary reduction in the money supply, it could issue and sell bonds for that purpose. It would be the government's duty to purchase on a falling market and sell on a rising market. In addition, dealing in securities in order to regulate the currency could also serve as a source of federal government revenue. He implied that the government's activity with respect to the money supply would be of a defensive nature as opposed to offensive. In other words, Smith did not propose what might be termed an expansionary monetary policy. The price level was the criterion by which the government would regulate the money supply. If the price level remained stable, no action would be forthcoming.

Smith suggested another method by which the government could regulate the currency: buying or selling gold or silver instead of securities. If there was too much money and prices had risen, the government could offer to sell gold or silver for slightly below the market price in order to induce the desired reduction in the currency. In order to expand the money supply, the government could buy the metals at slightly above their market prices. This method could be used to contract the currency if the supply of securities was inadequate and there was no desire to issue new ones and if the government's stock of the precious metals was sufficient to affect the desired reduction (Smith, 1896:210).

Either method by which the contraction of the money supply took place would ultimately take the form of taxation. The government would have to pay interest and principal on the bonds it issued in order to contract the currency. In addition, its stock of the precious metals would have to be maintained with later purchases at possibly higher prices. These costs of regulating the currency would, in the long run, have to be provided for out of taxation.

Smith suggested that by itself the taxing power of the government could be used to regulate the money supply. If the monetary unit had depreciated, the government could collect more in tax revenue than it spent thus absorbing excess money. Expansion of the money supply would require only that government expenditures exceed government revenues. "The circulating medium under this scheme," wrote Smith, "would be issued directly and exclusively by the government and the volume of money would at all times correspond to the actual needs of commerce" (Smith, 1896:214). Smith's ideas have a very modern ring to them. In effect this is what can be done through modern monetary policy and fiscal policy. Some of Smith's insights appear to have been in advance of his times.

3. *Thomas E. Will*

Another person who advocated a tabular standard, but one of a more simple variety, was Thomas E. Will, the Populist economist from Kansas State Agricultural College. He believed that some remedy had to be applied to the monetary situation of the United States at the end of the nineteenth century. He also believed that the more control the people had over the remedy, the more efficacious it would be in relieving the situation. It was on the criterion of popular control that he ranked the better-known monetary standards. From worst to best they were gold, international bimetallism, and national bimetallism. The remedy or standard he desired, however, was one in which the government scientifically controlled the volume of legal-tender money. If the people controlled the monetary system, they would control the general level of prices (Will, 1898:91).

The general level of prices would be established through an index-number system. The volume of money would be regulated by the fluctuations in the price index. Will believed that such a system would work because of the direct relationship between prices and all means of exchange. He wrote, "Given, then, this balance wheel, regulating at the same time the volume of our exchange medium and the movements of the price line, we shall enjoy, for the first time in our history, if not in the history of the modern world, an equitable standard of deferred payments, a money of uniform purchasing power and an honest dollar" (Will, 1898:92). Will's proposal is Populist in nature because the people were to control the money supply. Whether the people would actively work to maintain a stable price level instead of advocating continual and unnecessary increases in the money supply is another question.

IV. SUMMARY

The monetary-standard-of-value controversy in the United States generated much excitement and enthusiasm. Many individuals, both economists and noneconomists, penned their views. They proposed other standards besides gold, silver, and bimetallism. The generating force behind all of these concepts of the monetary standard of value appears to have been a general concern over the level of prices and the effect of price changes on economic activity.

Of the other metallic standards proposed, the most familiar is joint metallism, in which gold and silver jointly backed the supply of money. Joint metallism was not dissimilar from bullionism, of which John Rogers Commons was an advocate. Bullionism has the attributes of a gold-exchange standard. Silver alone could serve as the standard, but only at its market price. The other metallic standard discussed was the globe standard, in which both gold and silver would be subject to free coinage, but the new coins were to be used for international settlements and were to be passed by weight rather than by tale.

All of these other metallic standards were devised to make greater use of silver for monetary purposes but not to disturb the existing preeminence of gold. Prices would still be gold prices. In effect there would be no change in the situation. The owner of silver bullion would be no better off by converting his silver into money under these proposals than if he had merely disposed of the silver via regular market channels.

The nonmetallic standards which were proposed fall into two categories; those offered by noneconomists and those offered by economists.

The former category consisted of monetary standards based on the revenue-producing powers of the federal government and out-and-out John Lawism.

The first type suggested that the money supply would be regulated by tax revenue. When anticipated revenue was high, the money supply would be large and vice versa. This had procyclical connotations which are unacceptable in light of modern economic theory. The "John Lawism" proposed in this country would also be unacceptable, for it permitted additions to the money supply by simply pledging any form of tangible property as the basis of a loan from the federal government.

The second category, nonmetallic standards proposed by economists, applied economic theory, other than supply-and-demand analysis, to the monetary-standard problem. Value theory with respect to the new theory of marginal-utility analysis was being applied to the monetary-standard problem. The price level was still of great importance, but only in the manner in which it was used to derive utility.

Another economist, E. Benjamin Andrews, also made more extensive use of economic theory and statistics (the use of index numbers) in the formulation of a tabular standard for money. James A. Smith furthered this concept in his multiple money standard. In addition, the positive role of the central government in establishing and maintaining nonmetallic standards was also being advocated boldly. The greater use of value theory and the bold suggestions that active government participation in the establishment and maintenance of the monetary standard strike modern chords with respect to our current monetary and general economic policies.

REFERENCES

Andrews, E. Benjamin (1889), "An Honest Dollar." *Publications of the American Economics Association* 4(November):401–41.

Bagehot, Walter (1892), "A New Standard of Value." *Economic Journal* 2(September). (Reprinted from *The Economist,* November 20, 1875).

Buell, C. J. (1893), "The Money Question." *The Arena* 8(July):191–200.

Clark, John B. (1894), "An Unfinished Study by Mr. Merriam." *Annals of the American Academy of Political and Social Science* 4(May):969–72.

——— (1895), "The Gold Standard of Currency in the Light of Recent Theory." *Political Science Quarterly* 10(September):389–403.

Commons, John R. (1893), "Bullion Notes and Elastic Currency." *Annals of the American Academy of Political and Social Science* 4(September):299–301.

Davis, Hon. John (1892), "The Money Question." *The Arena* 5(April):543–55.

Dawson, Miles M. (1892), "The True Basis of Currency." *The Arena* 6(June):84–93.

Department of the Treasury (1889), *Annual Report of the Secretary of the Treasury.* Washington, D.C.: U.S. Government Printing Office, p. lxxiv.

Fetter, Frank (1895), "The Exploitation of Theories of Value in the Discussion of the Standard of Deferred Payments." *Annals of the American Academy of Political and Social Science* 5(May):882–96.

Harter, Michael D. (1894), "The Kind of Money That Would Rule the World." *The Forum* 17(July):603–08.
Jevons, W. Stanley (1875), *Money and the Mechanism of Exchange*. New York: D. Appleton and Company.
Marshall, Alfred (1887), "Remedies for Fluctuations in General Prices." *The Contemporary Review* 51(March):355–75.
Merriam, Lucius S. (1893), "The Theory of Final Utility in Its Relation to Money and the Standard of Deferred Payments." *Annals of the American Academy of Political and Social Science* 3(January):483–501.
Navarro, Jose F. de (1893), "Bimetallic Parity Under a Gold Standard." *The Forum* 15(April):225–31.
Ross, Edward Alsworth (1892), "The Standard of Deferred Payments." *Annals of the American Academy of Political and Social Science* 3(November):293–305.
——— (1893), "The Total Utility Standard of Deferred Payments." *Annals of the American Academy of Political and Social Science* 4(November):425–41.
Smith, James Allen (1896), "The Multiple Money Standard." *Annals of the American Academy of Political and Social Science* 7(March):173–232.
Stokes, Anson Phelps (1896), *Joint-Metallism*, 5th ed. New York: G. P. Putnam's Sons.
Webb, Anson J. (1895), "Outline of a New Philosophy of Money." *The Arena* 13(July):199–208.
Will, Thomas Elmer (1898), "Stable Money." *Journal of Political Economy* 7(December):85–92.

THE NEW ECONOMIC HISTORY AND CAPITALIST GROWTH: THE MORAL PERSPECTIVE

Stephen T. Worland

I. NEH: ORIGINS AND METHOD

"A revolution," wrote Douglas C. North in the pages of the *American Economic Review* some years ago, "is taking place in economic history" (North, 1963:128). This revolution, so Robert Fogel reported a year later in the same journal, has produced a New Economic History—a discipline which uses new and distinctive methods to arrive at a new and distinctive understanding of the economic past (Fogel, 1964). The difference between the new style of economic history and its older predecessor emerges clearly in a comparison between two editions, three decades apart in their dates of publication, of one of the social scientist's and historian's basic research sources.

Variations in Business and Economic History:
Essays in Honor of Donald L. Kemmerer
Research in Economic History, Suppl. 2, pages 191–209.

ISBN: 0-89232-262-4

Writing in the 1931 edition of the *Encyclopedia of the Social Sciences,* J. H. Clapham had described economic history as "a branch of general institutional history" which employs a methodology that "differs in no way from that of history in general." Admitting that the effort (exemplified in the work of Gustav Schmoller) to replace deductive economic theory with inductive historical generalizations had not succeeded, Clapham nevertheless emphasized the incommensurability of pure theory—which abstracts in order to isolate economic forces—and the actual historical process where such forces interact with other cultural, social, and psychological factors (Clapham, 1931). Writing some thirty years later in the *International Encyclopedia of the Social Sciences,* North took note of a "distinct change" in the study of economic history. Whereas Clapham had insisted that economic and general history employ an identical method, North emphasized that the two are in fact sharply distinguished, the former being characterized by "its appeal to a systematic body of theory as a source of generalization and by the equally systematic use of quantitative methods" (North, 1968). In Clapham's 1931 perspective, economic history and economic theory—the latter a body of timeless, abstract deductions, the former an empirical record of successive, complex events—cannot be related in any meaningful way to one another. For North, on the contrary, the two are strongly complementary. It is the systematic use of a body of standardized theory which both differentiates the work of the economic historian from that of other students of the past and enables him to achieve a deeper, more accurate understanding of the process of historical development. Making the same point in 1965, Fogel expressed the conclusion that the extended hiatus which for over half a century had separated the intellectual efforts of the historian and the economist had at last been closed. The New Economic History, Fogel reported, had emerged on the academic scene, and its emergence had been produced by the "reunification of economic history and economic theory" (Fogel, 1965:94).

The reunification referred to by Fogel was clearly explained by Meyer and Conrad in 1957 in a pathbreaking article that came to be recognized as one of the classic sources for the New Economic History. Drawing upon the work of philosophers such as Carl Hempel, they argued that, despite differences between the two disciplines, the same rules of explanation hold for history as for science.[1] They went on to argue that it is the function of the economic historian, not merely to describe or narrate, but to find those "conjunctions" among historical facts which are rich in "causal fertility"—that is, to differentiate between accidental and "constant conjunctions" so as to find the "causal ordering" connecting the facts observed in history. The mere accumulation of facts would not, in their view, contribute to understanding unless such information could be subsumed "under appropriate causal regularities" and analyzed with the "proper use of theoretical generalization" (Meyer and Conrad, 1957:525, 532–33).

Making a clear distinction between "exogenous variables" (causes) and "endogenous variables" (effects), Meyer and Conrad suggest a way to deal with the methodologically disturbing fact that theory deals with timeless abstract regularities while history must consider the sequence of nonregular, unique events. The impact of historically unique, accidental factors on particular events can be allowed for by adopting the econometrician's practice of including an "error" term in the equations expressing the structural relationships of the system being analyzed. The "constant conjunctions" that endure through time and that reflect the "causal ordering" between elements of the system are expressed in the relationship between exogenous and endogenous variables. The accidental factors that differ from one historical situation to another are to be treated as random and allowed to influence the endogenous variables only through the error term. Leaving the concern for the exceptional and unique factors to the social or political historian, the economist thus concentrates on "the systematic, repetitive aspects of behaviour." His objective is to discover stable relationships between exogenous and endogenous variables so as to "establish theories with at least some generality" (*ibid.*:539). Meyer and Conrad thus combine theory and history, using historical fact plus the distinction between random and exogenous variables to test theories and employing the "constant conjunctions" revealed in the tested theory to explain—locate the causes of—historical developments.

The procedure outlined by Meyer and Conrad seemed to lead the New Economic History to a series of immediate and impressive results. Commenting on the new approach in 1963, North pointed out that its use had already led to a basic modification of what had once been received as "accepted 'truths'" about the economic past—e.g., the belief that antebellum slavery was unprofitable, that railroads played an indispensable role in nineteenth-century development, that the Civil War accelerated U.S. industrialization (North, 1963:129). In a similar vein, Fogel pointed out in 1964 that the new history had "frequently resulted in dramatic re-evaluations of the economic impact of past events and institutions" (Fogel, 1964:93).

However, there is one factor in the understanding of the early accomplishments of the New Economic History that calls for special emphasis. In his 1964 discussion of the relationship between economic theory and history, Fogel points out that those working in the New Economic History had made use, not only of advances in statistics and computer technology, but also of sophisticated innovations and extensions of theory—such as imput-output analysis, CES production functions, and even the "rarified construct" of the Von Neumann-Morganstern utility index

(Fogel, 1964:93). However, though it may be the case that the new breed of historian sometimes utilizes sophisticated, high-level developments in theory, the basic theory presupposed in their work is in fact the standard neoclassical model. That is, their search for an explanation of historical events is based upon the assumption that economic decisions are made by rational individuals whose behavior is governed by a calculated desire to maximize net utility or net benefit. For example, Peter Temin used the standard neoclassical theory of a cost-minimizing, profit-maximizing firm to explain how shifts in the technology of iron production occurred in response to changing factor prices and transportation costs (Temin, 1964). In their attempt to weigh the impact of canals and railroads on the development of the economy, Ransom and Fogel employed a model of the economy which presupposes that the system makes a rational, cost-minimizing adjustment to changes in the transportation infrastructure (Ransom, 1964). In the 1965 assessment of the state of economic history, North is critical of much of the work done, not because it fails to employ the latest sophisticated refinements in theory, but because the causal implications in much of the work "run counter to basic economic propositions"—such as those having to do with the money supply and price level, demand elasticity and tax incidence, and the relationship between social and private rates of return on investment (North, 1965:87ff). Finally, it should be noted that the New Economic History's most widely acclaimed accomplishment—the strongly persuasive case it makes for a drastic revision of the traditional interpretation of slavery—is in fact based upon a very simple model of the process of economic decision making. The rate of return on investment in slaves is calculated according to standard procedure: by comparing the net stream of income produced over the life of the slave with the amount of capital invested in buying and maintaining him in production. This rate of return was found to be competitive with that available from alternative investments—a finding which led to the revolutionary conclusion that, contrary to both folklore beliefs and much scholarly opinion, antebellum slavery was in fact an economically rational, viable institution (Fogel and Engerman, 1974:60–75). Basic to the whole analysis is the finding that slave owners were not an aristocracy who owned slaves because such a practice provided symbolic reinforcement for romantic social values; on the contrary, slave owners are found to be "hard, calculating businessmen who priced slaves . . . with as much shrewdness as could be expected of any northern capitalist" (*ibid.*:73).

The preceding observations suggest that, although the New Economic History may be quite innovative in the way it combines statistical technique and computer technology to make use of historical data, and although its scholarly accomplishments may have led to a decisive modification of our understanding of the historical development of the economy, the New Economic History employs a basic model of the economy which corresponds closely in fundamental outline with that utilized in orthodox, mainstream neoclassical economics. Whereas a Marxist interprets capitalist development in terms of ideology and class warfare; whereas an Institutionalist tries to explain history by referring to processes understood in terms of social psychology; the New Economic History conceives of economic activity as motivated by a single-minded desire for wealth and governed by a rational, calculated effort to maximize benefits and minimize costs. The "constant conjunctions" and "causal regularities" which, according to the Conrad-Mayer methodology, are to be used to explain the facts observed in economic history are "constant" and "regular" because the economic process conforms through time to stable forces and tendencies—e.g., of resources to move from low-price to high-price markets; of supply and demand to settle at equilibrium; of entrepreneurs to adapt product lines and techniques so as to minimize costs.

Within fifteen years of the first systematic efforts to utilize a combination of theory and statistics, the New Economic History could be said to have "come of age" (Robertson, 1972:1210). The achievement of maturity was marked by the publication, in 1971, of Davis and North's innovative book *Institutional Change and American Economic Growth* (1971). With the publication of this work, two pioneers in the new branch of study made a tentative effort to enlarge the range of enquiry and to achieve a wider range of generalization. Whereas earlier work had concentrated on analyzing economic processes as they take place within a given institutional framework (Redlich, 1965:482), Davis and North intend, not only to analyze the working of economic forces within a stable structure, but also to explain shifts taking place through time in the structure itself. Noting that typical economic models treat the "state of existing institutional arrangements" as "given" and constant, they propose "to change that constant . . . into a variable" by developing a theory that will endogenize and "explain" the historical emergence and development of economic institutions (Davis and North, 1971:40).

Davis and North distinguish between the *institutional environment*—the "set of ground rules that establishes the basis for production, exchange and distribution"—and the set of *institutional arrangements*. The institutional environment includes such factors as the federal Constitution, its judicial interpretation, and the community's accepted "norms of behavior and values." An institutional arrangement is an economic practice or procedure adapted to facilitate economic activity which functions within the confines provided by the institutional environment. Thus an institutional arrangement is a pattern of stability that functions at a level between the basic ground rules of the institutional environment and the particular, day-to-day economic transactions entered into by individuals. Shifts in such arrangemental patterns occur in response to disturbances. And these arrangemental adjustments are the endogenous variables which Davis and North propose to "explain" or "predict" with their model of institutional change. "It is the process of innovation of these institutional arrangements that the model of 'institutional change' is designed to predict" (Davis and North, 1971:6–10, 44).

Three features of their model call for special comment. The theory takes note of the distinction, standard in neoclassical welfare economics, between innovations that improve efficiency or increase aggregate income—e.g., those that take advantage of economies of scale—and institutional shifts, such as the creation of a cartel or enactment of a tariff, that merely redistribute income from one group to another (*ibid.*:25–26). Also, the theory of institutional innovation is meant to be part of a larger whole—to be a "first step toward a useful theory of economic growth" (*ibid.*:4, 6). Finally, and of most importance for present purposes, the theory that is designed to explain the process of institutional change is formulated as an extension of, not a substitute for, standard neoclassical theory. Davis and North intend, as they indicate in their preface, "to integrate standard economic analysis with an explanation of the emergence and decline of institutional arrangement" (*ibid.*:vii).

Thus, in the Davis-North model, the agents responsible for bringing about a shift in the pattern of institutional arrangements are assumed to be rational profit maximizers. Institutional innovation will occur, according to their explanation, because "individuals or groups hope to capture some profit which is unattainable under the old arrangement," or when it is discovered that for a particular innovation "the expected net gains exceed the expected costs" (*ibid.*:10). When the profit possibilities available under a given set of institutional arrangements have been fully exploited, the system will settle down in an institutional equilibrium with economic activity and market adjustments taking place in a pattern determined by the given structure. But if the stable system is subjected to an exogenous shock that opens up new profit possibilities—e.g., a change in technology or a constitutional amendment that shifts the balance of political power—then a series of equilibrating adjustments in the pattern of institutional arrangements will begin to take place (*ibid.*:40–41). Thus, "it is the possibility of profits that cannot be captured with the existing arrangemental structure that leads to the formation of new institutional arrangement" (*ibid.*:39). Although they are careful to note that "money profit maximization" is not the only goal of social life (*ibid.*:30, n. 2), Davis and North take as the "basic assumption" of their model of institutional change the proposition that "the motivating factor in arrangemental change is the desire to gather the greatest amount of all possible profit'' (*ibid.*:40).

The fundamental significance of the profit motive in their theory is underscored by the way Davis and North use the model to interpret the American past. Adoption of the corporate form of business organization is explained as an institutional adjustment brought about by the effort to capture profits emerging from the discovery of a technology that permits economies of scale. Such technological change also gave rise to another source of profit—that associated with the shift of income from consumers to producers through monopolistic price fixing. And discovery of this second source of profit generated its own institutional adjustment. The corporate trust was introduced by Rockefeller to capture the profits to cartelization. Expansion of the market through growth of the West led to the development of new financial intermediaries designed to lower transactions cost. Adoption of the Seventeenth Amendment, an exogenous change which reduced the cost of political action, led naturally to a rational adjustment. In this case, the institutional adjustment involved greater use of the political system in the effort to shift income from the few to the many (*ibid.*:12–14, 42, 67, 168–71, 173–74).

II. NEH: POLITICAL PHILOSOPHY AND THE MORAL DIMENSION

As recommended by Meyer and Conrad, and as practiced by their successors, the New Economic History relies upon a systematic combination of logical inference and empirical observation, of deductive theory with attempts to test the theory against the data of experience. Among economists, such a view of methodology is quite often associated with the belief that economics is "a positive science . . . a body of . . . generalization . . . that can be used to predict the consequences of changes in circumstances'' (Friedman, 1953:39). Such a view in turn typically implies the more or less explicit acceptance of a basic philosophic principle: Hume's Law, or the belief that value judgments cannot be derived from statements of fact. If it is true, as the point was once put in a well-known essay on economic method, that "between the generalizations of positive and normative studies there is a logical gulf which no ingenuity can disguise,'' if the economist agrees that "propositions involving the verb 'ought' are different in kind from propositions involving the verb 'is''' (Robbins, 1935:148–49), then it follows that the economic historian's task is completed when he has succeeded in discovering the causal sequence that underlies the process of capitalist development. However, economists need to reflect on the fact that among philosophers who specialize in such matters Hume's Law is no longer unanimously accepted as universally valid (MacIntyre, 1966:264). Furthermore, raising doubt about the validity of Hume's Law leads to an immensely interesting question concerning the New Economic History.

The "new" history purports to use neoclassical theory extended to endogenize institutional change to explain the process of capitalist development.[2] But if the dichotomy between fact and value required by Hume's Law can no longer be taken for granted, the question emerges of the moral or ethical properties of the developmental process that the New Economic History tries to analyze. What kind of *moral* evaluation can be offered for the process of economic growth—motivated by a rational desire to maximize and characterized by rising per capita real income—that the New Economic History seeks to explain? Is the sequence of institutional change envisaged in the Davis-North model, for instance, the kind of historical development that warrants moral approval as good and conducive to human well-being? Or is capitalist economic growth perhaps a species of historical disease—susceptible of rational explanation in terms of underlying causes, but nevertheless recognized as an evil to be cured or avoided rather than a good to be pursued?

The answer to this fundamental question is not at all obvious. The Fogel-Engerman finding that human slavery is the natural outcome of rational economic decision making certainly provokes the strong intuitive judgment that the capitalist mechanism must involve immense and shameful evil. In the Marxian perspective, capitalistic development appears as a compulsive, neurotic process that thrives on systematic exploitation. The outlook on nature and society presupposed in the neoclassical economic model is a special case of a mind set sometimes characterized as "functional rationality." And there are those who argue cogently that such a mind set, allowed to function in the context of economic development, can produce social destruction and immense human suffering (Berger, 1976).

With reference to the moral evaluation of the capitalist growth process, Davis and North frequently refer to developments in political philosophy that, in their view, complement their own efforts to explain the course of economic history. For present purposes, there is special significance in their repeated references to what in its day was a highly original and innovative work in political theory—Buchanan and Tullock, *The Calculus of Consent*. In their opening chapter, Davis and North point out that their basic theory of institutional change "draws heavily" on Buchanan and Tullock (Davis and North, 1971:3n). So far as procedure and methods are concerned, there is indeed a striking parallel between the Buchanan and Tullock exercise in political analysis and the Davis-North effort to reinterpret the historical development of the U.S. economy.

The Calculus of Consent is designed to provide a scientific explanation for the emergence of political institutions—especially for changes in the community's basic political structure or "constitution." Adopting an individualistic (as opposed to "organic") conception of the social community, Buchanan and Tullock make the fundamental assumption that political behavior is motivated by the same kind of rational self-interest that, in economic theory, is supposed to give rise to division of labor, specialization in production, and contractual exchange (Buchanan and Tullock, 1965:12–13). According to their basic postulate, man is taken to be "a utility-maximizer in both his market and his political activity" (*ibid.*:23). When given an opportunity to make a political choice, the individual as envisioned in their model will make his decision not out of a regard for tradition nor by appeal to abstract moral principle. On the contrary, it is assumed that an "individual will . . . choose 'more' rather than 'less' when confronted with the opportunity for choice in the political process, with 'more' and 'less' being defined in terms of measurable economic position" (*ibid.*:29). "We have assumed that the rational individual, when confronted with constitutional choice, will act so as to . . . maximize his expected 'utility' from social interdependence' " (*ibid.*:49).

The Calculus of Consent and the Davis-North theory of economic development both presuppose as basic to their models the crucial assumption that decisions are made by rational, utility-maximizing individuals. The difference between them has to do with the range of endogenous variables, or the set of observed phenomena, that they purport to "explain." For Davis and North, the facts to be explained are shifts in the pattern of economic institutions, such as property rights, tariffs, and the creation of new market structures. For Buchanan and Tullock, the *explananda* are political institutions and rules, such as the principle of majority rule. Whereas Davis and North take the institutional environment as given and seek to endogenize changes in the pattern of institutional arrangements, Buchanan and Tullock move to a yet higher level of generality and seek to explain changes in the basic political structure.

Furthermore, in moving to a higher level of abstraction, Buchanan and Tullock encounter precisely that *moral* question which, as indicated above, is crucial for understanding what has been accomplished by the New Economic History. The authors of *The Calculus of Consent* not only propose to develop a "scientific explanation" of the results of political decision making; they also intend their work as an exercise in "normative social science" which will help the community decide which political institutions—or, more precisely, which *changes* in political institutions—are good and desirable and ought to be adopted. The formal symmetry between the explanatory model used in the NEH and that employed in *The Calculus of Consent*, taken in conjunction with the fact that the latter is intended to contribute to the *normative* evaluation of political institutions, suggests an interesting interpretive hypothesis. Could the moral theory implicit in the Buchanan-Tullock analysis of political decision making provide an adequate answer to the question: is the process of economic development as explained by Davis and North to be considered ethically desirable?

In their political theory, Buchanan and Tullock place a great deal of emphasis on the distinction between: (1) choices made at the constitutional level when the community must decide upon the operating rules to be followed in subsequent decision making; and (2) the rules themselves through which postconstitutional choices—e.g., of tax rates, of political candidates—are registered and implemented. The nature of the rules is taken as varying with the number of persons who, when the political system is put in operation, must agree in order to implement collective action. Thus the choice of rules at the constitutional level reduces to a choice of the number of persons who for a given type of decision must agree in order for collective action to take place. If "decision-making" costs were zero, it would be rational to insist that all choices, both constitutional and operational, be made by unanimous agreement (Buchanan and Tullock, 1965:85). But since such costs are positive, rational cost minimization requires that less than unanimity be allowed for many decisions. Thus, it is rational for those engaged in constitutional choice to adopt the principle of majority rule for some decisions, such as election to office. A plurality rule might be appropriate for other decisions. For still others, it might be rational to delegate operational authority, as to a public commission or the Open Market Committee of the Federal Reserve, and allow a smaller number of individuals to determine the course of collective action.

Thus, for the operating rules of the political system, the number of persons required to implement collective action can vary from a relatively small number, through a plurality or majority, to a larger number for decisions that might have an especially significant impact on the lives of individuals. However, it is of vital importance to note that, in the Buchanan and Tullock analysis, no such variation in the number required for collective decision is allowed when the community makes its basic constitutional choices. Majority rule, decision by plurality, or delegation of authority to a smaller group may be appropriate for different ranges of operational decision. But for those basic decisions made at the constitutional level, one and only one principle is allowed to operate. That principle is the *rule of unanimity*. It is instructive to consider why Buchanan and Tullock insist that decisions at the constitutional level must be unanimous.

In the opening stages of their analysis, Buchanan and Tullock warn that a discussion of collective decision making can easily slip into an infinite regress (Buchanan and Tullock, 1965:6). If collective decisions are to be made through the implementation of operational rules, but if such operational rules are to be chosen through a process of constitutional choice, then the question arises: how are the rules that govern constitutional choice to be selected? "In postulating a decision-making rule for constitutional choices, we face the problem, How is the rule itself chosen?" (*ibid.*:6). And to answer that the rule governing constitutional choice is itself to be selected by some kind of yet more fundamental collective decision merely pushes the analysis to a higher level of abstraction where the question emerges in a new form.

The rule of unanimity is introduced by Buchanan and Tullock as a way of avoiding this infinite regress. "One means of escape from what appears to be a hopeless methodological dilemma is that of introducing some rule of unanimity . . . at the ultimate constitutional level" (*ibid.*:6). In a democratic society, the direction and extent of collective action are to be determined by the free choice of individuals. These individual choices are to be processed through a decision-making mechanism which, operating according to established rules, will combine the individual choices so as to yield the community's collective decision. For example, individuals vote. The votes are counted. And the principle of majority rule is invoked to select the winning candidate. The principle of majority rule itself is also the product of individual choice as such choice functions at the higher, constitutional level. But in order to avoid an infinite regress, it is stipulated that the ultimate rule governing constitutional choice is to be taken as given. And the rule that is to be taken as given is the principle of unanimity.

Once introduced, the principle of unanimity comes to play a vital and fundamental role in the Buchanan and Tullock model. It not only serves to avoid the logical difficulty of an infinite regress but also provides the normative basis for deciding which changes in the social structure are to be considered good and desirable. As Buchanan and Tullock put it, "conceptual unanimity" provides the "criteria" for deciding whether an activity should be moved to the public sector. "Agreement among all the individuals in the group becomes the only real measure of 'improvement' that may be accomplished through change" (*ibid.*:6–7). With reference to modifications in government—that is, to the question of whether a change will "make things 'better'"—Buchanan and Tullock hold that "the rule of unanimity provides us with an extremely weak ethical criterion for 'betterness.'" Their evaluation of political institutions, they point out, is not intended "to go beyond welfare judgments deductible from rigorous application of the unanimity rule" (*ibid.*:13–14). Pareto optimality and the compensation principle, two concepts that play a key role in neoclassical welfare economics, are taken by Buchanan and Tullock as special variants of the unanimity rule. That is, a shift toward a Pareto optimal allocation of resources, or a movement of resources that would permit the payment of compensation, is a special case of the kind of modification of the system that would command unanimous approval (*ibid.*:90–92). In the last analysis, a modification of the political structure can be said to be desirable if and only if it can be shown to derive from the community's fundamental constitutional choice, and such a choice must be unanimous.

To relate these considerations to the New Economic History, it has been suggested that the Buchanan and Tullock analysis of political institutions might well be considered an extension or generalization of the theory of capitalist growth developed by Davis and North. In both models, a community of rational, utility-maximizing individuals is assumed to introduce basic changes—in decision-making rules in the one case, in economic institutions in the other—whenever doing so would conduce to net advantage. This relationship between the two models suggests that the ethical principles implied in the more comprehensive theory—that of Buchanan and Tullock—might also be said to be implied in the second theory also. Rational political decision making will bring about changes in the endogenous variables of the Buchanan and Tullock model. Such shifts are consistent with the unanimity rule governing constitutional choice and are therefore to be considered ethically desirable. In a similar vein, one might argue that the institutional changes explained by the Davis and North theory, motivated by the same utility-maximizing psychological forces as those at work in the Buchanan and Tullock model, are also to be considered the product of unanimous choice and, for this reason, are to be considered morally good and desirable. Thus, conflating the New Economic History with the normative political theory offered by Buchanan and Tullock leads to a conclusion that would seem to be immensely significant for understanding the former. According to such a conclusion, a community of reasonable and virtuous men who wish to construct a good, just, and moral society should adopt the unanimity rule as a basic ethical norm and should then devise a social structure that will facilitate capitalist growth, as the latter is explained in the Davis and North model.

The significance of this latter conclusion depends, of course, upon the persuasive force of the rule of unanimity. To suggest that a process of institutional change is to be considered ethically desirable because such a process conforms with the rule of unanimity leads naturally to the further question: what is the logical or philosophical justification for such a rule? Buchanan and Tullock indicate that, as an ethical postulate, the rule of unanimity is "an extremely weak ethical criterion for 'betterness''' (*ibid.*:13). Their approach, so Buchanan indicates, is one that "requires a minimum of ethical premises" as opposed to alternative theories which do not employ the unanimity rule and therefore require "a stronger ethical postulate" (*ibid.*:312–19). They also emphasize that their theory is to be considered "individualistic" in the sense that the individual is taken to be the "essential philosophic entity" and as opposed to the view that employs an "organic" conception of the state (*ibid.*:265; cf. pp. 172, 312). Apparently, with their rejection of the "organic" conception, Buchanan and Tullock mean to emphasize that the state cannot be considered a substantial entity capable of existence and thus of goodness or perfection in its own right. By insisting that the unanimity rule is a "weak" postulate they seem to mean that those who employ such a postulate as a normative premise need not try to specify in detail wherein the good lies but can leave such a specification to the free choice of the community's members. Such a justification for the rule of unanimity indicates that the basis of their model is a conception of social decision making that coincides closely with one of the classic formulations of social-contract theory.

According to such a version of contract theory, social norms (such as the decision-making rules endogenous to the Buchanan-Tullock model or the institutional changes that, for Davis and North, generate economic growth) derive from an ultimate, fundamental act of consent embodied in the original social contract. This primordial act of consent provides the moral basis for the evaluation of social practices and institutions. In Buchanan's terminology, the original act of consent comes to function as an "ethical criterion of 'betterness.'" The decisions included in the contract or in constitutional choice are ultimate—they constitute the final, sovereign authority in the community's decision-making process—because in the nature of the case there is no more basic standard against which such choices can themselves be evaluated.

Such a conception of social decision making (e.g., as exemplified in Hobbes's variant of contract theory) typically presupposes a deeper, philosophic notion, a particular and definitive conception of what constitutes the ethical good, or of what is the source of moral value. According to such a conception, a judgment as to the good or a judgment of value must in the last analysis be taken to derive from an ultimate act of will—of command, of consent, or of choice. The ultimate act of will is in itself definitive and not subject to critical evaluation or correction (Taylor, 1967). When such a conception of the good operates in social philosophy, the basic question becomes that of specifying which act of choice is to be considered ultimate and sovereign—shall it be the command of the monarch? the decision of a legislature? or the *vox populi?* Social-contract theory settles this question by designating the community at large as the relevant agency whose act of will, embodied in the original agreement, is to constitute the community's ultimate moral authority. It guarantees that such a collective act of will is to be accepted as final—so that there can be no higher standard in terms of which the contractual choice can be judged right or wrong—by insisting, as in the Buchanan-Tullock model, that the original act of constitutional choice be unanimous.

Such an understanding of the unanimity rule poses an important problem for appreciating the accomplishments of the New Economic History. One can note the complementarity between the Davis-North model of growth and the social-contract theory as exemplified in *The Calculus of Consent* and conclude that the institutional changes envisioned in the former would comply with a unanimity rule and therefore qualify as morally praiseworthy. However, reaching such a vital conclusion by such a route demands a very high price. The procedure seems to require the economic historian to accept a definitive, extreme, and ultimately dubious ethical theory. He must concur in a sophisticated form of moral agnosticism and agree that, at ground and fundamentally, decisions on ultimate values finally reduce to an arbitrary act of choice.

Fortunately, there is an alternative tradition in moral philosophy which also indicates that the institutional changes explained by the New Economic History are indeed worthy of moral approval, but which does not require acceptance of the philosophy of values implied in the Buchanan-Tullock unanimity rule. The alternative moral tradition is exemplified in the thought of Aristotle.

III. ARISTOTLE AND THE MORAL DIMENSION OF CAPITALIST GROWTH

In accordance with his teleological reading of nature, Aristotle presupposes that human behavior is goal-oriented. Holding that an infinite regress of means-to-ends would be incompatible with the observed fact that people undertake deliberate action, he concludes that there must be a terminus for human desire, an end which "we desire for its own sake, everything else being desired for the sake of this." Psychologically, the quest for this ultimate end provides the basic motive force underlying all human activity. Ethically, this ultimate end—*eudamonia* or happiness—must be the "good and the chief good" for man (*NE,* 1:2).

In keeping with his belief that the good or perfection of any natural object lies in a pattern of development determined by its characteristic structure or natural form, Aristotle tries to specify the nature of human happiness by isolating that particular function or activity that is distinctive for the human species. Taking note of those biological processes that are common both to man and other organisms, he finds that it is the exercise of a *rational principle*—either in the work of reason itself, or in the subordination of psychological inclinations to reason—that is the distinctive function or species-characteristic activity for mankind. From such considerations he concludes that *human good*—the perfection which constitutes happiness and which provides the terminal point for human desire—"turns out to be activity of soul in accordance with virtue" (*NE,* 1:7).

According to a modern authority (Hardie, 1968:357), if one were to find one word which for Aristotle best describes the highest human good, that word would be *theoria*—the exercise whereby man fastens his capacity for pure thought on the consideration of sublime truths. Such an activity, Aristotle holds, seems to "aim at no end beyond itself." It is also nearly self-sufficing and "is thought to offer pleasures marvellous for their purity and enduringness" (*NE,* 10:7). Having isolated the highest good as the life of contemplation, however, Aristotle goes on to indicate that, when all is said and done, such a life may be "too high" for man and "more divine than human." Not willing to reduce man to pure spirit or intelligence, he comes finally to the conclusion that an active life, involving the exercise of a range of intellectual and moral virtues in addition to the contemplative activity of philosophic wisdom, may be the kind of activity which more appropriately "befits human nature" (*NE,* 10:7). Employing a multi-drive psychobiological model of human behavior, and having defined the good as the terminus for natural desire, Aristotle holds that human perfection involves a horizontal dimension—the bringing to fruition of each element in the full range of human capabilities.

Thus "noble and good deeds"—which would include the exercise of moral, political, and artistic excellence—may conduce to the further end of contemplative wisdom. But, Aristotle finds, performance of such deeds is also "a thing desirable for its own sake" (*NE,* 9:6). Good acts are those that contribute to happiness, but not merely as means to an end. For to qualify as morally good, a human act must be performed "for the sake of the act itself" (*NE,* 2:4). Moral virtue moderates the passions so that fear or pleasure will not interfere with the command of practical reason and so distract from the attainment of contemplative perfection. But it is also true that moral virtue, and pleasure also, are instances of the kind of goods that "if nothing resulted from them, we should still choose each of them" (*NE,* 1:6).

According to Aristotle's political philosophy, the state is that "perfect society" which virtuous men create because of their desire to "dwell together." Such a desire, however, is not reducible to a merely utilitarian need to establish law and order so as to achieve the productive advantages of social cooperation (*Pol.,* 3:9). At a far deeper level the impulse toward political life derives from the desire of virtuous men to exemplify and contemplate the good and beautiful, to create good through their common endeavor and to share through discourse in the appreciation of such good. Political life requires unanimity, and, as in the Buchanan and Tullock model, such unanimity obtains when all men "have the same opinion about what is to their interest . . . e.g., when all the citizens think that . . . offices should be elective" (*NE,* 9:6). But such unanimity also extends beyond an agreement as to what is useful, to a shared conception of the good and noble achieved through the exercise of friendship (Clark, 1975:109–10).

As previous remarks indicate, Aristotle develops a complex, twofold conception of ultimate human well-being. On one view, the good life consists in the exercise of philosophic wisdom. On a second view, the good life involves virtuous (temperate and just) social and political activity, including the exercise of the special virtue Aristotle refers to as "magnificence." For an economist, it is vitally important to note that, in Aristotle's view, either conception of the "good life" requires a material base in an *efficient* economic system. The exercise of philosophic wisdom requires a moderate amount of *external goods,* and such wealth must be available before contemplative activity can take place. Furthermore, and much more significantly, the life of philosophic wisdom requires *leisure*—and leisure in the sense of freedom from burdensome toil is one of the most valuable by-products of an efficient economic system. As for the life of virtuous political and social activity, such a life requires a supply of "external goods." The virtuous man needs such goods in order to survive and also as "instruments" to be used in the practice of justice and liberality. To come to a much deeper point, social life is based upon the human need to exemplify and communicate in a shared conception of the good and the beautiful. Practice of the virtue of magnificence—such as the creation of works of art or the performance of artistic public ceremony—is one of the crucial ways such communication in the good and beautiful can be achieved (*NE,* 4:2). And the exercise of magnificence requires a flow of external goods—a level of wealth production—far in excess of what would suffice for utilitarian subsistence.

These observations lead finally to a vital conclusion—one that would seem to be crucial for understanding the New Economic History and its implicit theory of economic development. According to Aristotle's moral and political philosophy, the process of institutional change which the NEH purports to explain is a good and worthy and morally eligible objective for social policy—because such a drive toward economic efficiency is finally contributory to ultimate human good, to (1) a life of philosophic contemplation; and to (2) the life of active virtue. As is well known, Aristotle's political theory presupposes the institution of slavery as essential to provide leisure and material goods so that an aristocracy of noble men can practice the "good life." Perhaps economic progress as envisioned in the NEH can be considered a substitute for Aristotle's slavery—making leisure and material goods and a chance to share in the communication of the true and beautiful available to the entire community.

The above conclusion, however, needs to be qualified in two crucial respects. Social life is to exemplify the community's shared vision of potential beauty and perfection. Therefore, although it may be true that economic activity requires rational maximization, it is also true, and vitally so, that maximization is geared, not merely to the production of an ever-enlarging stream of "useful" goods, but ultimately to the exemplification of the beautiful. For Aristotle, to overlook this vital fact is to make a fatal mistake—for it involves reduction of the "good life" to the life of "sensual pleasure" and is thus morally retrogressive. In this connection, it might be noted that Aristotle warns that a society plentifully supplied with material goods will be in especial need of the virtues of temperance and liberality—lest they give way to the pursuit of mere sensual pleasure (*Pol.,* 7:15). In other words, according to Aristotle's conception of the good life, affluence and consumerism are morally dangerous. Furthermore, communication in a shared conception of the beautiful and good requires that men are able to communicate and to "tell their stories to one another." The pursuit of rational maximization must not, by allowing such rationality to obtrude beyond its proper place in economic activity, destroy the communal life it is meant to serve.[3]

Finally, to state a summary conclusion, Aristotle's complex moral philosophy rests on a conception of the good life and on a conception of political activity which provides strong support for the belief that economic progress—the process of rational institutional change which the NEH seeks to explain—is morally good, desirable, and worthy of choice.

The founders of the New Economic History, of course, may not have been aware of the implicit connection between their work and that of the Stagirite. But, as may be said of many great and innovative scholars, whether economists, historians, or economic historians, they "builded better than they knew."

NOTES

1. North (1969, p. 469) was to insist on this same point in his IESS article ten years later.

2. The Davis and North model, with emphasis on evolving property rights as the most significant form of institutional change, has been extended from its application to the

United States to an analysis of the history of Western civilization—to an effort to explain "that unique historical achievement," the attainment of the "affluence of Western Man" (North and Thomas, 1973, p. 1).

3. Cf. Marcuse's warning (Marcuse, 1964, pp. 146–48) that exclusive reliance on a rational, technological view of nature (an attitude he finds typical of an advanced industrial society) can deprive men of a sensitivity to values and the good.

REFERENCES

Aristotle, *Nichomachean Ethics*. In Richard McKeon (ed.), *The Basic Works of Aristotle*. New York: Random House, 1941, pp. 935–1127. (Referred to in the text as *NE*.)

Aristotle, *Politics*. In Richard McKeon (ed.), *The Basic Works of Aristotle*. New York: Random House, 1941. (Referred to in the text as *Pol*.)

Berger, Peter (1976), *Pyramids of Sacrifice*. Garden City, N.Y.: Anchor Press.

Buchanan, James M. and Gordon Tullock (1965), *The Calculus of Consent*. Ann Arbor, Mich.: University of Michigan Press.

Clapham, John H. (1931), "Economic History as a Discipline." In E. R. A. Seligman (ed.), *Encyclopedia of the Social Sciences*, vol. 5, pp. 326–30. New York: Macmillan Co.

Clark, Stephen R. L. (1975), *Aristotle's Man*. Oxford: The Clarendon Press.

Conrad, Alfred H. and John R. Meyer (1958), "The Economics of Slavery in the Ante-Bellum South." *Journal of Political Economy* (April):95–130. (Reprinted in Conrad and Meyer, *The Economics of Slavery and Other Studies in Econometric History*. Chicago: Aldine, 1964)

Davis, Lance (1968), "And It Will Never Be Literature." *Explorations in Economic History*, 2nd series, 6(Fall):75ff.

Davis, Lance and Douglas C. North (1971), *Institutional Change and American Economic Growth*. Cambridge: Cambridge University Press.

Fogel, Robert W. (1964), "The Reunification of Economic History with Economic Theory." *American Economic Review* (May):92–98.

——— (1964), "Discussion." *American Economic Review* (May):377–89.

——— (1966), "The New Economic History: Its Findings and Methods." *Economic History Review* (December):642–56.

Fogel, Robert W. and Stanley L. Engerman (1974), *Time on the Cross*. Boston: Little, Brown and Co.

Friedman, M. (1953), "The Methodology of Positive Economics." In *Essays in Positive Economics*. Chicago: University of Chicago Press, pp. 3–43.

Hardie, W. F. R. (1968), *Aristotle's Ethical Theory*. Oxford: Clarendon Press.

MacIntyre, Alasdair (1966), *A Short History of Ethics*. New York: Macmillan and Co.

Marcuse, H. (1964), *One-Dimensional Man*. Boston: Beacon Press.

Meyer, John R. and Alfred H. Conrad (1957), "Economic Theory, Statistical Inference and Economic History." *Journal of Economic History* (December):524–44.

North, Douglas C. (1963), "Quantitative Research in American Economic History." *American Economic Review* (March):128–30.

——— (1965), "The State of Economic History." *American Economic Review* (May):86–91.

——— (1968), "Economic History." In David L. Sills (ed.), *International Encyclopedia of the Social Sciences*, vol. 6, pp. 468–73. New York: Macmillan Co., and The Free Press.

——— (1974), *Growth and Welfare in the American Past*. Englewood Cliffs, N.J.: Prentice-Hall.

North, Douglas C. and Robert P. Thomas (1973), *The Rise of the Western World*. Cambridge: Cambridge University Press.

Ransom, R. L. (1964), "Canals and Development: A Discussion of the Issues." *American Economic Review* (May):365–76.

Redlich, R. (1965), "'New' and Traditional Approaches to Economic History and Their Interdependence." *Journal of Economic History* 25:480–95.

Robbins, L. (1935), *An Essay on the Nature and Significance of Economic Science*, 2nd ed. London: Macmillan and Co. Ltd.

Robertson, Ross M. (1973), "Review of *American Economic Growth* by Davis, Easterlin, Parker, et al., and *Institutional Change and American Economic Growth* by Davis and North." *Journal of Economic Literature* 10(December):1210–12.

Taylor, R. (1967), "Voluntarism." In Paul Edwards (editor in chief), *The Encyclopedia of Philosophy*, vol. 3, pp. 270–72. New York: The Macmillan Co., and The Free Press.

Temin, P. (1964), "A New Look at Hunter's Hypothesis about the Antebellum Iron Industry." *American Economic Review* (May):344–51.

Selected Publications of Donald L. Kemmerer

Books

Path to Freedom: The Struggle for Self-Government in Colonial New Jersey, 1703–76. Princeton, N.J.: Princeton University Press, 1940.

Economic History of the American People. New York: Longmans Green Co., 1942; revised, 1947 (with Ernest L. Bogart).

ABC of the Federal Reserve System, 12th ed. New York: Harper and Brothers, 1950 (with E. W. Kemmerer).

Economic History of the United States. Ames, Ia.: Littlefield Adams, 1953; revised, 1962 (with Merlin H. Hunter).

Comparative Economic Development. New York: McGraw-Hill Book Co., 1956 (with Ralph H. Blodgett).

American Economic History. New York: McGraw-Hill Book Co., 1959 (with C. Clyde Jones).

The Life of John E. Rovensky, Banker and Industrialist. Champaign, Ill.: Stipes Publishing Company, 1977.

Chapters in Books

"Allied Military Currency in Constitutional and International Law." In *Money and the Law*. New York: New York University School of Law and Economists' National Committee on Monetary Policy, January 15–16, 1945.

"The Federal Reserve System." In Herbert V. Prochnow, *American Financial Institutions*. New York: Prentice-Hall, 1951.

"A Proper Central Banking System." In James W. Bell and Walter E. Spahr (eds.), *A Proper Monetary and Banking System for the United States*. New York: Ronald Press, 1960.

"Preface." In Joseph Van Fenstermaker, *The Development of American Commercial Banking, 1782–1837*. Kent, Ohio: Bureau of Economic and Business Research, Series 5, Kent State University Press, 1965.

"Foreword." In Melchior Palyi, *The Twilight of Gold, 1914–1936: Myths and Realities*. Chicago: Henry Regnery Co., 1972.

"The Role of Gold in the Past Century." In G. Carl Weigand (ed.), *Toward a New World Monetary System*. New York: McGraw-Hill Book Co., 1973.

"The Gold Standard and Economic Growth." In *World Monetary Disorder*. Malibu, Calif.: Center for International Business, Pepperdine University, 1974.

"The Role of Gold in the Past Century." In Hans F. Sennholz (ed.), *Gold Is Money*. Westport, Conn.: Greenwood Press, 1975.

"Discussion." In Henry G. Manne and Roger LeRoy Miller, *Gold, Money and the Law*. Chicago: Aldine Publishing Co., 1975.

"American Devaluation Revisited." In G. Carl Weigand (ed.), *Inflation and Monetary Crisis*. Washington, D.C.: Public Affairs Press, 1975.

"The Case for Gold." In G. Carl Weigand, *The Menace of Inflation: Its Causes and Consequences*. Old Greenwich, Conn.: Devin-Adair Co., 1977.

"The Gold Coin Standard Reconsidered." In Tullio Bagiotti and Giompiero Franco (eds.), *Pioneering Economics: International Essays in Honor of Giovanni Demaria*. Padua, Italy: Cedam, 1978.

"Abolish the Gold Standard and Prime the Pump." In G. Carl Wiegand (ed.), *Inflation and Unemployment*. Old Greenwich, Conn.: Devin-Adair Co., 1980.

Journal Articles

"The Suffrage Franchise in Colonial New Jersey." *Proceedings of the New Jersey Historical Society,* (no date).

"Judges Good Behavior Tenure in Colonial New Jersey." *Proceedings of the New Jersey Historical Society,* January 1938.

"New Material on the Stamp Act in New Jersey." *Proceedings of the New Jersey Historical Society,* July 1938.

"Neglected Source Material on Colonial New Jersey." *Proceedings of the New Jersey Historical Society,* January 1939.

"The Missing Journal of Governor Cornbury's Council." *Proceedings of the New Jersey Historical Society,* May 1939.

"The Colonial Loan-Office System in New Jersey." *The Journal of Political Economy* 47(6), 1939.

"Inflation after World War I." *The Economic Future,* Spring Quarter, 1945.

"The Coming Inflation." *The Economic Future,* Summer Quarter, 1945.

"How Much National Income in the Light of Economic History." *The Economic Future,* Fall Quarter, 1945.

"Are the Social Scientists Backward?" *American Association of University Bulletin* 34(3), 1948.

"The Pre-Civil War South's Leading Crop: Corn." *Agricultural History* 23(4), 1949.

"Reasons for the Growth of the Knights of Labor in 1885–86." *Industrial and Labor Relations Review* 3(2), 1950 (with Edward W. Wickersham).

"Perspective on the Recent Actions of the Federal Reserve Authorities." *The Analysts' Journal,* Fourth Quarter, 1950.

"Federal Reserve vs. Treasury." *Journal of the American Society of Chartered Life Underwriters* 5(3), 1951.

"Let's Use More Economics in Teaching Economic History." *Social Studies for Teachers and Administrators* 63(1), 1952.

"The Marketing of Securities, 1930–52." *Journal of Economic History* 12(4), 1952.

"War and Inflation—The First World War." *Current History* 24(141), 1953.

"Financing Illinois Industry, 1830–1890." *Bulletin of the Business Historical Society* 27(2), 1953.

"United States Labor Policy—Mine Workers: A Labor Monopoly." *Current History* 27(155), 1954.
"Taxation before 1914." *Current History* 27(156), 1954.
"A History of Paper Money in Colonial New Jersey, 1668–1775." *Proceedings of the New Jersey Historical Society* 74(2), 1956.
"The Changing Pattern of American Economic Development." *Journal of Economic History* 16(4), 1956.
"L'Election Presidentielle aux Estats-Unis." *Revue des Sciences Politiques,* 2nd series, no. 2, 1960.
"The Recent Outflow of Gold." *Delphian Quarterly* 44(3), 1961.
"The European Common Market." *Delphian Quarterly* 45(1), 1962.
"The Silver Coin Crisis." *Delphian Quarterly* 48(4), 1965.
"Impressions of European University Education by a Visiting American Professor." *Delphian Quarterly* 49(1), 1966.
"Restoring 'Gold Clauses' in Contracts." *American Bar Association Journal* 60(August), 1974.
"John E. Rovensky, 1880–1970, Industrialist and Banker." *Business and Economic History,* 2nd series, 6(February), 1977.

Articles in Periodicals

"The Problem of Too Much Gold." *Opinion and Comment* 38(February), 1941.
"Economic History of American Wars." *Opinion and Comment* 39(February), 1942. (Reprinted in *The Director's Digest* 2(2), 1943; U.S. Savings and Loan League, Chicago, Ill.)
"The Plight of the Small Investor." *Opinion and Comment* 40(November), 1942 (with Burton C. Hurd).
"The Tariff Issue is Important Today." *Opinion and Comment* 41(November), 1943.
"The Prospect of Serious Inflation." *Opinion and Comment* 41(August), 1944.
"Does Inflation Still Threaten?" Unsigned editorial, *Illinois Business Review* 1(9), 1944.
"Allied Military Currency in Italy." *The Commercial and Financial Chronicle,* September 21, 1944 (with T. Eugene Beattie). (Reprinted by the Economists' National Committee on Monetary Policy, New York.)
"Possibilities of Deflation." Unsigned editorial, *Illinois Business Review* 1(10), 1944.
"Postwar International Aviation." Unsigned editorial, *Illinois Business Review* 1(12), 1944.
"The Recent International Civil Aviation Conference." *The Commercial and Financial Chronicle* 161(4358), 1945.
"What is the Best Hedge against Inflation?" *Opinion and Comment* 42(May), 1945.
"The British Loan." *Opinion and Comment* 43(May), 1946.
"How to Buy Stocks and Bonds." *Opinion and Comment* 45(May), 1948 (with Burton C. Hurd). (Reprinted in *The Commercial and Financial Chronicle,* July 8, 1948.)
"Are the Social Scientists Backward?" *Opinion and Comment* 46(August), 1948.
"Where Are We Going?" *Opinion and Comment* 46(November), 1948.
"For Long Term Investment: Stocks or Bonds?" *The Commercial and Financial Chronicle,* February 1, 1951.
"The Gold Standard, the People and the Gold Mining Industry." *The Commercial and Financial Chronicle,* February 15, 1951. (Reprinted by the Economists' National Committee on Monetary Policy, New York.)
"Have We Completed a Cycle of War Bond Selling?" *Current Economic Comment* 13(3), 1951.

"Our Financial Health at the Outset of Four Wars." *Current Economic Comment* 14(1), 1952.

"Gold Coins More Important Than Increase in Price." *The Northern Miner* 41(19), 1953.

"We've Waited Too Long for Return of the Gold Standard." *The Commercial and Financial Chronicle,* April 22, 1954. (Reprinted by the Economists' National Committee on Monetary Policy, New York.)

"The Gold Standard in Historical Perspective." *The Commercial and Financial Chronicle,* August 5, 1954. (Reprinted by the Economists' National Committee on Monetary Policy, New York.)

"Economic Trends and Elections." *Current Economic Comment* 17(1), 1955.

"A Closer Look at Money." *Challenge, The Magazine of Economic Affairs* 6(5), 1958.

"Dr. Kemmerer Answers Mining Record." *The Mining Record* 72(14), 1961.

"What Should be the Attitude of the Gold Mining Industry." *The Commercial and Financial Chronicle,* June 8, 1961. (Reprinted by the Economists' National Committee on Monetary Policy, New York.)

"Comments: Money, Public Good or Private Good?" *Gold Standard News* 3(8), 1979.

"The Gold Coin Standard: What It Is and Why the U.S. Should Return to It." *Illinois Business Review* 37(1), 1980.

"The Rotting Fabric of Trust." *The Freeman,* March 1980.

"How to Cut Taxes." *Barron's,* July 7, 1980 (with Rene A. Wormser).

Encyclopedia Contributions

"Confiscation of Property," "Federal Deficits," "Balance of Trade," "Banking," "Banking Branch and Group," "Capitalism." In *Dictionary of American History*, 6 vols. New York: Charles Scribner's Sons, 1940.

Brief biographies of Clarence Birdseye, Alfred Fuller, Amadeo Giannini, Will H. Hays, Conrad Hilton, Samuel Insull, Hugh S. Johnson, Eric Johnston, Alfred Krupp, John W. and Clarence H. Mackay, Andrew W. Mellon, Hjalmar H. G. Schacht, Ellsworth M. Statler, Charles Edward Wilson (of General Electric), and Owen D. Young. In *World Book Encyclopedia*, 19 vols. Chicago: Field Enterprises, 1958.

"Abram Piatt Andrew," and "George McClelland Reynolds." In supplementary vol. 2 of *The Dictionary of American History*, 21 vols. New York: Charles Scribner's Sons, 1958.

"Balance of Trade," "Bank Deposits," "Bank Failures," "Capitalism," "Export-Import Banks," "Banking," "Banking: Branch and Group," "Federal Reserve System," "Gold Standard," "Investment Banks," "Savings and Loan Association," "Trusts." In *Dictionary of American History*, 7 vols. revised. New York: Charles Scribner's Sons, 1962.

"The Business Cycle." *Standard Reference Works*. New York: Columbia University Press, 1964.

"Alexander Dana Noyes," and "Daniel Richard Crissinger." In supplementary vol. 3 of *The Dictionary of American History*, 21 vols. and 3 supplementary volumes, 1928–73. New York: Charles Scribner's Sons, 1973.

"Balance of Trade," "Bank Deposits," "Bank Failures," "Bank for International Settlements," "Banking," "Banking, Branch and Group," "Banking, State," "Banks, Export-Import," "Banks, Savings," "Capitalism," "Check Currency," "Deficit, Federal," "Federal Reserve System," "Gold Standard," "Hard Money," "Independent Treasury System," "International Monetary Fund," "Investment Banks," "Limping Standard," "Managed Money," "Panic of 1907," "Repudiation of Public Debt," "Savings and Loan Associations," "Surplus, Federal," "Trusts." In *Dictionary of American History*, 8 vols. New York: Charles Scribner's Sons, 1976.

Monographs

The Case for Resumption of Specie Payments in the United States, 1954. New York: Economists' National Committee on Monetary Policy, 1954. (Also reprinted and distributed by Hugh W. Long Co., Inc., Elizabeth, N.J., 1954.)

"Newspaper Accounts of the Resumption of Specie Payments in the United States on January 2, 1879," *Monetary Notes* 22(5), New York: Economists' National Committee on Monetary Policy, 1962.

"Resumption of Specie Payments: Three Foreign Experiences, 1861–1890." Monetary Notes 22(6), New York: Economists' National Committee on Monetary Policy, 1962.

"The Gold Standard and Economic Growth," Monetary Tract No. 6 (January). Greenwich, Conn.: Committee for Monetary Research and Education, 1975.

"Restoring Gold Clauses in Contract," Monetary Tract No. 7 (January). Greenwich, Conn.: Committee for Monetary Research and Education, 1975 (with Rene A. Wormser).

"Why a Gold Standard and Why Still a Controversy?" Monetary Tract No. 25 (January). Greenwich, Conn.: Committee for Monetary Research and Education, 1979. (Abridged and reprinted by the American Educational League, Buena Park, Calif.)

"The Relationship between an Economy and Its Money," occasional paper. Greenwich, Conn.: Committee for Monetary Research and Education, 1979.

"Under a True Gold Standard the Free Market Does Not Fix the Price of Gold," occasional paper. Greenwich, Conn.: Committee for Monetary Research and Education, 1979.

Testimony before Congressional Committees

Hearings before a Sub-Committee of the Committee on Banking and Currency, U.S. Senate, 83rd Congress, 2nd session on S. 13, S. 2332, S. 2364, and S. 2514. To permit the sale and resume the redemption of gold, to establish a sound monetary system, etc. (pp. 293–94) March 29–April 1, 1954. Washington, D.C.: U.S. Government Printing Office.

Hearings before the Committee on Banking and Currency, U.S. Senate, 90th Congress, 2nd session on S. 1307, S. 2815, and S. 2857 relating to repeal of the gold reserve requirements for U.S. currency (pp. 115–16) January 31, 1968. Washington, D.C.: U.S. Government Printing Office.